1 BEST SELLING GUIDE BOOK IN TURKEY

SAFFET EMRE TONGUÇ
FATİH TÜRKMENOĞLU

BOYUT
PUBLISHING GROUP

ISBN: 978-975-23-0450-5

1 Best Selling Guide Book in Turkey

101 Must-See Places in Turkey

Saffet Emre TONGUÇ
Fatih TÜRKMENOĞLU

Editor in Chief
Bülent ÖZÜKAN

General Manager
Nilgün ÖZÜKAN

General Art Director
Murat ÖNEŞ

Translation
Melis ŞEYHUN

Editor
Pat YALE

Co-editors
Nil YÜZBAŞIOĞLU
Zahide BİLSAY
Harry G.TZIMITRAS
Leila BISHARAT

Art Director
Bülent USTAOĞLU,
Yıldız ERTAN, Ümit VURGUN

Assistant General Manager of Advertising
Yaprak Üner

Project Manager in Advertising
Aslı Balımtaş

Photography
Saffet Emre TONGUÇ
Boyut Publishing Group Archives

Yüzyıl Mah. Matbaacılar Sitesi,
1. Cadde No:115 34204 Bağcılar - İstanbul
Phone: (212) 413 33 33 pbx Fax: (212) 413 33 34

www.boyut.com.tr
e-mail: info@boyut.com.tr

Print
Boyut Printing House

contents

101 Must-See

Alphabetical order

Places In Turkey

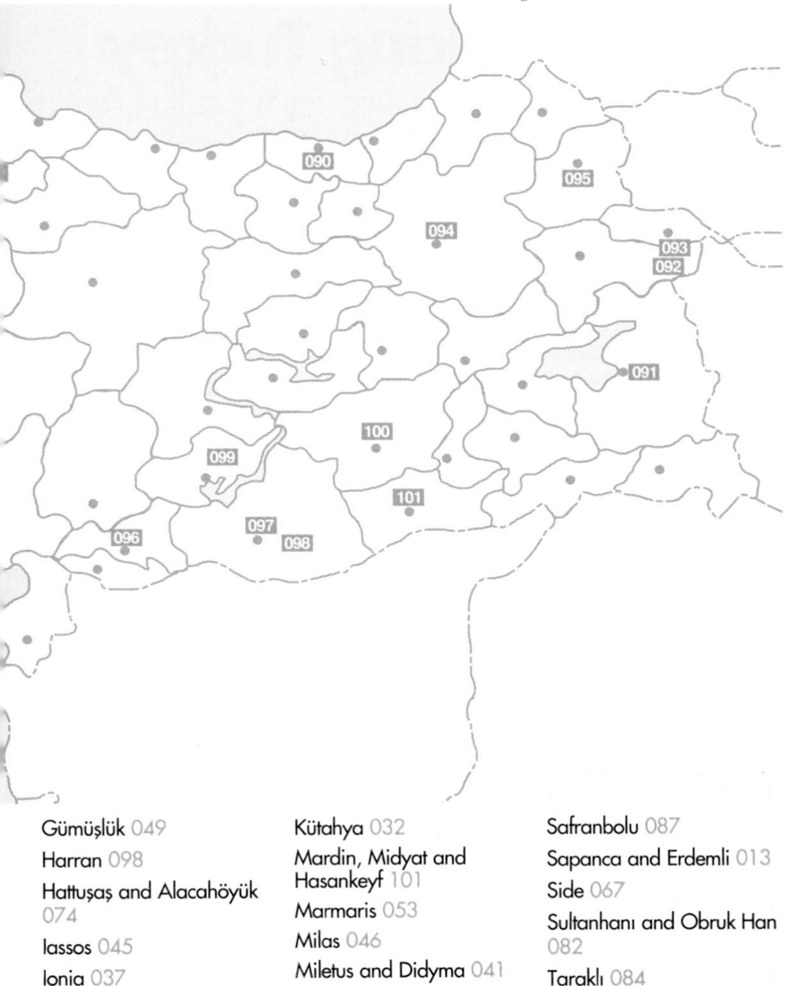

Introducing Turkey

It may be a cliché to describe Turkey as the bridge between east and west, but it's none the less true for all that. It's not just that the country crosses the geographical divide, with one foot in Europe and the other firmly in Asia, but that psychologically it also straddles what is commonly thought of as the West and the East. Nowhere, is this more apparent than in İstanbul, the glorious city on the Bosphorus, which is Turkey's capital in all but name and where a vibrant modern lifestyle sits side by side with ways of thinking and behaving that come straight from the Middle East.

This is a country that has it all – thousands of miles of glorious Aegean and Mediterranean coastline; towns and villages where history lurks in every gatepost; soaring mountains with ski resorts clinging to their sides; long-distance walking trails that meander through tiny, half-forgotten settlements; and more ancient ruins than Greece and Italy put together. It's a country, where you can ski one day and sunbathe the next; where you can watch the dervishes whirl one evening, then go clubbing the next; and where you can shop in atmospheric old bazaars or in the most modern shopping malls, depending on your taste.

History in a nutshell

Piecing Turkey's history together is immensely complicated, because its geographical location has ensured that almost every ancient civilization has had some part to play in it. Amongst the earlier civilizations to have left their mark on the country were the Hittites whose capital was at Hattusaş, north-east of Ankara; the Phrygians, who had their base at Gordion, south-west of Ankara; and the Urartians, who made Van in the far east their center. Later, came the Lydians, who gave the world its first coinage; the Lycians, who left tombs like mini temples cut into the rock; and the Carians, who left behind them the Mausoleum of Halicarnassus, one of the Seven Wonders of the Ancient World.
Eventually, the Ancient Greeks sent colonists to settle the coast of Asia Minor, then dotted the country with temples to their many fractious gods and engaged in warfare with their Persian rivals. In their footsteps, Alexander the Great passed through on his way to invade India. Then came the Romans, who took over and expanded the old Greek colonies and left their mark in marble all along the Aegean and Mediterranean.

When the Roman Empire eventually overreached itself and split into two, the old East Roman capital of Constantinople (modern İstanbul) became Byzantium, the capital of the Byzantine Empire, which left a legacy of glorious mosaics, frescoes and rock-cut churches as far inland as Cappadocia. The Byzantines soon found themselves battling for supremacy against the Arabs, who came pouring up through the Middle East, bringing Islam to areas which were, at that time, mainly Christian. Then came the first of the Turkic tribes, the Seljuks, who marched in from the east and established a kingdom centered in Konya. The Seljuks stamped their mark on the country with a network of caravanserais to accommodate the camel caravans that plodded slowly across the land bringing trade from east to west and vice versa. But eventually they, too, met their match in the Mongols under Tamerlane, who shattered their kingdom, permitting a myriad splinter emirates to pop up all over the country. Amongst those splinter groups the most important was the one that developed in the north-west around Bursa under the leadership of Osman Gazi. This group was to go on to force out the last of the Byzantines when, Sultan Mehmed the Conqueror broke through the land walls of Byzantium in 1453. The Byzantine emperor died defending his city, which duly became İstanbul, the capital of the great and growing Ottoman Empire.

At its height, the Ottoman Empire extended as far north as Hungary and as far west as Morocco. At one point the Ottomans even threatened to occupy Vienna, but then they, too, overreached themselves. By the time of the First World War, the Sultan, esconsed in the Baroque splendour of the Dolmabahçe Palace on the Bosphorus, was a beleaguered soul, his power already a shadow of what it had been. When he made the mistake of throwing in his lot with the losing side, he left the door wide open for the war hero Mustafa Kemal Atatürk to launch the Turkish War of Independence. By 1922, this had succeeded in forcing out all the foreign invaders, who had tried to grab pieces of the old Ottoman heartlands for themselves. Atatürk went on to rebuild Turkey as a modern republic, moving the capital from İstanbul to Ankara, changing the alphabet from the Arabic to the Latin script, downplaying the part of religion in all aspects of life and generally laying the foundation for everything that has happened since. Little surprise, then, that he is revered as the country's founding father and that his image crops up in every office and every town square.

Turkey Today

For Turkey these are exciting times. After a long period in the economic and political doldrums, the country is now moving forward at a cracking pace. Everywhere you go, you will see new infrastructural projects underway and new buildings shooting up as the younger generation opts to set up home on its own rather than with mum and dad. The money is coming in from tourism, from textiles, from farming and from a growing manufacturing base. Development still lags behind in the east, which remains the most exotic and least visited part of the country from the point of view of foreign visitors, but the mental line separating west from east seems to move that little bit further east with every passing year, especially now that the political turmoil that tore the east apart during the 1990s has mostly settled down.

Greater prosperity means that modern Turkey has a growing army of domestic holidaymakers, many of whom migrate *en masse* from the cities to the coast for the summer just like the French. Popular television programmes set in remoter parts of the country have also helped interest the Turks themselves in what is happening away from the İstanbul-Ankara-İzmir population centres.

This lovely new guidebook is a reflection of the changes that have been taking place. Originally written by Turkish travelers for other Turkish travelers, it offers an insider's look at what the country has to offer. Its two authors, both of them award-winning seasoned travelers and travel writers, take you behind the scenes, describing not just places such as Ephesus, which everyone has heard of, but also unearthing little-known places like Taraklı, which are only just starting to make a name for themselves. They know the Turkish poets, novelists and film-makers, who have left their mark on the different localities, they know the local dishes that can add spice to a visit, they know the anecdotes that bring a smile to the lips of the reader. In short, they know what makes Turkey tick.

Let them take you by the hand and show you round their country.
We don't think you'll regret it!

Pat Yale
Editor

Melis Şeyhun
Translator

So many places
to see...

When the idea for this book first cropped up, we both knew that, as two travelers-cum-writers, we would have no difficulty coming up with "101 Places" to see. One of us is a professional guide, historian and travel writer, the other one a TV broadcaster, journalist and, yes, travel writer.

Despite that, we didn't realize we would encounter quite such an abundance of places, and that some would have to be eliminated with great reluctance. Nor did we think that we would have to put other places onto a reserve list for a second book.

In some sections of this book, you will find anecdotes, stories, and small human intrusions alongside the more conventional guidebook information. You will read our advice about "what to do" in the places that you visit, and will be able to share our past experiences as regards "where to stay" and "where to eat".

Still, we would like to underline one thing, which is that no two journeys are ever alike; no travel experience ever exactly the same as someone else's. After setting off with your own personal luggage of experience, knowledge, and expectations, you will return with your own personal memories. Perhaps a restaurant we loved will not satisfy you, or perhaps you will discover some little hotel that, for one reason or another, escaped our attention. A pension we suggest may have changed hands, a restaurant we raved about may have closed down, phone numbers may have changed, internet sites may have folded, or a wonderful walking trail may have been converted into the garden of a hotel since we last visited; who knows?

Of course, every place in the world undergoes change. Yet, Turkey is one of those countries where change is almost on overdrive. Which may be why every journey in Turkey can evolve into a discovery, or an adventure.
We look forward to your suggestions for places, you would like us to include in future editions and in our upcoming books.
You can contact us by e-mail:

tonguc@saffetemretonguc.com
mektup@fatihturkmenoglu.com

Life is a long journey. We hope you will have a pleasant one, with many stops along the way.

Good luck and bon voyage!

Saffet Emre TONGUÇ
Fatih TÜRKMENOĞLU

Dara Ruins

Saffet Emre **Tonguç**

Saffet Emre Tonguç was born in 1966. Between 1983 and 1987, he studied, at Boğaziçi University in Istanbul, in the departments of Psychology, Management, and the Atatürk Institute for Modern Turkish History. He graduated from the Tourism and Hotel Management, Political Science and International Relations, and Ottoman Social History departments. Tonguç received his Master's degree from the same institution and wrote his thesis on "The Jews and the Ottoman Social Structure". Between 1990 and 1992, he pursued a PhD with Wirtschafts Universität's Business Administration Program in Vienna.

Tonguç started a career as a professional guide, while he was still a student in the Tourism Department at Boğaziçi University. Over 20 years, he has guided many influential people including statesmen and celebrities. By 1990, his photographs were being published in various international magazines and on Internet sites in the United States, Australia, and elsewhere. His first photo exhibition took place in a 1500-year-old cistern. Following his participation in a series of competitions held by the Turkish Ministry of Tourism and Culture, some of his photographs were purchased by the Ministry.

Tonguç has also designed countless houses and gardens, a number of which have been featured in magazines such as *Maison Française, House Beautiful, Home Art,* and *Elele.*

He has participated in various panels and seminars focused on the promotion of Turkey abroad, and has appeared as a guest speaker on CNN International's "Earth Matters" program, during a special broadcast about Turkey. He has also worked as a presenter on the celebrated US television channel ABC's "Good Morning America."

In 2005, Tonguç was granted the "Professional Supremacy Award" by the Rotary Club. He has traveled to more than 100 countries, both professionally and for fun, and was selected as "Turkey's Most Traveled Guide" by TUREB (the Turkish Association of Tourist Guides); in 2006, he was given "The Travel Writer of the Year" award by the same association. In 2007, he received a "Travel Writer" award in the "White Crystal Awards", and "Best Tour Guide of Turkey" award by SKAL CLUB. In an interview he gave to *Hürriyet* newspaper's famous columnist and interviewer Ayşe Arman, he was introduced as "The man who has traveled to the strangest places in the world". Aside from his articles that appear regularly in *Hürriyet*'s travel section and in *Voyager* magazine, Tonguç has been widely published in various magazines, newspapers, and bulletins on Turkey, including *Milliyet, Cumhuriyet, Sabah, Conde Nast Traveler, Hillsider, Skylife, On Air, Gezi Traveller, Cosmopolitan, Boğaziçi, Maviology, Nokta, Asklepios, VW, Elit, Formula 1,* and *Travel and Leisure.*

Fatih **Türkmenoğlu**

Fatih Türkmenoğlu was born in Istanbul, in 1968. He graduated from the Psychology Department of Boğaziçi University in İstanbul and received his Master's degree in Business Administration and Human Resources from New York University. In 1994, he started working as a journalist for the Sabah Media Group; his articles and interviews have appeared in *Aktüel, Cosmopolitan, Yeni Yüzyıl* and *Sabah*. He has also been producing and presenting a radio talk show for the last two years. In 1996, as NTV, one of Turkey's most prestigious news channels was getting ready to launch, he moved on to television. In the course of a five-year career at NTV, he has produced and presented "Sesler ve Renkler" (Sounds and Colors), "Hindistan'da Düğün ve Cenazeler" (Weddings and Funerals in India), "Yolcu" (Passenger), "Her Mevsim Bahar" (Spring in All Seasons), and "Sevgi İle" (With Love). He continued to broadcast news and worked as a presenter at the NTV News Center. At the same time, he started preparing the news from Turkey for CNN International. Over the next five years, he took part in annual educational programs and seminars on "international television journalism" for the CNN Center in Atlanta. From NTV, he moved to CNN Turk, and co-produced and co-presented "Sesler ve Renler" with Pınar Demirkapı. The following year, he worked as CNN's Turkish producer and correspondent. His column "A Day Out in Istanbul" appeared regularly in the *Turkish Daily News*. He has interviewed many international celebrities, and traveled to 45 countries, pursuing countless stories. In 2003, Türkmenoğlu was awarded a Knight-Wallace Fellowship which allowed him to live in Ann Arbor, Michigan, for a year and a half. While at Michigan University, he presented a series of lectures and seminars on "The Last Decade for the Turkish Media." He took classes on Italian Cinema, International Politics, Middle Eastern History and French Literature. Upon his return to Turkey, in 2004, he began working at *Milliyet* newspaper, where he currently conducts interviews and writes the "Gezmek Gerek" (Travel is a Must) page, introducing a new destination every week. He also produces and presents "Sahil Günlüğü" (Coast Diary), and the culture and arts program "Afiş" (Billboard) for CNN Turk. Türkmenoğlu also gives seminars on "Presentation Techniques" and "Media Communication" for private corporations.

His first book, *Üç Kuruş Fazla Olsun Kırmızı Olsun* (Make it Red for a Few Cents More) was published by Epsilon Publications in 2003. His second book *Amerikan Rüyası Tabirleri* (Interpretations of the American Dream) was published in 2005. He received the "Travel Writer of the Year in National Media" award in 2006 and the "Best Travel Writer" award from TUREB (the Turkish Association of Tourist Guides) in 2007. Fatih Türkmenoğlu is married to İdil and has a daughter.

26 MUST-SEE PLACES
IN THE MARMARA REGION

THE MARMARA REGION

ER CAPITAL AND HOME TO
N'S MASTERPIECE
rne

MENOĞLU

One of Turkey's most delightful small cities, Edirne, on the Greek and Bulgarian borders, is a bit like an open-air museum of Ottoman architecture.

Edirne was originally named after the Roman Emperor Hadrian.

Nil Yüzbaşıoğlu

Adorned with several magnificent mosques, including famous architect Mimar Sinan's masterpiece the Selimiye Camii, Edirne boasts some graceful stone bridges, the remains of an early Ottoman palace and a museum of medicine in a beautiful riverside location. It is also the setting for the annual oil-wrestling championships, an orgy of greasy, testerone-fuelled one-upmanship.

Beautifully located on the banks of the Meriç, Arda and Tunca rivers, Edirne served as the Ottoman capital for 92 years.

Edirne became the second capital of the Ottoman Empire after Bursa. The Roman Emperor Hadrian, who visited Thrace in 124 AD, bestowed his name on the city, calling it "Hadrianapolis". In time, Hadrianapolis evolved into the modern name of Edirne.

As a result of its geographical position, Edirne has changed hands many times over the centuries. While the Ottomans were trying to occupy what is now Greece, Edirne served as a military base, and Ottoman Sultan Yıldırım Bayezid (r. 1389–1402) conducted the first siege of İstanbul from here. Later, Sultan Mehmed I ruled the empire

The interior of the Eski Cami (Old Mosque).

Nihal Yuvakuran

Selimiye Mosque.

Nihal Yuvakuran

from this city for eight years. Edirne was captured by the Russians during the 1877-1878 Ottoman-Russian War, but was reclaimed in 1879. It remained under Bulgarian rule during the Balkan Wars and Greek rule after the First World War. Under the terms of the Treaty of Lausanne, it was finally incorporated into modern-day Turkey in 1923.

Mimar Sinan was 84 years old by the time he finished the Selimiye Camii. You can get a superb look at it from the Yalnızgöz Bridge.

Selimiye Mosque – the crooked minaret

Walking through the streets of Edirne is almost like attending a crash course on Ottoman history.

By far the finest building in town, the Selimiye Mosque, a masterpiece of the famous Mimar Sinan, demands several hours of your time. It was built between 1569 and 1575 for Sultan Selim II. Some of its priceless tiles were ripped out and carried off to Russia during the Ottoman-Russian war, but those that remain are still magnificent.

Apparently, all sorts of curious incidents took place during the building of the mosque. One story goes like this:

After construction work was complete, Sinan crossed the street and looked proudly at his masterpiece. Then he started chatting to an old woman and asked for her opinion. After scrutinizing the mosque for some time, she replied: "It's nice, my son, but one of the minarets is crooked."

Sinan immediately sent one team of men up the supposedly crooked minaret while another group waited below. The team at the top then threw a thick rope to the one below, who started to pull. Sinan kept asking the old woman if the

The amazing dome of the Selimiye Camii rises 43m from the ground and has a diameter of 31m.

Nil Yüzbaşıoğlu

minaret was straight yet, and after a few "a little to the right, a little to the left", she finally conceded that it was.

Sinan thanked the old woman and bid her farewell. Once she was gone his men surrounded him and said: "You are one of the greatest architects in the world. Why would you take the words of an old woman seriously? And a 71-meter-high minaret, built to stand the test of time, will surely not straighten itself up after a few workers tug on it with a rope!"

Sinan simply replied: "Of course she was wrong and the minaret was not crooked. And of course you can't straighten it by pulling on a rope. But if I hadn't put a stop to her gossiping, everyone would say forever that, this minaret is crooked."

The 263-meter-long Meriç Bridge was built in 1842

An open-air museum of Ottoman architecture

The Selimiye Camii may be Edirne's most beautiful mosque, but it's also worth dropping into the Eski Cami (Old Mosque), which dates back to 1414, as well as the mid 15th-century Üç Şerefeli Cami which has four different minarets, one of them with three balconies, hence the name meaning "Mosque with Three Balconies". Yet another wonderful mosque forms part of the II. Bayezid Külliyesi (complex), a late 15th-century structure standing in water-meadows within walking distance of Sarayiçi. It houses a museum of medicine showing how sounds and smells were already being used to help with healing, long before the present fad for aromatherapy. Edirne's other small museum contains the finds made at recent excavations around the Macedonian Tower, a partially Roman structure that served as a clock-tower in the 19th century.

It's well worth heading south to look at the lovely Ottoman bridges over the Tunca and Meriç rivers. Here, you'll also find the town's most popular waterside restaurants, where wedding parties take place over the summer.

Meriç River
Nil Yüzbaşıoğlu

WHERE TO **STAY?**

Selimiye Taş Odalar
Phone: (0284) 212 35 29
Newly-opened hotel, which drips with history, sandwiched between the Selimiye Camii and Edirne Museum.

Karam Hotel
Phone: (0284) 225 15 55
Hotel in a restored townhouse with a garden restaurant and live music some nights of the week.

Efe Hotel
Phone: (0284) 213 60 80
www.efehotel.com
Homely atmosphere and reasonable facilities. You can hang out at the English Pub in the evening.

Pera Konuk Evi (Guest House)
Phone: (0532) 361 42 02
A restored Greek house with only two rooms which might suit those who prefer unconventional places to stay. The owners also organize small-group dinners.

Edirne Synagogue
Nil Yüzbaşıoğlu

WHERE TO **EAT?**

Ağa Köşkü II
Phone: (0284) 213 82 82
Near the Meriç river. Good food and live music.

Çiçek Tava Ciğer Salonu (Liver House)
Phone: (0284) 225 20 80
The best place to sample Edirne's famous liver (ciğer).

Edirne Ciğercisi (Liver House)
Phone: (0284) 212 12 08

Murat'ın Yeri
Phone: (0284) 212 34 03
Small, cozy place in Karaağaç opposite the train station. The fish and meat are delicious.

Reis Et ve Balık Restaurant
Phone: (0284) 214 50 85
One of the best places in town for fish and meat suppers. The mezes (appetizers) are great and you wash them down with the famous Tekirdağ rakı.

Park Restaurant
Phone: (0284) 225 56 57
Ideal for kebab-lovers.

Lalezar Restaurant
Phone: (0284) 213 06 00
If you prefer somewhere that serves alcohol, this meat and fish restaurant is located by the river on the road to Karaağaç.

Hocaoğlu Köftecisi
Phone: (0284) 214 73 00
Eat as many meatballs as you can. Who's counting?

London Café
Phone: (0284) 213 80 52
Youthful hangout on Saraçlar Street.

HOW TO **TRAVEL?**

If you take the TEM motorway, Edirne is 230km from İstanbul. Should you pass through Çorlu, stop at the Dörtler Restaurant at the Çorlu exit, opposite the Orion Shopping Center. It is one of the best places to eat meatballs (köfte) in Turkey.
Phone: (0282) 673 14 24

WHAT **TO DO?**

The Kırkpınar Yağlı Güreşi (Oil Wrestling) competitions have been held at Sarayiçi in Edirne at the end of every June for the last 650-plus years. In front of the stadium stand statues of the golden names in oil-wrestling history: Koca Yusuf, Kurtdereli and Kel Aliço. This is the one time of year when you should be sure to reserve a hotel room well in advance.

Shop till you drop in the bazaar. Try Ulaş Şekerleme (Phone: (0284) 225 58 83) or Keçecizade (Phone: (0284) 225 24 81) for badem ezmesi (marzipan) and lokum (Turkish delight). Edirne is also famous for a type of candy called "deva-i misk" and for its "Gaziler helva" (Veteran's helva, a delicious mixture of butter, flour, milk, sugar and almond), as well as for an extremely popular feta cheese. Edirne rag dolls are on sale in the Ali Paşa Bazaar, as are a selection of fruit-shaped soaps and brooms set with blue-eye beads.

002 A TREKKERS' FAVORITE Kıyıköy

Fatih TÜRKMENOĞLU

Set between two rivers, Kıyıköy is a peaceful fishing village overlooking the rough waters of the Black Sea. It's a world away in atmosphere from İstanbul, and a great escape for people, who enjoy long walks and seafood.

The view from Kıyıköy is fantastic from every angle.
Fatih Türkmenoğlu

On the little-visited northern shore of Thrace, lovely Kıyıköy perches on a high hill between the Pabuç and Kazan rivers - the view is simply breathtaking. Otherwise known as Midye (Mussels), modern Kıyıköy (Village on the Coast) boasts a natural harbor that provides a safe haven for fishermen. The locals make a living from fishing and forestry as well as from running pensions and restaurants.

The scattered ruins indicate that there have been settlements in Kıyıköy since antiquity.

Surrounded on three sides by the rough waters of the Black Sea, the village is accessed via a ruined Byzantine gateway.

The main street consists of a chain of lovely old houses, all of them dilapidated. From the road that leads down to the sea, you can reach a sheltered, sandy bay where fishermen drop anchor and people swim in the summer.

As you explore caves which are rumored to have been the haunt of pirates in the past, your imagination will run away with thoughts of the shenanigans that may have gone on inside them. It's also worth looking out for the remains of a tunnel which enabled villagers to escape to the sea unseen, whenever enemies approached the village. On weekends, Kıyıköy fills up with keen İstanbul walkers. Do yourself a favor and visit mid-week.

Monastery of Hagia Nikola

Kıyıköy seems to have been settled in the 6th century and expanded in the 13th and 14th centuries. Until the 1923 population exchange it had a largely Greek population, which has since been replaced by settlers from Bulgaria.

Most of the ruins at Kıyıköy date from the Middle Ages but, fortunately, a philanthropic villager decided to set about preserving the Monastery of Hagia Nikola (St Nicholas) which is set apart from the other ruins. Constructed in the 6th century, during the reign of Justinian, Hagia Nikola is one of the best surviving examples of a rock monastery, although it is in sore need of restoration and decent lighting.

The main things to do in Kıyıköy are eat lots of fish and take long walks. You can also admire the old houses lining the narrow streets.

Fatih Türkmenoğlu

HOW TO **TRAVEL?**

Head towards Edirne on the TEM motorway and take the Çerkezköy exit towards Saray. The 23 km road from Saray has lots of bends but is still beautiful. Kıyıköy is 165 km from İstanbul. If there is no traffic, you can easily get there in two hours. Alternatively, you can take the old road via Avcılar, Çatalca, and Saray. This takes longer but is bound to be more enjoyable.

To get there by public transport, take a Saray bus from İstanbul's Esenler terminal. Minibuses connect Saray with Kıyıköy.

WHERE TO **STAY?**

Kıyıköy Hotel Endorfina
Phone: (0288) 388 63 64
Architect-designed hotel on a headland with great views. Excellent seafood restaurant.

WHERE TO **EAT?**

The fish caught off the nearby island of İğneada is always delicious. Depending on the season, red mullet, turbot, bluefish, black bream, salmon, mussels and crabs abound.

Deniz Feneri
Phone: (0288) 388 60 73-74
Kıyıköy's most famous fish restaurant has a spectacular view and idiosyncratic décor.

City walls

WHAT **TO DO?**

Rent a boat and put to sea, heading for the island of İğneada (Needle Island).

Don't miss the sunset from Kartaltepe (Eagle Hill).

Visit the Kastro creek, 18 km away from Kıyıköy, where it's possible to enjoy nature in complete solitude. The fresh air, the greenery and the soothing sound of water will help you relax, ready for the return to the big city.

Take a bus to nearby Vize, which has the remains of a Byzantine church, bath-house and towers, and a 9th-century cave monastery.

This is a great area for long walks so make sure to pack those extra socks and sturdy shoes. If you prefer, you can also join an organized tour.

Arnika
Phone: (0212) 245 15 93
www.arnika.com.tr

THE NORTHERN AEGEAN'S BEST - KEPT SECRET

003 Enez

Fatih TÜRKMENOĞLU

Because of its proximity to the Greek border, until January 2004, Enez, on the Gulf of Saros, was forbidden territory. This prohibition has finally been lifted but, contrary to expectations, Enez has not yet filled up with tourists. The 4-kilometer-long pristine beach and the wonderfully blue sea are still waiting to be discovered.

In antiquity, Enez was known as "Ainos". This is an exceptionally beautiful area where the Aegean merges with the Meriç River.
Fatih Türkmenoğlu

If you want a complete escape from the stress of İstanbul, a visit to Enez, a little town on a peninsula where the river Meriç flows into the sea, should leave you feeling as if a great weight has been lifted from your shoulders.

Enez has a population of only 3,500, although the number rises in summer, especially when vacationers drive in from İstanbul. Recently, visitors from Greece have also started to come here. Greece is a mere 10 minutes away by sea and it is actually possible to pick out the town of Alexandroupoulis (Dedeağaç) in the distance. However, without a marina and Customs office to welcome them, Greek holidaymakers must still embark on a more circuitous land journey to reach Enez.

It is thought that the first settlements in this area date back to 3000 BC. In Antiquity, Enez was known as Ainos and, as such, crops up in Homer, Herodotus and Thucydides. Towards the end of the Byzantine era, it was briefly held by a Genoese family who had acquired it through a dynastic marriage. In 1456, during the reign of Sultan Mehmed II, the Ottomans besieged the town which gave up without a struggle. In his Kitab-ı Bahriye (Book of Seas), the celebrated 16th-century cartographer Piri Reis, described it as a trade center with two ports; most of its trade appears to have been with the Aegean islands.

If you are after complete peace, Enez should fulfil your needs perfectly.

Military "occupation"

Unfortunately, its location, very close to the Greek border, meant that Enez had to endure a long period in the doldrums as a closed military zone. However, as a probable hangover from those days, anyone who is not from town is still seen as an outsider in the eyes of the locals.

Recent years have seen a sad influx of illegal immigrants,

many of them Afghanis and Iraqis heading for Europe.

The four-kilometer beach is an amazing sight. Unfortunately, the roads still need maintenance, and there is no water at the beach, hence no showers. However, recently the town was awarded a grant of 450,000 €, so things could soon change.

Sightseers will want to look at the old Byzantine walls into which some ancient tombstones are set; İngiliz Kışlası (British Barracks), an Ottoman caravanserai converted for reuse by the British during WWI; and the Fatih Cami which started life as a Byzantine church. The delta, where the Meriç River flows into the sea, is also well worth a look.

Enez Beach
Fatih Türkmenoğlu

HOW TO TRAVEL?

If you are driving from İstanbul, head towards Tekirdağ and then to Keşan. From İstanbul to Enez is about 280km. If you prefer to take a bus, head for Keşan and then take a minibus to Enez. The road to Enez wends its way past fields full of sunflowers; in spring-time the roadsides are also awash with wildflowers.

WHERE TO EAT?

Since this is an area where a river joins the sea, both the fresh and seawater fish are delicious. Try the grey mullet or the eel at Ayı Ahmet taverna or Emre Restaurant. Prices are very reasonable and the fish very fresh.

WHAT TO DO?

Visit Tuz Gölü (Salt Lake), Peso Gölü and Gala Gölü, all of which are popular stopover points for migratory birds.
Take a walk in the Hisar Dağları (Mountains) and gaze down on Turkey and Greece sitting peacefully side by side.

The İngiliz Kışlası (British Barracks)
Fatih Türkmenoğlu

A PEARL ON THE GULF OF SAROS
004 Erikli

Fatih TÜRKMENOĞLU

Erikli is a pleasant small seaside resort 260 km from İstanbul. The sea is clear, there's always a breeze in the evenings, and the fish suppers are delightful. It's the perfect getaway for a short break.

Erikli, which was known as Xeros and Melas in ancient times, is the largest village on the Gulf of Saros.

Fatih Türkmenoğlu

In summer Erikli (which means "with a plum") swells to become the largest settlement on the Gulf of Saros although in winter its population contracts to a few locals, a couple of retirees and a dog. The center of the village is full of summer houses, quite a few of them available for rent; with the first sign of spring, the "for rent" signs pop up all over the place. The pensions and hotels are very reasonably priced and most are either right on the beach or on a road running parallel to it.

The best thing to do in Erikli is to enjoy the sea and the sand.

The Gulf of Saros is the saltiest part of the Aegean Sea. It is said to be able to cleanse itself, although in reality the strong currents and relatively low level of industrialization locally are probably responsible for its clarity. The sand here is beautiful, and the sea deepens almost immediately, but somehow the beach stays relatively uncrowded. A gentle breeze in the afternoon helps alleviate the oppressive heat.

A tranquil holiday

The island of Gökçeada lies immediately across from Erikli; with a boat, you can get there in 45 minutes; without one, it's still nice to be able to dream about it from afar. You can go scuba diving, surfing and sailing in Erikli. The diving schools are open throughout the summer season, although this is very short; Erikli only really fills up during July and August when Turkish schools are closed. Because of its proximity to Greece, Erikli also hosts some holidaying Greeks.

When you've had enough of the sea and the water sports, you can explore neighboring villages such as sleepy İbrice, Danişment, Koruklu, Çeltik and Beyköy. In a part of Turkey that is very close to Greece, the "meyhane" (taverna) tradition is very much alive, which means that you can stretch out a leisurely meal for many happy hours. What's more, the surrounding forests offer several enjoyable walking trails.

This corner of Turkey is perfect for a peaceful holiday. There are no tour boats blasting out music and the bars of the beach hotels (there are only two), turn down the music before midnight. It's wonderful to be able to take long walks on the beach and watch the moon and stars. With no noise pollution to speak of, the only thing that can disturb you is the sound of the waves.

Erikli makes a great base for a holiday involving lots of walking, swimming and good food. It's close to İstanbul and getting here is easy. If you can visit in September, you will find the weather milder and the beach less crowded.

Erikli is only crowded during July and August. Otherwise, this vast beach and this lovely sea are all yours.

Fatih Türkmenoğlu

HOW TO **TRAVEL?**

With a car, drive to Keşan via the İstanbul-Tekirdağ road, then take the Erikli exit (230 kilometers), and drive for another 30 kilometers to reach the village. Buses go to Keşan whence minibuses leave for Erikli every half hour.

WHERE TO **EAT?**

The fish is absolutely fantastic, with plenty of bluefish, sea bream, red sea bream, red mullet, grey mullet, sea bass, black bream and octopus, all fresh from the sea.

Local restaurants also offer sardines, stuffed vine leaves, olives and a hard type of white cheese from Edremit. You'll want to eat non-stop!

WHERE TO **STAY?**

Erikli Hotel
Phone: (0284) 737 35 65
The service is excellent; in summer, they hire enthusiastic, young university students. The hotel's garden is quite popular with young people. With candles lit at night, the beach looks extremely romantic.

İşçimen Hotel
Phone: (0284) 737 31 48
Erikli 's oldest hotel, dating back 30 years.

Sevim Pansiyon
Phone: (0284) 737 30 94
Owner Mrs. Sevim, also runs the local grocery store.

A WINE-LOVER'S BOLTHOLE
005 Mürefte

Fatih TÜRKMENOĞLU

The seaside village of Mürefte lies in an area of rich, fertile soil which is perfect for wine-growing. The sea is glorious, the wines divine. It's a great place to come for a long weekend break from İstanbul.

Keep an eye on the lovely scenery as you drive to Mürefte.

Mürefte is a small settlement, 51km southwest of Tekirdağ. It probably dates back to around 2000 BC and according to ancient sources, the name Mürefte came from the Greek word "miryefton", meaning "of 10,000 fragrances", a name, which makes perfect sense if you visit in spring, when every field will be awash with wild flowers of every hue giving off the most wonderful aroma.

Mürefte offers the perfect getaway for wine lovers.

The drive to Mürefte

The drive to Mürefte is reason enough for a visit, especially in spring. On the way it's worth stopping off in Uçmakdere to have a drink in the teahouse in the village square. Afterwards you can take a quick look at the old wooden houses and at the venerable old plane trees which wear proud plaques identifying them as ancient monuments.

The wineries

The wines produced in this area are legendary and it is small wonder that most of the major wine producers in Turkey have vineyards in Mürefte. Several wine producers offer "degustation" sessions to let you sample their products. Some, but not all of them, charge a fee.

THE DOLUCA STORY

Doluca is one of the best-known names in Turkish wine production. The company started life in the 1930s when Nihat A. Kutman returned from Germany and set up a small plant in Galata in İstanbul. At the time this was a very brave move since until then this was an industry that was traditionally dominated by Turkey's non-Muslim minorities. At first Kutman used only local varieties of grapes for his wines, but then he moved production to Mürefte and started growing Cinsault, Semillon, Gamay and Riesling grapes.
In the 1960s the Mürefte facilities were modernized and Nihat Kutman was joined in the business by his son Ahmet who had studied in California. Together they started growing Anatolian grapes inland from the Sea of Marmara, and gradually names like Villa Doluca, Moskad, Nevşah and Antik carved out a name for themselves in the wine market.

Today, Ahmet Kutman's daughter Sibel has joined the family firm, representing the third generation of a wine-loving family to work at Mürefte. Doluca, now produces 12 million bottles of wine every year, and recently started growing Sauvignon Blanc, Chardonnay, Cabernet Sauvignon and Merlot grapes at its Sarafin vineyard on the Gulf of Saros. Sarafin wines arrived on the market in 1998 and have been selling well ever since.

HOW TO **TRAVEL?**

Leave İstanbul on the Tekirdağ road and then follow the coast road towards Şarköy.

WHERE TO **EAT?**

Fish, shrimps and grapes, accompanied with lots of wine! The coastal restaurants are good, as are the cafés and restaurants on the beach.

WHERE TO **STAY?**

There is no accommodation in Mürefte, so if you want to stay the night in the area, you will have to continue on to Şarköy, 13km away.

Yapıncak Turistik Tesisleri
Phone: (0282) 528 84 44

Sohbet Motel
Phone: (0282) 518 11 40

Sedef Motel
Phone: (0282) 518 10 94

WHAT **TO DO?**

Take photographs of the old houses that survived the earthquake of 1912.
Visit Hoşköy and Hoşköy Hora Feneri (Lighthouse).
Eriklice is a lovely place to picnic.
Visit Tekirdağ, which has a pleasant sea-facing promenade and two small museums. One is a straightforward archaeological collection, the other a memorial to Prince Francis II Rakoczy (1676-1735), a rebellious Hungarian prince, who was exiled to Turkey and given asylum by Sultan Ahmet III. The museum is housed in an old wooden house and contains some lovely watercolors of old Tekirdağ.

ON THE TRAIL OF **THE OTTOMANS**

İstanbul

Saffet Emre TONGUÇ

The Ottomans competed with the Byzantines to adorn the new capital of their empire with architectural gems. There are reminders of their efforts all around the city but especially on the historic Sarayburnu (Seraglio Point) peninsula, often called Old İstanbul and listed by UNESCO as a World Heritage Site. There are so many Ottoman monuments in the city that this section is only a first taste focusing on the most outstanding buildings, including one of the masterpieces of the great 16th-century architect Mimar Sinan.

Süleymaniye Mosque: a view of the interior.
Bünyad Dinç

Süleymaniye Mosque

Designed by architect Mimar Sinan (c. 1497-1588), the Süleymaniye Mosque is one of the most spectacular reminders of the Ottoman Empire. Regarded by some as just the largest and by others as the most beautiful mosque in the city, the Süleymaniye crowns the third hill of İstanbul, the "City of Seven Hills", and can be seen from miles around. The Süleymaniye was commissioned by the celebrated Ottoman Sultan Suleyman the Magnificent (r. 1520-66) to celebrate his thirtieth year on the throne. Construction of the mosque started in 1550 and lasted for seven years. The four minarets indicate that Suleyman was the fourth Ottoman sultan to reign in İstanbul, and the 10 "şerefes", or minaret balconies, reveal that he was the tenth sultan since the establishment of the empire. The mosque complex consists of a number

Süleymaniye Mosque
Saffet Emre Tonguç

There are several cafés in the Grand Bazaar.

Saffet Emre Tonguç

of structures ranging from a caravanserai to a medrese (seminary), and from a hamam (bath) to a hospital. The tombs of Sultan Süleyman and his Ukrainian wife Hürrem Sultan (Roxelana) can be seen in the mosque's garden. In the opposite corner lies the modest grave of Mimar Sinan himself.

Grand Bazaar and the Spice Market

Dating back to 1461, Kapalıçarşı, the Covered or Grand Bazaar, has nearly 60 streets and 4,000 shops. It's one of the oldest and largest bazaars in the world and is set on the second hill of the city. The bazaar's main street houses countless jewelry shops while the myriad leather, carpet, textile, pottery, copper, antiques, and souvenir shops fill the labyrinthine back streets. In each shop, customers are offered freshly brewed tea – a symbol of Turkish hospitality – either on arrival or during the lengthy business of bargaining!

Eminönü features a smaller version of Kapalıçarşı: the Spice, or Egyptian, Market. Built to provide an income for the Yeni Cami (New Mosque) right beside it, this bazaar offers an introduction to the aromatic world of spices. Apparently, it was the last stop for camel caravans traveling along the Silk Road. From Turkish delight to precious saffron, from caviar to henna, you can find almost anything in this colorful and intoxicating place. They are both closed on Sundays.

Cağaloğlu Hamamı (Bath)

The Turks were inspired by the Romans when it came to building their own baths. Much like its Roman predecessors, a hamam (bath) consists of a frigidarium (soğukluk), tepidarium (ılıklık) and caldarium (halvet). Although modernity is doing its best to eliminate traditional hamam culture from daily life, İstanbul still houses many beautiful hamams that compete to entice customers into their hot and steamy atmospheres. Commissioned by Sultan Mahmud I in 1741 the Cağaloğlu Hamamı has welcomed many famous figures from King Edward VIII to Franz Liszt, and from

A view of the Spice Bazaar

Bünyad Dinç

The Sultanahmet Mosque was built over the grounds of the old Byzantine Palace of Daphne.
Saffet Emre Tonguç

famous nurse Florence Nightingale to actor Tony Curtis. Although it is İstanbul's best-known hamam, some may prefer the smaller, less pretentious baths that are hidden away in the back streets; the Zeyrek, Çinili and Beylerbeyi hamams are less touristy, and thus all the more authentic.

Sultanahmet (Blue) Mosque

Facing Hagia Sophia is the splendid architectural jewel called the Sultanahmet Mosque. Built by Sedefkar Mehmet Ağa between 1609 and 1616, the Sultanahmet Mosque dramatically changed the city's silhouette. When it was built, it was the only mosque in the world with six minarets, In addition to the painted wall decorations, the interior of the mosque boasts more than 20,000 blue-and-white İznik tiles, and is called the Blue Mosque by foreigners. Light streaming through 260 stained-glass windows also throws different shades of blue onto the carpeted floor. Sultan Ahmet, who commissioned the mosque, was laid to rest in a grand tomb beside the mosque.

İbrahim Paşa (Pasha) Palace

Currently used as the Museum of Turkish and Islamic Arts, what was once the palace of the grand vizier İbrahim Paşa stands in the Hippodrome. When his vizier's palace loomed larger than he thought appropriate, Sultan Süleyman the Magnificent ordered the pasha's execution - a fate İbrahim shared with many other Ottoman bigwigs! The museum was selected as European "Museum of the Year" a few years ago and the objects on display are fabulous. The portal brought from the Ulu Camii (Mosque) in Cizre, the Seljuk tiles and the enormous Uşak (Ushak)

Sultanahmet (Blue) Mosque
Saffet Emre Tonguç

carpets are particularly breathtaking. On the ground floor, a not-to-be-missed section is dedicated to the lifestyles and handicrafts of the nomads and other rural residents of Anatolia. The courtyard café is one of İstanbul's best-kept secrets; you stare at the Sultanahmet Mosque in awe as you sip your coffee. Closed on Mondays.

Topkapı Sarayı (Palace)

Topkapı Palace served as the seat of government and as a private home for the Ottoman Sultans for 400 years. The palace takes its name (which literally means Cannon Gate Palace) from a former gate in Sarayburnu, which used to be full of cannons. The sprawling complex encompasses Hagia Irene Church, the impressive Archeology Museum, and lovely Gülhane Park, while the palace itself is set around four courtyards. In the main part of the palace, the Chinese porcelain collection is breathtaking and the Pavilion of the Holy Mantle, which holds the so-called "Sacred Trusts", including the cloak, sword, and other relics of the Prophet Muhammad, is particularly intriguing for Muslim visitors.

You must purchase a separate ticket to visit the infamous Harem, which is accessed from the second courtyard; a visit takes you through the private quarters of the sultans' families. The Treasury, in the third courtyard, consists of four rooms full of priceless objects, including the 86-carat Kaşıkçı (Spoon-maker) Diamond, which first surfaced during the reign of Sultan Mehmed IV.

The views from the palace are spell-binding. From one terrace, you gaze down on the Bosphorus and the Sea of Marmara, while from the other you look all the way across the Golden Horn and the seven hills of the city. Closed on Tuesdays.

Topkapı Palace.
Bünyad Dinç

The Kaşıkçı Diamond in the Topkapı Palace Treasury

Favorites' Apartments in Harem
Saffet Emre Tonguç

Atatürk died at Dolmabahçe Palace on 10 November, 1938. The name of the palace literally means "filled garden" because the palace was built on land reclaimed from the sea.

Şemsi Güner

Dolmabahçe Palace

In order to prove that the Ottoman Empire was not the "Sick Man of Europe" that foreigners claimed, the later Ottoman sultans constructed a number of palaces along the Bosphorus even as their power crumbled around them. Completed in 1856, the Rococo Dolmabahçe Palace replaced the 400-year-old Topkapı as the imperial base. It was designed by the celebrated Balyan family of architects and completed in 13 years. The palace contains 285 rooms, 43 halls and 6 bathrooms. The most impressive section is the hall between the selamlık (men's quarters) and the harem (women's quarters) which contains an immense 4.5-ton chandelier made of Bohemian crystals and a stunning silk Hereke rug. Atatürk lived in this palace for several years and visitors can inspect the flag-draped bed in which he died in 1938.

The palace has its own 600-meter-long quay and an impressive clock-tower still showing Arabic numerals. The mosque at the entrance was built to commemorate Sultan Abdülmecit's mother Bezmialem Valide Sultan. Closed on Mondays and Thursdays.

WHERE TO **EAT?**

At several places on İstanbul 's historic peninsula you can enjoy a tasty meal while following in Ottoman footsteps.

Fes Café
Phone: (0212) 526 30 70
www.fescafe.com
The owners have two cafés, one in the Grand Bazaar on Halıcılar Street and the other on Ali Baba Türbe Sokak, a Nuruosmaniye back street. The decoration is unique, the tables are always decorated with fresh flowers, and the food and service are both great. They also have a shop called Abdulla where you can buy natural soaps, "peştemals" (hamam bath towels), and bedspreads. A refined combination of East and West, the cafes and shop come highly recommended.

Bahar Restaurant
Phone: (0212) 512 74 39
The Bahar serves delicious home-cooked dishes in the Yağcı Han, next to the Nuruosmaniye Gate into the Grand Bazaar.

Havuzlu Restaurant
Phone: (0212) 527 33 46
One of the few real restaurants inside the Grand Bazaar, the Havuzlu ("with a pool") is on the street behind the atmospheric Şark Kahvesi ("Oriental Coffeeshop").

Sultan Pub
Phone: (0212) 511 56 38
www.sultanpub.com.tr
Perfect for drinks. On the tramline in Sultanahmet.

Balıkçı Sabahattin
Phone: (0212) 458 18 24
Ideal for fish lovers. In the back streets of Sultanahmet.

Pudding Shop (aka Lale Restaurant)
Phone: (0212) 522 29 70
www.puddingshop.com
Historic café, much beloved of the hippies, where you can enjoy some Turkish specialties as well as international food.

Tarihi Sultanahmet Köftecisi
Phone: (0212) 520 05 66
Famous for its meatballs. Cheap and delicious.

Kurucu Ali Baba Kanaat Lokantası
Phone: (0212) 520 76 55
Try the kurufasulye-pilav (haricot beans and rice) with a magnificent view of the Süleymaniye mosque in the background.

Darüzziyafe
Phone: (0212) 511 84 14
The former soup kitchen of the Süleymaniye Mosque is now a lovely restaurant serving Turkish specialties.

Hamdi Restaurant
Phone: (0212) 528 03 90
www.hamdirestaurant.com
Both the kebabs and the view are great.

007 Byzantine İstanbul

Saffet Emre TONGUÇ

When the French want to suggest abundance, they say "C'est Byzance," meaning "it is Byzantine". Interestingly, the Turkish idiom "Bizans Entrikası" alludes to secret plots and scheming…

Mosaic of Empress Zoë and Emperor Constantine IX Monomachos in Hagia Sophia's southern gallery.

Saffet Emre Tonguç

The Byzantine Empire was one of the most significant and longest lasting empires in history, and what best exemplifies it is the wonderful city of İstanbul, which still preserves some of its Byzantine magnificence. King Byzas is thought to have been one of the founders of a settlement here in 660 BC. Later, the Roman Emperor Constantine established the city of Constantinople, which he named after himself. The city went on to become the capital of the Roman Empire. When the empire was divided into two in 395, the city continued to be the capital of the Eastern Roman Empire, better known as Byzantium. Following the Ottoman conquest in 1453, Sultan Mehmed II crowned the city as the new capital of the Ottoman Empire. The Byzantines always seem to have regarded themselves as Roman, yet after the 16th century, romantic European historians preferred to use the name "Byzantine Empire" in order to distinguish the Eastern Roman culture and civilization - which resembled Rome in terms of administration but chose Orthodox Christianity as its religion and Greek as its language - from the classical Roman Empire.

A majority of the mosaics in Hagia Sophia were created in the 9th century, after the Iconoclastic period.

How many cities in the world can boast that they have served as the capital of three major empires, are set on two continents, and are surrounded by seas on all three sides? İstanbul is surely the only one.

THE BOULEVARDS AND SQUARES OF BYZANTIUM

The present-day Sultanahmet Meydanı (Square) was once called the Augusteion. Byzantium was regarded as the center of the world, and so the Milion Stone was erected in this square. The Milion was used to calculate the distance from Byzantium to other cities of the Roman Empire and stands near the Basilica Cistern. Divanyolu, along which the tram passes today, was the main boulevard of the city and was called the Mese, or Middle Way. Çemberlitaş, then the Forum, housed the Column of Constantine which still survives today. Constantinople's largest square at the time was the Forum Tauri, also known as the Forum Theodosius, where present-day Beyazıt Square stands; what is left of the large monument that used to adorn the square lies scattered on the main street today. A few streets down from the Forum stands the Church of Mirelaion, now the Bodrum Camii (Mosque). Forum Bovis (Ox Square) was another important square; during the Ottoman Empire, settlers from the city of Aksaray near Cappadocia moved here and the square was renamed after their home town. The famous Via Egnatia once stretched all the way to Bakırköy, which is near the airport, and then onto Durres in modern Albania.

The Çemberlitaş or Column of Constantine is very close to the Grand Bazaar.

The Obelisk (Dikilitaş) in the Hippodrome (At Meydanı) was built by Thutmosis III of Egypt (1502-1448 BC) in 1450 BC to commemorate his victories in Asia. It was brought here from Egypt by Theodosius the Great.

Serhan Güngör

Underground Cistern
Saffet Emre Tonguç

BYZANTINE CISTERNS AND AQUEDUCTS

Basilica Cistern (Yerebatan Sarayı)

A magnificent masterpiece from the period of famed Byzantine emperor Justinian I, the Basilica Cistern resembles an underground palace and is therefore called the Yerebatan Sarayı (Submerged Palace) in Turkish. The 1500-year-old structure consists of 336 columns spread over a 140m by 170m space. After the Roman Empire embraced Christianity in the 4th century and wanted to demolish all pagan symbols, the two Medusa bas-reliefs on the column bases at the far end were reused in the building of the cistern. Since the Ottomans preferred drinking spring water rather than still water collected in cisterns, this particular cistern was used to irrigate the palace gardens. Today, the cistern has been restored and fitted out with suitably atmospheric lighting and music. It makes a great place for a visit.

There are over a thousand cisterns on İstanbul 's historic peninsula.

Further up Divanyolu from the Basilica Cistern, the 15-meter-high Philoxenos Cistern stands near the entrance to the Palace of Justice (Sultanahmet Adliyesi). Originally named after a Roman senator, the cistern contains only 224 columns despite its pet name, Binbirdirek (1001 Columns) Sarnıcı. These days it operates as a tourist establishment. Not far away from it is the Theodosius Cistern hidden inside Eminönü Belediyesi (Municipality/Town Hall).

There are several other Byzantine cisterns in İstanbul. Among these are, the Aetios Cistern in Karagümrük, named after a forgotten Byzantine governor; Aspar Cistern (Çukur Bostan) in Çarşamba; and the curiously-named Fil Damı (Elephant Roof) in Bakırköy. Another imposing cistern also lies beneath the Nakkaş carpet shop in Sultanahmet.

Aqueduct of Valens

Known as Bozdoğan Kemeri in Turkish, this aqueduct was built by the Roman Emperor Valens in 375. Approximately one kilometer in length, the aqueduct has double-tiered arches and is 20 meters high. It was once used to channel water from the Belgrade Forest into the Nymphaeum Maximum (the Great Fountain) near Şehzadebaşı. Part of the aqueduct is visible on the way to the Süleymaniye Mosque.

Aqueduct of Valens
John Armstrong

BYZANTINE MONASTERIES AND CHURCHES

Studion Monastery and Ayios Ioannis Prodromos Church

Built in the mid-5th century, the church of St John the Baptist of Studios is regarded as the oldest surviving Byzantine church in İstanbul and was once part of a very important monastic complex, the Studion. The church was converted into a mosque and given the name İmrahor İlyas Bey towards the end of the 15th century. Located in Samatya, which still preserves its Byzantine name (a corrupted version of İspomatheia), the church retains some of its floor mosaics, although the most beautiful ones are on display at the famous Benaki Museum in Athens. The gate of St. John Studites (Narlıkapı) in the city walls was used to provide access for the emperors when they visited the monastery.

Hagia Sophia (Ayasofya)

Hagia Sophia is, without doubt, one of the most important architectural structures in the world. Hagia Sophia (Holy Wisdom) and the Church of Hagia Irene (Holy Peace), behind it in the grounds of Topkapı Sarayı, represent the two most important attributes of Jesus Christ. Built by two of the most important architects of the time, Anthemius of Tralles and Isidore of Miletus, in a period of five years with the help of 10,000 workers and 100 masters, Hagia Sophia is an astounding achievement. The church was completed in 537 and was used as the center of the Patriarchate until the conquest of İstanbul in 1453 when it became a mosque. Later, it was converted into a museum during Atatürk's time. Today it stands as a witness to religious harmony. In one corner there is a huge calligraphic circular sign bearing Allah's name, and on another wall there is a mosaic of Jesus Christ flanked by the Virgin Mary. The priceless frescoes, which offer clues to the history of Christianity, greatly enhance the beauty of this 7500–square-meter structure.

From the gallery you can really appreciate what an immense structure Hagia Sophia is. Supported by 108 columns taken from other earlier structures, including the Temple of Artemis in Ephesus, Hagia Sophia was the largest church in

Hagia Sophia Museum

Saffet Emre Tonguç

the world for almost a thousand years. As you leave it, the mosaics of Emperors Justinian (who ordered the construction) and Constantine (who founded İstanbul) salute you.

Chora Church (Kariye Camii)

The original name of the Kariye Camii (mosque) was Chora, which means "country". The church's full name in Greek actually translates as the Church of the Holy Saviour in the Country, a name given to it because, when first built, it was outside the Constantinian city walls. Despite the 11th-century building's relatively small size, its mosaics and frescoes are superb. In the 1320s the celebrated Byzantine statesman Theodore Metochites bequeathed most of the sublime mosaics to the church and then added his own image to a mosaic of Jesus Christ. The building consists of an entrance hall (narthex), a main hall (naos), two corridors (exonarthex and esonarthex) and a parekklesion (side chapel), which contains the most vivid of the frescoes.

The mosaics on the walls depict the main events in the life of Christ, starting with the story of the parents of the Virgin Mary and ending with the Resurrection. There are only three mosaic panels in the naos; these show the Virgin Mary and the infant Jesus, Jesus Christ himself, and the Dormition of the Virgin. The remaining sections depict other interesting stories from the Bible.

Chora Church, details

Church of Saints Sergius and Bacchus (Küçük Aya Sofya Camii)

Often referred to as Little Hagia Sophia, this old church is located immediately inside the Çatladıkapı (the Bull and Lion Gate) which led to the harbor and the Bucoleon Palace. It was built by the Emperor Justinian in 527 and anticipates the architecture of the Byzantine church of San Vitale, Ravenna; completed in 547, San Vitale contains magnificent mosaics of Justinian and his infamous wife Theodora. Originally named after two saints, Sergius and Bacchus, who were tortured to death in the early

The parekklesion of Chora Church is richly decorated with frescoes.

Saffet Emre Tonguç

The Church of the Ecumenical Patriarchate of Constantinople (Fener Rum Patrikhanesi) is dedicated to St George.
Serhan Güngör

4th century, Little Hagia Sophia contains Greek inscriptions in the upper gallery, close to the dome.

Theotokos Panaghiotissa Church
(Mary of the Mongols)

As you wander through the streets of Fener and Balat on the Golden Horn (Haliç), you stumble upon an incredibly rich heritage, just waiting to be discovered. The whole place is saturated with history and the different layers of civilization blend neatly into one another. Unfortunately, most of the structures and monuments are crumbling and neglected. One of Mimar Sinan's baths is used as a shop, for instance, while Küçük Mustafa Paşa Hamamı, the oldest bath in İstanbul, has long been abandoned and the lead from its dome stolen. Even the enchanting wooden houses, the last surviving examples of local secular architecture, are starting to disappear.

Incredible riches wait to be discovered in the back streets of Fener and Balat.

Fener contains one striking structure, which resembles a fairy-tale castle. Most people mistake it for the Greek Orthodox Patriarchate, but in fact it is the Fener Greek High School, also known as "The Red School" because of the color of its bricks. Next to it is the Theotokos Panaghiotissa Church, otherwise known as St Mary of the Mongols. The only remaining Byzantine church preserved in its original state, Theotokos Panaghiotissa is a rare example of a trefoil church in İstanbul. In 1453 the architect, Atik Sinan (Christodoulos), a "Greek" who was responsible for Fatih Camii (mosque), pleaded successfully with Sultan Mehmed II. At his request, St Mary of the Mongols became the only church not to be turned into a mosque. A copy of the decree ensuring its survival is still preserved inside the building.

The church's name is as interesting as its history. Emperor Michael Paleologos sent his illegitimate daughter Maria to marry the Mongolian Khan Hulagu. By the time poor Maria reached distant Mongolia, she found that Hulagu had been killed. Instead, she was married to his son Abaka Khan, who was, in turn, killed by his brother, Ahmed Khan. The unfortunate Maria returned home and became a nun.

In front of the Church of the Pantocrator stand dilapidated wooden houses.

Saffet Emre Tonguç

St Theodosia Church (Gül Camii)

Near Kadir Has University on the Golden Horn (Haliç), this church, with its unusually tall dome, was once known as the Church of Hagia Theodosia. Legend has it that on the saint's day (29 May) preceding the Conquest, the locals filled the church with roses and prayed that the Turks would not be able to breach the city walls. History shows that their prayers went unanswered, but when Fatih's soldiers walked into the church and found it covered in petals, they renamed it the Gül Camii (Rose Mosque).

Beneath this 11th-century structure is a crypt reserved for the graves of the empire's most distinguished individuals. Opposite the church stands a library commissioned by Adile Sultan, a 19th-century Ottoman princess, and famous poet and philanthropist, who also built the Kandilli High School for Girls over on the Asian side of the city.

The name "Zeyrek" commemorates Molla Zeyrek Mehmet Efendi, a 15th-century scholar, who was instrumental in converting the church into a mosque.

Church of the Pantocrator (Zeyrek Camii)

"The Pantocrator" is one of the titles ascribed to Jesus Christ and means "Almighty" or "All-powerful." The 12th-century Church of the Pantocrator is on a hill to the right as you head from Unkapanı to the Aqueduct of Valens. Made up of three separate structures, it is the second largest Byzantine edifice in İstanbul after Hagia Sophia.

Although it was the former capital of Byzantium, İstanbul still lacks a Byzantine Museum and, the Pantocrator Church would make the perfect place for one. After centuries of neglect the poor church wreaks of mildew. The beautiful red bricks in the narthex are obscured by a white ceramic-tiled ablutions fountain but splendid mosaics lurk beneath the rugs and frescoes languish under the whitewash on the walls; the candlesticks were stolen some time ago.

Church of the Theotokos Pammakaristos (Fethiye Camii)
Bünyad Dinç

Externally, you are looking at a once-lovely Ottoman structure now nearing the end of its days. After the Conquest the church was used as a medrese (seminary) by Sultan Mehmed II. Today a lovely café with a view sits right in front of it.

Church of the Theotokos Pammakaristos (Fethiye Camii)

Briefly used as the seat of the Greek Orthodox Patriarchate in the mid-15th century, this church can be found in the back streets of Fatih. It was possibly built by Emperor John Komnenos and his wife in the 12th century. During the reign of the Ottoman Sultan Murat III in the 16th century, the church was converted into a mosque and was renamed "Fethiye" (Conquest) in honor of the Sultan's victories in Georgia and Azerbaijan. Its original name "Theotokos Pammakaristos" literally means "the all-praised Mother of God". The church's mosaics are regarded as some of the best in any of İstanbul's Byzantine churches, third only to Chora and Hagia Sophia.

Monastery of Constantine Lips (Fenari Isa Camii)

Located on Vatan Boulevard, close to the old Amusement Park this complex, with its seemingly extraordinary name, was originally built for Constantine Lips, a celebrated Byzantine admiral. Created by merging two separate structures, the monastery ended up with a grand five aisles as well as four roof chapels. Converted into a dervish lodge by Fenari Ali Efendi in the 15th century, it was later used by the eminent preacher, Sheikh İsa, hence the compound name "Fenari İsa".

Church of Theotokos Kyriotissa (Kalenderhane Camii)

Built in the 12th century, this church stands in front of the aqueduct on the way to Süleymaniye Mosque. The frescoes, depicting the life of St Francis of Assisi, are the jewels of this Byzantine church. Probably, painted a mere 25 years after his death, these are the earliest paintings of the saint to survive. Unfortunately, it is difficult to make out much detail as most of the cycle is hidden beneath the paint and plaster of the mosque.

Church of Theotokos Kyriotissa (Kalenderhane Camii)
Saffet Emre Tonguç

You can see the mosaics of the Daphne Palace in the Mosaic Museum next to the Arasta Bazaar.

Saffet Emre Tonguç

Daphne or the Great Palace

İstanbul was adorned with many palaces during the Byzantine era. One of the most important was the Daphne Palace which stood just where Sultanahmet (Blue) Mosque does today. The Hippodrome, immediately in front of it, was where horse races were held in Byzantine times. Here stood the Kathisma, a private box which allowed the emperor to watch the races, with a tunnel beneath it so he could make a speedy escape if necessary. Some remains of the original 400-meter-long Hippodrome can still be seen underneath the present-day Marmara University building. In Ottoman times the Hippodrome's name was changed to At Meydanı (The Square of the Horses), the name it still bears today.

In the Hippodrome stands a 3500-year-old granite Egyptian Obelisk (Dikilitaş), also known as the Column of Theodosius, which was brought here from Egypt in 390. Another Byzantine obelisk, the Column of Marcian, is tucked away in one of the Fatih back streets. Erected in honor of the Emperor Marcian in c. 450, this obelisk is called Kıztaşı (Maiden's Column) in Turkish because of the relief of Nike, the Greek goddess of victory, carved into it.

Inside the park attached to the Palace of Justice in Sultanahmet, you can still see the remains of the old Antiochos Palace. On the waterfront, near Ahırkapı, stood the Mangana and Bucoleon palaces. You will notice the walls and windows of the Bucoleon Palace as you head out to Çatladıkapı. The palace was restored during the reign of Justinian but was severely damaged during the Fourth Crusade of 1204. The ruins of the Magnaura Palace lie scattered around the Four Seasons Hotel. Next to the İstanbul Belediyesi (Municipality) building and above the Haşim İşcan Passage stand the remains of the Anicia Juliana Palace and its church, the Polyeuktos.

Tekfur Sarayı (Blachernae)

The Blachernae Palace complex was built in the 6th century. After the brief period of Latin government (1204-61), the palace became the permanent residence of the Byzantine emperors. What is left of the complex today is the Palace of Constantine Porphyrogenitus, known in Turkish as Tekfur Sarayı (the Palace of the Emperor). This building was used as a tile factory in Ottoman times. Cyrus Hamlin, who founded Robert College (present-day Bosphorus University) in the 1860s, actually considered incorporating the Tekfur Sarayı into the campus at the time.

Tekfur Sarayı (Blachernae)

Saffet Emre Tonguç

AND MORE...

City Walls and Gates

Old İstanbul had extensive land and sea walls, and long sections are still intact, stretching for nearly 20 km; they make one of İstanbul's most impressive sights. When the original walls built during the reign of Constantine could not meet the needs of the expanding city, the Emperor Theodosius II ordered the construction of the present-day walls in 413. Since it was next to impossible to conquer the city from the sea and there was already a heavy chain closing off the Haliç (Golden Horn), the sea walls needed to be less elaborate than the land fortifications. These included inner and outer walls with a ditch between them, as well as various gates to provide access for the military and the public. From the marble gate on the Marmara seafront to the shores of the Golden Horn, 13 gates were built along the coast. These include Yedikule, Belgradkapı, Silivrikapı (Selymbria), Mevlanakapı (Rhegium), Topkapı (St Romanus), Sulukule, Edirnekapı (Charisius), and Eğrikapı. After Sultan Mehmed II's conquest of İstanbul, Yedikule was partially reinforced with a tower and additional walls and was converted into a fortress; today it serves as a museum. At the entrance to Yedikule, you can still see the Byzantine symbol of the double-headed eagle.

The most important structure in this area is the gate the Byzantines called the Porta Aurea (Golden Gate), which was used by emperors and commanders to facilitate their triumphal return to the city after a victory. Yedikule was used first as the treasury then as a prison during the Ottoman period. At the turn of the 17th century, the Ottoman crown prince Genç Osman was executed here after attempting to slash the power of the Janissaries.

Prison of Anemas

This prison, which bears the name of an Arab commander who served the Byzantine Empire, held many important captives, including half-a-dozen emperors. It is located on the Golden Horn, inside the walls overlooking Fatih Bridge, next to Tekfur Sarayı.

Galata Tower

Built by Genoese traders in 1348 during the Byzantine era, this structure was initially called the Tower of Christ. Following restoration work in the 1950s, a roof was added to the tower and a restaurant opened on the top floor. The tower is 61 meters tall and offers a spectacular view of İstanbul with the seven hills of the old town on one side and the Bosphorus on the other. In 1453, when the Ottomans had conquered İstanbul, the keys to the tower were handed to Sultan Mehmed II. The tower was used as a prison thereafter.

İstanbul City Walls
Saffet Emre Tonguç

WHERE TO **EAT?**

Four Seasons Hotel
Phone: (0212) 638 82 00
This former prison-turned-luxury-accommodation was selected as the best hotel in Europe for several years in a row. The food in the courtyard restaurant is magnificent and the Sunday brunches are simply divine.

Yeşil Ev
Phone: (0212) 517 67 85
www.istanbulyesilev.com
The garden offers a shady oasis in summer.

Ayasofya Konakları
Phone: (0212) 513 36 60
www.ayasofyapensions.com
As you eat on the terrace of the hotel restaurant, you can flirt with Hagia Sophia right in front of you.

Develi
Phone: (0212) 529 08 33
www.develikebap.com
The celebrated kebab house is still a favorite Samatya hotspot.

Asitane
Phone: (0212) 534 84 14
www.kariyeotel.com
Ever wondered what kind of food would have been served at the circumcision ceremony for Sultan Süleyman the Magnificent's sons? Then take a look at Asitane's menu which probably offers the best Ottoman cuisine in the entire city. The world-famous Zagat Survey cites it as perfect for a dinner worthy of a sultan. It is right next to the Kariye Mosque (Chora Church).

NBUL ISLAND HIDEAWAYS

e Princes' Islands

RKMENOĞLU

When an İstanbul resident talks of "the Islands" they usually mean the Princes' Islands, a cluster of nine islands, only five of them inhabited, in the Sea of Marmara, where the lucky few still maintain summer homes. Imagine walking amid pine trees, riding a bike, smelling the fresh air, looking at beautiful houses, and even listening to İstanbul from far, far away... The Islands, especially Büyükada, Heybeliada, Burgazada, and Kınalıada, are an echo of the past, the last stand of an elegant lifestyle, now all but lost.

The Princes' Islands are the pearls of İstanbul, a must-see for anyone staying in this beautiful city.

Saffet Emre Tonguç

Büyükada (Prinkipo)

Büyükada is the largest (hence the name "büyük", meaning "large", and "ada", meaning "island") and most dashing of the islands. The beauty of the streets, the houses, the trees, the flowers and even the cats suck you in immediately. This is a place where mimosas burst into flower in spring and where the blossoming Judas trees invite you to stop and take pictures. Best of all, with motorized vehicles barred from the island, it is the music of clip-clopping horse hoofs that you hear in the background instead of the roar of traffic.

Büyükada was called "Caria" in Byzantine times and it was the place that held out longest during the conquest of İstanbul in 1453. Later its name was changed to Prinkipo. During the 700 years of the Byzantine Empire, Büyükada was famous for its prisons; several important figures were sent into exile here either because of rivalry or because of "Byzantine" dirty tricks. Later, the Russian revolutionary Leon Trotsky lived here in exile from 1929-33, a period he is said to have greatly enjoyed.

In 1861 Sultan Abdülaziz set up the "Adalar Belediyesi" (the Municipality of the Islands), with Büyükada as its administrative center. The island suffered considerable damage in the 1894 earthquake and from fires in the early 20th century. After the 1940s, there was a considerable increase in the number of people buying or renting summer homes on the island.

Every visit to the Islands will feel like the first one. Their beguiling beauty will astound you every time.

In 1984, it was declared a historic site and was brought under state protection.

Büyükada is a sizeable island where you can rent bikes to get around. A much nicer – and lazier! – option is to hire one of the horses and carriages that stand waiting near the main

A seagull flying in front of Büyükada

Saffet Emre Tonguç

square. Most offer fixed tours of the island but if you want something more specific the drivers may be open to negotiation.

This is a place where it pays to go the extra mile. The Monastery of St George (Aya Yorgi) sits near the top of one of the highest hills on the island and as you climb up to visit it you will spot pieces of cloth tied to tree branches, usually by women who are praying for a child. Each year on April 23 (St George's Day), some people ascend the steep hill on bare feet, so deep is their faith that their prayers will be answered. No matter when you visit, though, the views out towards İstanbul will be magnificent.

"If you wonder what old İstanbul was like, spend some time on Büyükada..."

Büyükada has always held an important place in Turkish literature and old Turkish movies. Each little street holds another surprise and it is a delight to come face to face with houses in which famous literary figures and politicians have lived. It's also worth looking out for the Con Paşa and İzzet Paşa mansions, as well as the choicest hotel of a bygone era, the Splendid. Then, there's the dilapidated Greek Orphanage and Hristo Tepesi (Hill of Christ)...

Dil Burnu (Cape) and Yörük (Nomad) Ali beach are great places to explore. Should you happen upon football legend Lefter Küçükandonyadis (ex of Fenerbahçe) cycling round the island, then your Büyükada tour will be complete.

A not-to-be-missed pleasure of Büyükada: the horse-carriage tour.

Bünyad Dinç

WHERE TO **STAY?**

Splendid Hotel
Phone: (0216) 382 69 50
Not quite as splendid as in its heyday but still very comfortable. Some rooms have lovely sea views.

Aya Nikola Pension
Phone:(0216) 382 41 43

WHERE TO **EAT?**

After a long and tiring day of cycling, wonderful mezes (appetizers), fish and rakı await you in the İskele (Harbor). Afterwards, the Lunapark Coffeehouse is very pleasant as is the Portofino Patisserie in the main square.

Alibaba Restaurant
Phone: (0216) 382 37 33
www.buyukadaalibaba.com

The Greek Orthodox Seminary on Heybeliada
Nil Yüzbaşıoğlu

Heybeliada (Halki)

According to the locals, Büyükada is the "city" whereas Heybeli is just the "island." Its former name was "Halki" which was probably derived from the Greek word "Halkos" (copper), because there was a copper mine on the island in antiquity. The Turkish name Heybeli ("with saddlebag") may have been chosen because of the island's shape - we don't know for sure.

In the 16th century, the island provided shelter for rich Christians who wanted to escape an outbreak of plague in İstanbul. Later, it suffered considerably from a fire and a series of earthquakes in the early 20th century. In 1924, a new sanatorium helped revive the island's fortunes. İsmet İnönü, the first prime minister and later second President of the Turkish Republic, spent some time in the sanatorium and always kept his ties with the island, which helped increase its popularity even more. The sanatorium finally closed down in 2006.

It would be wonderful to visit the church of Haghia Triada (the Holy Trinity) but this is attached to what was a Greek Orthodox theological seminary until the 1970s and you need to get permission to do so in advance. If you can get permission from the Commandant of the Naval College near the landing stage you could also visit the small church of the Blessed Virgin Kamariotissa, the last church

to have been built in the area before the conquest of İstanbul in 1453. Failing that you can take a look at the Çam Limanı (Pine Grove Harbor) and Değirmen Burnu (Cape Mill) or take a stroll to Sadık Bey Beach.
Both Hüseyin Rahmi Gürpınar (1864-1944), a celebrated writer and politician, and Ahmet Rasim (1865-1932), a journalist, writer and historian, lived on Heybeli. Before leaving the island, it's worth recalling the famous verses of Rıfat Ilgaz (1911-93) which sum up the island perfectly:

Don't forget to visit the house of Hüseyin Rahmi Gürpınar, the celebrated writer and politician. His personal belongings are preserved exactly as he left them...

"How can you not like Heybeli?
I have neither a house, nor a garden
Nor a rowboat at the pier
Nor money to spend.
The pines, the sea, the moonlight are mine.
I have no strength to climb the asphalt.
I do have a share in the wind
Though only for a mouthful of air..."

WHERE TO **STAY?**

Merit Halki Palace Hotel
Phone: (0216) 351 00 25
A stay here is rather like a trip back in time to the 1950s. Great pool and restaurant.

Naval High School.
Saffet Emre Tonguç

You can eat meat cooked in a tandır (clay oven) at Kalpazankaya on the far side of the island. Don't return to the city without sampling the food at the Barbayani, Mehmet Usta or Antigoni restaurants to the left of the landing stage.

Burgazada

Although it is only two square kilometers in size, Burgaz is the third largest of the islands. Since it provided sheltered anchorage for boats, it was known as "Panormos" (safe harbor) in ancient times. Later it was called "Antigone". Following the conquest of İstanbul in 1453, it was renamed Burgaz after the Greek word "pigros" (bastion).

Referred to as "Burgazlu" in famous 15th-century admiral and cartographer Piri Reis's book, Burgaz is a beautiful island.

The loveliest houses on Burgaz are in Gezinti, Gönüllü and Mehtap streets. You can also visit celebrated writer Sait Faik's house and the Aghios Ioannes Prodromos (St John the Baptist) Church. On the far side of the island, Kalpazankaya offers the best access to the sea.

Until 2003 the island was heavily wooded but unfortunately a bad fire has left the landscape largely barren.

Kınalıada

Kınalıada, originally called "Proti" (meaning "first" in Greek), is the closest of the islands to İstanbul and it was probably this proximity to the city that led to its being attacked by pirates during the Byzantine era. Like the other islands, Kınalı served as a handy prison. After the Battle of Malazgirt (Manzikert) in 1071, the defeated Byzantine Emperor Romanos IV Diogenes was held captive on this island.

The island was named "Kınalı" (Henna Island) because the old iron and copper mines give the soil a reddish hue.

At one point Kınalı was home to three important monasteries. Two of them were demolished before the conquest of İstanbul. The third, which Diogenes had built and which later served as his prisc still survives.

Beautiful Kınalıada Camii (Mosque) was built in 1964 by architects Turhan Uyaroğlu and Başar Acarlı. The dome, the triangular minarets and the glass exterior make this a rare modern mosque that stands out for its architecture. There is also an Armenian church on the island.

Should your visit happen to fall on 6 August, head straight for the Christos Monastery, where you will be met with an incredible feast of meats, rice, salads and wine and with a festival of music and dance.

The sea is cleaner than it used to be although you may prefer to take a dip at the Ayazma Kamo Tesisleri (Club) or at the Su Sporları Kulubü (Water Sports Club). Kınalı is the calmest of the islands. Unfortunately, in recent years, the concrete apartment blocks have begun to swamp its old romantic beauty.

Şemsi Güner

WHERE TO **EAT?**

The fish and mezes (appetizers) at Mimoza Restaurant and Kınalı Sofrası are exquisite although prices are not cheap.
A particular Kınalı tradition is to buy a rose-shaped ice cream from Dondurmacı (ice cream maker) Yücel. Yücel makes the ice cream entirely from fresh fruit without using any preservatives. After walking and swimming, it tastes really excellent.

And the rest...
Of the remaining islands, Yassi ("Flat") is at least worth a footnote as the place where prime minister Adnan Menderes was tried and sentenced to death in 1961. It's not a lot more cheering to learn that Sivri ("Pointed") Island was where several sultans attempted to abandon the city's stray dogs. Once they were saved by a storm at sea. On another occasion fires that broke out in the city were taken as a bad omen and the dogs were brought back home again.

ɹUL FROM THE WATER

ɹosphorus Boat Ride

JRKMENOĞLU

ɹnaps the best way to get a feel for İstanbul is to take ˎ boat ride along the Bosphorus, accompanied by wonderful waterside yalıs (mansions), glorious Ottoman palaces, a tower with a fairy-tale history, and the constant screech of seagulls. It doesn't matter how often you've done this trip before – it's guaranteed to have you falling in love with the city all over again.

A Bosphorus cruise offers an unforgettable intercontinental boat ride.

Saffet Emre Tonguç

The Bosphorus ("Boğaz", or "throat" in Turkish) is that magnificent stretch of water that separates the European and Asian shores of İstanbul. It extends 30 km all the way from Sarayburnu, the city's historic peninsula with all its magnificent monuments to times gone by, to the Black Sea at Anadolu Kavağı. Even now, when many of the wonderful wooden "yalıs" (waterside mansions) that used to line the shores have been ripped or burnt down, the beauty of the Bosphorus is still absolutely magnetic and few things can be more enjoyable than taking a day trip all the way along it, looking out for historic palaces and ancient castles, and floating beneath the twin modern bridges without which the İstanbul traffic would grind to a complete halt. At Anadolu Kavağı you can stop for a fish lunch and climb up to the remains of a castle with a view down to the Black Sea. Then it will be time to hop back into the ferry for the return journey via Kanlıca, well-known to İstanbulites for its thick and tasty yoghurt.

If the Judas trees are in bloom, a Bosphorus cruise will be even more of a delight.

Why the Bosphorus?

According to Greek mythology, the king of the gods, Zeus lusted after a priestess called Io. Afraid of getting caught by his jealous

Hekimbaşı Salih Efendi Yalı in Anadolu Hisarı

Saffet Emre Tonguç

wife Hera, he decided to turn her into a cow. Of course Hera was not fooled by this ruse, and sent a gadfly which tormented poor Io into wandering the earth until eventually she crossed what is now known as the Bosphorus and gave it its name which means "ox passage" in Greek. The story had a happy ending because Io eventually escaped to Egypt where Zeus had the decency to restore her to human form.

Yalıs old and new

In Greek, the word "yalı" is used to refer to the waterfront in general, although in Turkish it means a large waterside house. The Bosphorus yalıs are graceful wooden mansions that sit right beside the water with landing-stages for boats to tie up at them. The first yalıs were built in the early 18th century, during the so-called Tulip Era, but most date back to the 19th and early 20th centuries. Unfortunately, as population pressure made land along the Bosphorus more valuable, many were either demolished or caught fire in sometimes suspicious circumstances. Those that still remain are aptly described by the locals as "the pearls of the Bosphorus".

History on both sides... Eminönü to Bebek

Shortly after leaving Eminönü, where ferries for the Bosphorus tours depart, you will see the old sheds that now house the İstanbul Modern Art Museum on the European shore. Immediately opposite, there is a magnificent view of Sarayburnu (Palace Point) with the Topkapı Palace, Hagia Sophia and Sultanahmet (Blue) Mosque giving it a wonderful silhouette. A little further along, you will spot Kızkulesi (Maiden's Tower), just off Üsküdar on the Asian shore. This tower boasts the perhaps predictable story of a young princess locked away to protect her from the threat of early death, which finds her out anyway, when an old lady arrives with a fruit basket containing a snake.

The elaborate 19th-century

Boasting mythological origins, historical mansions and great natural beauty, the Bosphorus is a symbol of İstanbul.

Serhan Güngör

A FIVE-STAR BOAT ON THE BOSPHORUS

A growing number of Bosphorus tours are being organized, and the extra demand has resulted in the arrival of better and more luxurious boats. Keyif Style is one of these more luxurious crafts. Many visiting heads of state have been hosted on this boat, which offers superb service. The company has 14 boats in its fleet, and according to Altan Tuzluoğlu, PR Manager for Keyif Organization, 50% of their clients are foreigners. The most popular reason for hiring one of their boats is to hold a wedding at the point where the two continents meet on the Bosphorus. At almost 50% of these weddings, either the bride or the groom or both are foreign. Rates start at €35 per person. Phone: (0212) 277 43 63 www.keyiforganizasyon.com

The Küçüksu Pavilion was commissioned from famous architect Nikogos Balyan by Sultan Abdülmecit, Construction was completed in 1856.
Saffet Emre Tonguç

Dolmabahçe Palace then looms up on the European side, followed shortly afterwards by the pretty early 20th-century Beşiktaş landing stage, which was recently given a makeover. A little further along you will see the Four Seasons Bosphorus Hotel and the luxurious Çırağan Palace Hotel, with its wonderful swimming pool right on the water's edge. On the opposite shore is the late 18th-century Pink Yalı, more correctly called the Fethi Ahmet Paşa Yalı.

As you approach the Bosphorus Bridge look out for Ortaköy (Middle Village) on the European shore; this is one of İstanbul's liveliest nightlife hubs. Facing it, and almost immediately beneath the bridge, is Beylerbeyi Palace, which looks like a cut-down version of the Dolmabahçe and was once the home of Sultan Abdül Aziz (r. 1861-76). Still on the Asian side you will also spot the twin towers of the Kuleli Miltary School which was built in 1860.

Some days the seagulls are particularly greedy; the more you feed them, the more they want.

Back on the European side of the strait, the boat will sail past lovely Arnavutköy (Albanian Village) which retains many of its wonderful wooden houses, some of them turned into restaurants and cafes but others still occupied. A little further along you pass the beautiful Art Nouveau building in Bebek that used to house the Egyptian Consulate.

Rumeli Hisarı to Anadolu Kavağı

Over on the Asian shore you should keep your eyes peeled for the white Kıbrıslı Mustafa Emin Paşa Yalı, Küçüksu Palace and the late 17th-century Köprülü Amcazade Hüseyin Paşa Yalı which is the oldest surviving wooden mansion on the Bosphorus. Shortly before İstanbul's second bridge, the Fatih Sultan Mehmet Köprüsü, will loom up with the unmissable ruins of Rumeli Hisarı on the European shore. This castle was built in 1452 as Mehmed the Conquerer readied himself to drive the Byzantines out of the city for good. These days it serves as a museum. On the opposite shore are the less dramatic remains of Anadolu Hisarı, its older and smaller twin.

The boat continues past Kanlıca and then, on the Asian shore, you'll see, high on a hill, the Hıdiv Kasrı, a wonderful Art Nouveau summerhouse built for the last khedive (Ottoman governor) of Egypt in c.1900. On the European side the boat skirts Emirgan and the pretty harbour at İstinye before coming to Yeniköy (New Village), a particularly upmarket suburb where you'll see the 19th-century Sait Halim Paşa Yalı, now restored for use as a banqueting hall.

Further still, you pass Tarabya and Sarıyer before arriving at Rumeli Kavağı where some people will want to disembark to sample the fish restaurants. Otherwise you can continue to Anadolu Kavağı on the Asian side and the end of the run.

"A boat takes off from İstanbul, with İstanbul on all sides of the boat

The boat is İstanbul from one end to the other

A boat

A shackle

An İstanbul..."
(Aydın Hatipoğlu).

Fatih Sultan Mehmet Bridge
Saffet Emre Tonguç

WHERE TO EAT?

The crew of the Bosphorus ferries come round at regular intervals touting tea, fresh orange juice, toast and Kanlıca yoghurt. The best places to disembark for a fresh fish lunch are Rumeli Kavağı on the European side and Anadolu Kavağı on the Asian side.

Rumeli Hisarı (Fortress)

HOW TO TRAVEL?

İDO (İstanbul Sea Buses) has two boats that leave from Eminönü in the morning. The 10:35am service stops at various landing stages and then docks at Anadolu Kavağı where it waits for three hours before returning to Eminönü at 4:30pm. The 1:35pm boat gets to Anadolu Kavağı at 3pm and returns at 5pm. Phone (0212) 522 00 45 or (0212) 444 44 36. For online information or reservations: www.ido.com.tr.

If you don't want to take the whole cruise it is still possible to take a "poor person's cruise" (i.e. just to catch a ferry from one place to another). Whatever route you choose, this will still let you get a taste of the Bosphorus and its fantastic scenery. The İDO company operates 15 ferries, 47 passenger boats and 20 service boats. Board one of their ferries from any one of the 56 landing stages, including Eminönü, Karaköy, Kadıköy and Beşiktaş, and you will see crowded İstanbul from a very different perspective. Schedules change at weekends and in winter but tickets are very cheap.

If you don't have much time, you can hop on a boat from Arnavutköy landing stage and sail to Bebek, Kandilli, Anadolu Hisarı and Emirgan. After a while, the boat returns, stopping at the same places. Bebek Pier: Phone (0212) 263 60 23. Departures Office: Phone (0212) 249 16 95.

Private motorboats to tour the Bosphorus leave from Eminönü, Beşiktaş, Kadıköy, and Ortaköy, especially in summer and over weekends. At weekends, boats leave from Ortaköy every 20 minutes after 1pm (hourly on weekdays). A tour lasts for an hour. Phone: (0212) 236 27 38.

The Presidential Summer Palace in Tarabya

To rent a luxury boat:

- Süreyya III, Süreyya V and Bebi boats
  Phone: (0216) 575 47 75
  www.adaturizm.com
- For The İstanbul and The İstanbul 2
  Phone: (0212) 326 11 00/82 72
  www.swissotel.com.tr
- For imperial caïques worthy of sultans
  Phone: (0212) 296 52 40
  www.sultankayiklari.com
- Taşkent Yachts
  Phone: (0216) 492 23 93
  www.taskent.com.tr

To rent a regular boat

Turyol
Phone: (0212) 251 44 21
www.turyol.com.tr
Lüfer
Phone: (0212) 229 64 64
www.lufer.net
Yat Atilla
Phone: (0216) 422 52 97
www.yatlatilla.com
Küçük Prens
Phone: (0212) 227 95 72
www.kucukprens.com
Gümüş Damla
Phone: (0212) 23 40 10
www.gumusdamla.com

DAY TRIP ESCAPES FROM İSTANBUL

010 Poyrazköy and Anadolu Kavağı

Fatih TÜRKMENOĞLU

Tuck into a fish lunch at Anadolu Kavağı, then climb up to the remains of a castle which overlooks the Black Sea. Watch the ships on the Bosphorus from Anadolu Feneri and go swimming at Poyrazköy. Technically speaking, you are still in İstanbul, but this day trip is a world away from the inner-city hustle.

A small İstanbul suburb with a village atmosphere right at the point where the Bosphorus meets the Black Sea, Anadolu Kavağı is a heaven for lovers of fish lunches with more than 10 restaurants vying to offer competitive prices. There's not a lot to do here apart from tucking into a meal sustaining enough to ready you for a climb up the steep hill behind the village. This leads to the remains of Yoros Castle, a Byzantine structure, possibly built on the site of a temple to Zeus, which the Genoese used as a watchtower in the 14th century. Today the, ruins are unremarkable, but in its heyday this castle was bigger than the one at Rumeli Hisarı on the other side of the strait. Not surprisingly, it offers a breathtaking view out over the Bosphorus and towards the Black Sea. Who knows? If you're lucky, you might spot one of the dolphins, who have recently returned to the Bosphorus.

Pristine beauty which could be hundreds of kilometers away from İstanbul.

Lighthouse and beach

Once past Anadolu Kavağı, you are venturing into a part of Turkey that most people completely overlook, even though some of the bays in the area are inviting and completely secluded.

After exploring the castle, you can drive on to Anadolu Feneri (Lighthouse) where a lighthouse and mosque look very picturesque together. A little further along the road is Poyrazköy, so named after the poyraz, the chilly north-easterly wind that whips down the Bosphorus in winter. Its one specific monument is a small 18th-century fortress. The Greeks were the first to settle here. Then came the Byzantines, then the Ottomans, and finally immigrants from the distant Black Sea settlements of Trabzon and Rize. Poyraz has a lovely beach overlooking the crystal-clear sea; unfortunately you may find it covered in litter. A small café sells all sorts of food and drinks, and the fish in the restaurants is as fresh as it comes.

On the way back to İstanbul, it's worth popping into Akbaba village which boasts a great coffee house beneath a majestic plane tree: Café Barbi. The Turkish classical music played there and the refreshing tea will set you up for the rest of the day. In Beykoz, you can visit the tomb of Yuşa Hazretleri, a famous Muslim holy man. Legend has it that Yuşa Hazretleri and Telli Baba, who is buried on the European side of the Bosphorus, jointly protect the strait.

The sea off Anadolu Kavağı and Poyrazköy is really clean. This area is rarely busy except over summer weekends. But this is the Black Sea where dangerous undercurrents are common. It's best not to swim too far off-shore.

HOW TO **TRAVEL?**

Regular ferries serve the Anadolu Kavağı-Rumeli Kavağı-Sarıyer route.

Other ferries also run direct from Sarıyer to Anadolu Kavağı and Poyraz. Alternatively, you can get there by using the excursion boats from Eminönü. There are also three daily ferries between Kavak and Poyraz.
If you are using buses, take the no 15 from Üsküdar which serves the Kavacık-Anadolu Kavağı route. To get to Poyraz, take the no 135F from Beykoz.
If you are driving, it's 34km from Kavacık to Poyrazköy. The road is narrow but fun. It takes a while to get there but the journey is certainly worth it.

WHAT TO **EAT?**

Fish, fish, and more fish! Both Poyrazköy and Anadolu Kavağı are filled with fish restaurants, and the mussels are a particular delicacy. The local ice cream is also a must. Watch out for all those extra calories!

WHAT **TO DO?**

If you visit in the summertime, you can swim, sunbathe, and play beach volleyball at Poyrazköy. The beach is open from 8:00am to 7:30pm daily. Showers are available, and beach umbrellas can be rented.

THE SPA AMID THE PLANE TREES

011 Yalova Termal

Fatih TÜRKMENOĞLU

The thermal springs of Termal, near Yalova, have been healing patients since c. 2000 BC. Today they still welcome visitors who want to bathe amid the giant plane trees or try out a thermal version of the Turkish bath. The walking trails and the arboretum are equally alluring.

According to legend, the thermal springs at Termal first sprang to life after an earthquake in c. 2000 BC. The region then developed into a spa during Roman times. The 17th-century Ottoman travel writer Evliya Çelebi reported that the main Kurşunlu Banyo (Leaded Bath, so named because of its lead roofing) was constructed by a grateful father when his daughter was cured of scabies after bathing in the local water. The bath-house was repaired by Sultan Abdülhamit in 1900 and has been given yet another face-lift recently. There are few places nicer to swim in all of Turkey than its outdoor pool, which is surrounded by verdant fir trees. Look carefully at the outside of the bath-house and you'll see Roman tombstones reused in its décor.

Termal offers the perfect breathing space for those who want to escape the stress of İstanbul.

Atatürk at Termal

Turkey's first president, Mustafa Kemal Atatürk, visited Termal in 1929 and was very taken with it. He had an arboretum planted on the slopes rising up behind the baths and then had a summer house built for himself too. Finally, he ordered work to start on construction of the Termal Hotel in 1936, although this has since gone the way of so many other old buildings in Turkey. These days Atatürk's house is open to the public, although you must visit it on a guided tour, alas given in Turkish only. The house is stuffed with Yıldız porcelain and other extravagant items that seem very ill at ease with the generally austere furnishings.

Healing waters

Experts agree that the waters of Termal are good for helping rheumatism, sciatica, gastro-intestinal problems, and gall bladder diseases, regardless of whether you drink it or bathe in it. Aside from swimming in it at the Kurşunlu Banyo, you can also rent a private bathroom in the Sultan Banyo or undergo the familiar Turkish bath routine, but with the chance to take a dip in piping hot water as well at the Valide (Mother Sultan) Banyo. No matter which option you decide to go for, it's bound to be enjoyable.

A tale of martyrdom and miracles

A sign in front of the Çınar Hotel tells the tragic story of the virgin sisters Menodora, Metrodora and Nymphodora who lived here in the early 4th century and pursued a life of Christian contemplation, healing the sick through prayer. The local prince of Bithynia heard of the women and summoned them to see him. His efforts to convert them to his own religion or to get them to marry his noble friends were unsuccessful, whereupon he had them tortured to death. But as soon as he ordered their burial, the heavens opened and fire consumed the prince and the torturers. A sudden rainfall then extinguished the flames so that the locals could bury the women.

The Atatürk Pavillion
Fatih Türkmenoğlu

HOW TO **TRAVEL?**

It's easy to get from İstanbul to Yalova with or without a car on the İDO sea-buses from Yenikapı. Frequent minibuses run from Yalova bus station to Termal, 12km away.

WHERE TO **STAY?**

There are many small hotels and pensions, all offering thermal water, in the uninviting, nearby village of Gökçedere. They mainly cater to visiting Arabs.

Çamlık Hotel
Phone: (0226) 675 74 00
Averagely good hotel in a great location, right in the middle of Termal. The rooms at the back are cheaper than those in the front. The Çınar in the centre of the village is under the same management.

WHAT **TO DO?**

Visit the Sudüşen Waterfall, 6km away inside the forest. The road is rather rough, but the waterfall is beautiful and there's a 2 km-long walking trail.

Don't miss Hayrettin Karaca's arboretum on the Yalova-Termal road (Phone: (0226) 833 77 67).

Drop into the potato-bread shop of Georgian baker Seyfi Baba in Gökçedere. Seyfi Görürü is known locally as "Philosopher Seyfi" because he has come up with more than 2,500 aphorisms or pithy sayings, most of which take quite a lot of translating.

A HILL FOR ALL SEASONS

012 Kartepe

Saffet Emre TONGUÇ

In the outskirts of Maşukiye, near İzmit, Kartepe welcomes trekking fans from April to the end of November and then hosts skiers in the winter. Whether you want to escape the summer heat of the city or to enjoy a few hours of skiing, it makes the perfect getaway from İstanbul.

Once you bypass the İstanbul traffic, and the İzmit industrial zone, you will quickly come to Maşukiye and the green route leading to Kartepe. A lovely road curves out of the forest and carries you up to the top of the hill; on a clear day, you can see all the way to Lake Sapanca and the Gulf of İzmit. If you come in winter, you can strap on your skis immediately and lose yourself in a ski resort set in a sprawling 3.5 million square meters of land.

Kartepe and its environs are very attractive with waterfalls and creeks on one side and hidden paths on the other…

The 'Kartepe' (Snow-capped Hill) at 1700m dominates everything, and you will soon feel yourself caught up in its enchantment, especially at that time of year when the leaves turn to reds, oranges and browns.

For skiing and snowboarding enthusiasts, Kartepe offers 4 ski lifts and 42-kilometers of ski runs on 14 slopes. Beginners can enjoy the easy runs, while more accomplished skiers can go off-ski runs and ski among the trees on the steep hillside. As you get better, you will be directed to the more difficult

runs among the trees. A special baby-lift area is reserved for children and beginners.

If you are into ski touring, you can join the trainers on a 25-km course, which offers all sorts of modern equipment, including GPS. Then, in the afternoons, you can join the après-ski parties held at Kadıkonağı, at the bottom of the ski runs. A glass or two of mulled wine, soft music drifting from the loudspeakers, and cozy chats with friends ensure that the long day of physical exertion soon seems a long way away!

Nor is that the only way to recover. The hotel has a great fitness center, complete with sauna, steam bath, and indoor pool. Experienced masseurs are on hand to give you a relaxing massage.

Kartepe is worth visiting even at snow-free times of year. Nearly 3,000 species of plant grow on the hillside, and deer, bears, coyotes, and rabbits lurk amid the trees. Tennis courts, volleyball pitches and two soccer fields that meet FIFA standards are available for use throughout the year.

One of the biggest advantages of Kartepe, formerly known as Keltepe, is its proximity to İstanbul.

HOW TO **TRAVEL?**

If you are leaving İstanbul, follow the TEM motorway towards İzmit. After driving for 94 kilometers, take the "İzmit Doğu Çıkışı" exit. Maşukiye is about 10 kilometers from the tollbooths. Once you pass through it, it's a 17km drive to Kartepe. The whole trip should take about two hours.

WHERE TO **STAY?**

The Green Park Resort
Phone: (0262) 315 47 00
www.thegreenpark.com
This lovely 250-room hotel houses the open-buffet Şimşek Restaurant, as well as à la carte Italian and Ottoman restaurants. For those who want to prolong their evening, the Roof Bar on the top floor is perfect. The hotel also offers seven meeting rooms, a ballroom and a congress hall suitable for meetings.
Next to the hotel are 50 apartments, each with two bedrooms and a living room which makes them ideal for families.

WHERE TO **EAT?**

There are several trout farms and restaurants in Maşukiye and near Alabalık Vadisi (Trout Valley) where the Yayla Creek flows down from Kartepe. Baked on brick with butter and mushrooms, the trout here is finger-lickin' good!

Some of the restaurants on the way to Kartepe offer a beautiful view of Lake Sapanca. Vadi (Phone: (0262) 354 22 02) and Motali (Phone: (0262) 354 32 38) restaurants in Maşukiye are very good. You can also enjoy meat specialties at Kadıkonağı Restaurant in Kartepe or try some "sucuk-ekmek" (garlic-flavored sausage and bread) at Geyikalanı (Phone: (0262) 315 47 00) restaurant on the summit.

A LAKE AND A WALKER'S PARADISE

013 Sapanca and Erdemli

Fatih TÜRKMENOĞLU

Just half an hour's drive from Sapanca brings you to the village of Erdemli where the creeks, waterfalls, fish restaurants and walking trails are perfect for shedding all that big-city stress.

Sapanca Erdemli village house.
Fatih Türkmenoğlu

The village of Erdemli, near Lake Sapanca, is so small and lovely that it is hard to resist its charm.

The village consists of a single mosque and a handful of houses, and is surrounded by a spectacular forest. The Şelale Creek wends its way down to Lake Sapanca through this forest; in places it's little more than a ripple but sometimes the water cascades over sizeable waterfalls. No Hollywood movie could hope to match this scenery.

A four-hour walk

A trekking trail starts on the Soğucak Plain and takes about four hours to complete, there and back.

As you walk through enchanting forest the chestnut, oak, linden and beech trees sometimes grow so close together that they almost block out the sky.

After admiring Lake Sapanca, you can walk for hours around Erdemli.

It's as well to come prepared as you may need to wade through some of the creeks.

If all that sounds too much for you, there are other shorter forest walks out of the village and these will take you across creeks and cute little wooden bridges.

Afterwards you can tuck into a superb trout supper at the İstanbul Balık Evi (Fish House).

Lake Sapanca

Six kilometers across at its widest point, Lake Sapanca is one of Turkey's larg stretches of inland water. It is connected to the Sea of Marmara and drained by .. Sakarya river. Very beautiful from a distance, it is starting to suffer from the various new uses to which it is being put, amongst them serving as a drinking-water reservoir for İstanbul and providing water for local industrial plants. There are many hotels and restaurants beside the lake, as well as lots of villas under construction as weekend cottages.
The lake is a magnet for waterfowl and you should be able to see common and red-crested pochards as well as coots on the water.

HOW TO **TRAVEL?**

Leave İstanbul on the TEM motorway and take the Sapanca exit; continue along this road without entering Sapanca itself. The village of Erdemli is only 6km from Sapanca and the road there is very beautiful. The journey is about 140km from the center of İstanbul. You can also get there by bus with Ağa Tur (Phone: (0264) 582 79 10)

WHERE TO **EAT?**

İstanbul Balık Evi
Phone: (0264) 582 67 39
www.istanbuldere.net
Of the several trout farms with restaurants in Erdemli, the most famous is İstanbul Balık Evi. The trout is brought from local breeding farms and casseroled with butter, grilled, or deep-fried. The owners also bake their own special bread and serve home-made village baklava for dessert. Prices are very reasonable. If the weather is good, you can enjoy your meal in the terraced garden or by the lake; if it's bad they have plenty of space inside as well. By the time you read this there may be a few wooden chalets for rent as well.

WHERE TO **STAY?**

There is no accommodation in Erdemli itself. Most people come for the day, but if you do want to stay, there are plenty of hotels and pensions in Sapanca.

Sakarya University Education and Accomodation Facilities
Phone: (0264) 582 25 30
Seven kilometers from Sapanca town center and close to the lake. Apartments offer a double room and living room.

Club Lale Hotel
Phone: (0264) 582 89 30
www.laleotel.com

Kedikaya Aparts
Phone: (0264) 592 28 94
www.kedikaya.net
No food available here.

Richmond Nua Wellness Center
Phone: (0264) 582 21 05
www.richmondnua.com
If you really want to spoil yourself the Richmond offers one of Turkey's finest spas.

Zeliş Çiftliği
Phone: (0264) 592 05 85
Pleasant small guesthouse in Kurtköy, at the west end of the lake, with a great reputation for its food.

WHAT **TO DO?**

Lots of walking. Bring extra clothing, socks and even shoes (it gets pretty muddy out here). Pack a raincoat just in case it rains, which it does – a lot!

Eat plenty of the delicious locally-reared trout.

Try some of the chestnut honey made by residents who have moved here from from Artvin. It is surprisingly bitter but still delicious.

Buy a basket from one of the many roadside hawkers.

OME OF A THOUSAND TILES
ik

KMENOĞLU

Set on the shores of a peaceful lake, İznik is a wonderful old walled town with an extraordinary history. Tree-lined streets are dotted with monuments to Turkey's pre- and early Ottoman history. Come here to learn about the ancient art of tile-making and maybe to pick up a piece or two to take home.

Three nouns sum up what İznik has to offer - history, a lake and tiles.

İznik was originally founded by Antigonius, one of Alexander the Great's generals, in 316 BC. However, in 301 BC, Lysimachus took the city from him and gave it his wife's name: Nicaea. During the reign of King Zipoites gold coins were minted here, gaining the town the nickname "the Golden City".

Nicaea soon rose to prominence as one of the most important towns of the Eastern Roman Empire. Churches, cisterns and aqueducts were built, and in 325 Nicaea played host to the first Ecumenical Council of the Christian world; this drew up the Nicene Creed which summarizes the basic tenets of Christianity to this day. In 1075, Kutalmışoğlu Süleyman Şah seized Nicaea and five years later the city was crowned the capital of the Seljuk Empire and renamed İznik. After the Crusaders drove the Byzantine emperor out of İstanbul in 1204, İznik served as the capital of a short-lived, so-called Nicaean Empire for 57 years.

İznik was finally conquered by the Ottomans in 1331 during the reign of Sultan Orhan Bey, who built mosques, inns, religious schools and baths in the area. It became a major stopover point for caravans on the road leading from İstanbul to Anatolia. Several scholars and poets were born here, and most of the celebrated academics of the period taught at the İznik seminaries. After the conquest of İstanbul, however, the town fell from importance and its wonderful monuments were left to rot.

After dipping a toe in Lake İznik, soak up the town's fascinating history and then shop for tiles.

The historic core

The most striking reminder of İznik's historic importance is the five-kilometer-long wall which still encircles much of the town center. It is still possible to walk along considerable stretches of this wall, especially between the Yenişehir and Lefke gates. Otherwise, the most striking attractions are the elaborate old entrances, the most important being the İstanbul, Yenişehir, Lefke and Göl gates.

Right in the town center stands Hagia Sophia (Aya Sofya), the church where the seventh Ecumenical Council convened in 787. These days, the building is just a shell sitting in a sunken garden but it would be hard to over-state its historic significance. Even the great architect Mimar Sinan is believed to have worked on it at one point.

Not far away is the Yeşil Cami (Green Mosque), which was built by Çandarlı Halil Hayrettin Paşa between 1378 and 1392; its minaret is decorated with turquoise tiles that look as if they have strayed from Iran. Across the road stands the İznik Museum which was originally built as an imaret (soup kitchen) by Sultan Murat I for his mother Nilüfer Hatun in 1388. Surprisingly, it is not as full of İznik tiles as you might expect (and hope).

Other monuments worth tracking down include the Hacı Özbek Camii, the first mosque built in İznik, and the 14th-century Yakup Çelebi Mosque and Medrese (Seminary). In Yeni Mahalle you can inspect the remains of an ayazma (sacred spring), once used for baptism rituals, and the Koimesis and Hagios Tryphon churches; the exiled Byzantine king Theodore Laskaris was buried in the Koimesis church which was later deliberately destroyed. Don't miss the remains of an aqueduct built by Emperor Justinian in 530 just outside the Lefke gate.

And if your children are tired of all the sightseeing you might want to take them to look for the so-called "Tomb of the Moodies" outside the İstanbul Gate. Legend has it that ratty kids who're brought here miraculously turn into little angels!

The splendor of İznik tiles...

On his way to Damascus in 1648, celebrated 17th-century traveler Evliya Çelebi stopped in İznik and wrote: "Here, they create such incredible tiles with intricate chameleon motifs that there are no words to describe them." İznik tiles were especially famous for their use of a coral-red glaze which was perfect for depicting tulips and carnations, the flowers most loved by the Ottoman sultans. However, by the 18th century the industry had virtually died out. Then in the early 1990s, a group of tile aficionados got together and set up the İznik Vakıf (Foundation) to revive the lost art; they have been so successful that they now have shops in İstanbul and elsewhere. It is possible to visit their workshop near the Saray gate; if they have space you may even be able to stay in one of their guestrooms.

HOW TO **TRAVEL?**

To get to İznik by car from İstanbul either take the İDO sea-bus from Yenikapı or the Eskihisar-Topçular ferry across the Sea of Marmara. From Yalova, follow the signs to İznik. There are also plenty of bus services between İstanbul and İznik. Call **Ağatur**: Phone: (0224) 757 15 17

WHERE TO **EAT?**

The local olives are delicious, as are the tomatoes and cucumbers. Shrimps, catfish and carp from the lake are also excellent.

Konak Lokantası
Phone: (0224) 757 13 07

WHAT **TO DO?**

The local market takes place on Wednesdays.

The best place to buy a new-look İznik tile is the İznik Vakıf. **The Adil Can-Nursan Atelier** (Phone: (0224) 757 65 29) opposite the İstanbul Gate sells lovely pottery.
Strolling along the lake-shore is always enjoyable and there are plenty of small cafes ready to serve you tea with a sunset view. Don't leave without viewing İznik from Abdülvahab Hill.

If you can persuade the İznik Museum to give you the keys, it would be good to visit the underground tomb in nearby Elbeyli. It dates back to the 4th century and contains remarkable Byzantine frescoes.

WHERE TO **STAY?**

Çamlık Motel
Phone: (0224) 757 1631
Pleasant lakeside hotel with decent restaurant

İznik Vakıf Konukevi
Phone: (0224) 757 6025
Stay with the tile-makers in a stylish small guesthouse with rose garden near the lake.

A FILM SET COMES TO LIFE

015 Cumalıkızık

Fatih TÜRKMENOĞLU

Cumalıkızık is a tiny picture-postcard village with an interesting 700-year history on the outskirts of Bursa. It looks like a cut-down version of more famous Safranbolu. Beautiful old wooden houses, narrow cobbled streets and a general air of rusticity make it a wonderful place to escape to when the Bursa traffic gets too much.

It is impossible to see Cumalıkızık and not fall in love with it. The village doesn't just look like a film set, but it is also a real one since it has been used in the making of numerous Turkish television series and movies. Even when there are no film crews about, it still feels as if a period movie is in permanent production as you amble about the narrow cobbled streets; shooting might have been going on for centuries.

An undamaged Ottoman villagescape

Cumalıkızık offers one of the loveliest surviving examples of an undamaged Ottoman villagescape, and each of the 270 houses (60 of them still inhabited) merits a viewing. None of them is excessively elaborate or ornate but they are perfectly designed for the life that used to be lived in them, when houses featured a great deal less furniture than they do today. Many of them are painted in jaunty pastel colors. An old auntie waves her handkerchief from a bay window on an upper floor. An old couple sell home-made jam at the door to their home. It feels very much as if you are stepping back in time.

Although some of the local houses are dilapidated, most of them are extremely photogenic.

Cumalıkızık was one of the first places, where the Ottomans settled in the Bursa area. Later, a group of Turcoman Kızıks came to live here, hence the suffix "kızık"

Historical Cumalıkızık houses
Fatih Türkmenoğlu

in the name it shares with five or six other nearby villages. Residents of all these villages would come to Cumalıkızık for Friday prayers, livening it up considerably for that one day, hence the prefix "Cumalı" (which roughly means "on Friday" in Turkish).

The local bath and the 700-year-old mosque are both worth visiting, as is the small and dusty museum whose contents were mostly in use until quite recently. There are also slight traces of a Byzantine church here. Do yourself a favor and visit mid-week when the streets will be deserted and the pension prices are lower.

Osmanlı Fırını (Ottoman Bakery) and Silor

Bread aficionados should hotfoot it straight to the Osmanlı Fırını (Ottoman Bakery) run by Rafet Yavuz to buy some delicious sourdough bread. The bakery also sells "silor" which is rather like a ready-made "mantı" (Turkish ravioli) although with an unusual shape and taste.

Fatih Türkmenoğlu

HOW TO **TRAVEL?**

After you leave İstanbul, take the Bayramoğlu exit on the TEM highway and keep going until you reach the Eskihisar-Topçular ferry which will get you to Bursa via Yalova. Alternatively, take the İDO seabus from Yenikapı to Güzelyalı-Bursa. From Bursa take the Ankara road towards Eskişehir and watch for "Cumalıkızık" signs. It's much easier to get there by public transport. Minibuses leave from the town-centre Santral Otobüs Garajı or you can take the hourly no 22 municipal bus to Cumalıkızık.

The Karagöz Travel Agency
Phone: (0224) 221 87 27 in Bursa also runs tours to the village.

WHERE TO **EAT?**

The locals make "tarhana" (a sun-dried dish of curd, tomato and flour) with stinging nettles which is both nutritious and delicious - nettles are supposed to be good for the skin and the digestive system.
Pension breakfasts usually include tomato paste with eggplant and walnuts, as well as thick, tasty bread, gözleme (Turkish pancakes), noodles, honey and home-made jam. They're absolutely delicious. Cumalıkızık is one of the only places in Turkey to grow raspberries and there is a Raspberry Festival every June.

WHERE TO **STAY?**

Both the village pensions are adorable.

Konak Pansiyon:
Phone: (0224) 372 48 69
Chestnuts, marmalade and honey are on sale here.

Mavi Boncuk Pansiyon:
Phone: (0224) 373 09 55
Cozy, traditionally-furnished pension where you can have lunch or dinner even if you are not staying. People from Bursa flock in for Sunday brunch around large samovars.

THE FIRST CAPITAL OF THE OTTOMAN EMPIRE

016 Bursa

Saffet Emre TONGUÇ

Uludağ, the ancient Mt Olympus, dominates bustling Bursa, a historic city full of wonderful monuments dating back to the early Ottoman period. Although it is still often called "Yeşil Bursa" (Green Bursa), industrialization has taken its toll on the city, which has paid its dues by shedding most of the greenery. Nonetheless, it's a wonderful place to linger for a weekend and receives far fewer visitors than İstanbul.

Ulu Cami (The Great Mosque)

Saffet Emre Tonguç

The first six Ottoman sultans are buried in Bursa, a city that was once central to the silk business and still does a roaring trade in textiles. Its name is derived from that of King Prusias I who lived here in the 2nd century B.C. Sources suggest that the Carthaginian king Hannibal, who was in Gebze at the time, helped Prusais I pick its location. Initially overshadowed by İzmit and İznik, the city rose to prominence as a result of the Roman proclivity for taking hot baths in its thermal waters. It also prospered with the silk trade, especially during the reign of the Byzantine emperor Justinian. Although the first Ottoman sultan Osman Gazi laid siege to the city, Bursa was only conquered during the reign of his son Orhan Gazi. Afterwards it was decked out with magnificent buildings as befitted the favorite residence of the first sultans.

Begin discovering Bursa at the Ulu Cami (the Great Mosque) in the town center. Commissioned by Sultan Bayezid I in the early 15th century, the mosque glories in 20 domes instead of the more normal one or two. Legend has it that the sultan promised to build 20 mosques in the city, but when he couldn't keep his word, he made do with

Bursa Yeşil Cami (Green Mosque)

Saffet Emre Tonguç

Entrance to historical Silk Market

Saffet Emre Tonguç

building one with 20 domes instead! The interior of the mosque is decorated with beautiful works of calligraphy, and there is a lovely fountain (şadırvan) in the middle for ritual ablutions.

Right next to the mosque lies the Kapalı Çarşı (Grand Bazaar), which has preserved its local color and is far less touristy than its İstanbul counterpart. In the nearby Koza (Cocoon) Han you can still find beautiful silk scarves on sale. Its courtyard is heavenly in summer; you can sit at one of the tables with a drink and think about the enterprising individuals who smuggled silk cocoons out of China in the 6th century and then started silk production in the Byzantine Empire. If you visit in June or July, you can still see farmers running white cocoons through their hands; they've come here to sell them.

Bursa houses several especially beautiful works of architecture from the early Ottoman period, including the Muradiye and Yeşil Cami (Green Mosque). The Yeşil Cami was built in 1424, during the reign of Sultan Mehmed I; it has a small fountain in the middle, rooms on either side of the prayer area, and an imperial pew upstairs which was reserved for the sultan and his family. As the name implies, the mosque is adorned with lovely green tiles. The tomb next to the mosque is known as the Yeşil Türbe, which means Green Tomb, although it is decorated with turquoise tiles; it's the burial site of Sultan Mehmed I and his family. The surrounding area is a particularly attractive part of town in which to while away a few hours.

Also well worth a look is the lovely Muradiye Complex which has 12 tombs in its sweetly-scented garden. Most of the occupants of the tombs were Ottoman crown princes murdered by members of their own families to prevent them from ascending the throne.

Finally, don't miss the tombs of Osman and Orhan Gazi, the first two Ottoman sultans, who are buried up high at Tophane near an old Ottoman clock-tower and a newly-restored stretch of the old city wall.

The cafés in the courtyard of the historic Koza Han are delightful.

Saffet Emre Tonguç

Mehmed I and his family are buried in the Yeşil Türbe (Green Tomb), which is famous for its turquoise tiles.

WHERE TO **STAY?**

Hotel Çelik Palas
Phone: (0224) 233 38 00
www.celikpalasotel.com
A carefully renovated hotel that still bears the imprint of the past. The hamam (Turkish bath) – a gift from Atatürk - is wonderful, and it is a joy to be scrubbed clean on the marble slab underneath the soaring dome.

Kervansaray Termal Hotel
Phone: (0224) 233 93 00
www.kervansarayhotels.com
Located in Çekirge, the hotel boasts one of Turkey's most beautiful hamams.

Authentique Club Hotel
Phone:(0224) 211 32 80
www.otantikclubhotel.com
A chic, retro hotel with 29 rooms inside Bursa's beautiful Botanical Park at Soğanlı. Its Şifne Restaurant is one of the best in town.

Efehan Hotel
Phone: (0224) 225 22 60
www.efehan.com.tr
Right in the town center, this recently-renovated three-star hotel offers a view of Uludağ from the upper-storey rooms.

Hotel Çeşmeli
Phone: (0224) 224 1511
Excellent city-center hotel run by women and named after a popular drinking fountain. Immaculately kept rooms and hefty breakfasts.

WHERE TO **EAT?**

Beceren
Phone: (0224) 211 52 60
Inside the Botanical Park. Mostly kebabs.

Balıkçı Reşat
Phone: (0224) 222 25 02
Arap Şükrü Sokağı in Bursa is filled with restaurants where you can sit outside and enjoy seafood, particularly in summer. Reşat is one of the best.

Yusuf Restaurant
Phone: (0224) 234 49 54
Open since 1953 in Bursa Culture Park, it offers especially good "kuzu tandır" (lamb cooked in a clay oven).

Çiçek Izgara (Grill)
Phone: (0224) 221 65 26
A Bursa classic, always full of Turkish families enjoying kebabs and other favorites.

Kitabevi
Phone: (0224) 225 41 60
An old Bursa house near the Tophane gate converted into a restaurant/bar/bookstore. In the summer it hosts exhibitions in the garden.

İskender Kebap
Phone: (0224) 221 46 15
City center favorite that dishes up the eponymous İskender kebab, supposedly 'invented' here in Bursa.

Soğanlı Botanik Park
Phone: (0224) 211 26 90
www.kebapciiskender.com.tr
Yavuz İskenderoğlu's restaurants offer delicious Bursa lamb dishes. Kebapçı İskender's menu includes İskender kebab and Kemalpaşa, a famous local dessert consisting of small, round pastries softened in syrup.

Uludağ Kebapçısı
Phone: (0224) 254 72 64
Cemal Usta's little shop in the former Santral Garajı (Central Bus Terminal) is very famous. Since 1964, it has been one of Bursa's best kebab joints.

Most well-off families live in or around Bademli, so several establishments have opened there:

Café de Paris serves as a restaurant (0224) 244 76 01, Pronto (0224) 244 72 26 as a café, and Boo (0224) 244 88 78 as a bar.

Balıkçı Nadir
Phone: (0224) 244 66 18
A good choice for seafood.

WHAT **TO DO?**

Don't leave Bursa without visiting a hamam. The best area for doing this is leafy Çekirge where most of the hotels boast their own thermal baths. The Yeni and Eski Kaplıca (Hot Springs) are open to the public; both are very attractive, although the men's sections are better than the women's.

Visit the TOFAŞ Anatolian Car Museum, the only example of its kind in Turkey - it's housed in an old silk-making factory. Bursa City Museum is a state-of-the-art establishment containing wax figures of the six sultans who lived in the city and much more.

Gümüşlü Café is an oasis in the heart of the city. Sit beneath the plane trees at this cool place, sheltered from the winds.

Buy some candied chestnut from Kafkas (www.kafkas.com)

In ancient İnkaya, a nearby village, there is a 600-year-old plane tree where you can sit and daydream about the past.

A RESORT FOR ALL SEASONS

017 Uludağ

Fatih TÜRKMENOĞLU

Uludağ gazes down on Bursa from a height of 2540 meters. You can go skiing here in the winter, pick flowers in the spring, or just enjoy some fresh air in the fall. No matter what the time of year, Uludağ will always be beautiful - and getting to the ski slopes by cable-car is sometimes half the fun!

View from Uludağ.

Refik Ongan

Literally "the Great Mountain" in Turkish, Uludağ really does live up to its name. With its snow-capped slopes and trees, it completely dominates the surrounding landscape, giving it an unforgettable majesty.

Uludağ is the highest mountain in Western Anatolia. In 1961, nearly 13,000 hectares of land were set aside as national park, a decision you will certainly feel like toasting as you explore the mountainside. Come here in the spring and you will feel as if you are walking on a grass carpet decorated with flowers. Come in summer and it will be refreshingly cool. Come in the fall and the red and orange leaves will astound you with their color. And that's before we get to winter which is when Uludağ really comes into its own.

If you are going to Uludağ in the winter you can rent or buy tire chains on the way up.

In Antiquity, Uludağ was called "Mt. Olympus" and the ancients believed that the gods who watched over them from above lived here. During the Byzantine period, so many hermits took refuge here that it came to be known as "Keşiş Dağı" (the Mountain of the Monks).

Today, Uludağ is one of the greatest places in Turkey to go skiing, take a long walk, join a trekking tour, watch beautiful scenery, or tuck into a delicious barbecue.

A floral feast

An important characteristic of Uludağ is that the surrounding vegetation keeps altering as you climb. Just as the climate changes with every other meter, so do the trees and flowers. The laurel, chestnut, elm and pine trees that grow here are all incredibly beautiful. There is also a special species of tree found only on Uludağ and so named the "Uludağ Göknarı". You'll see it, once you cross the 1000-meter point.

BBQs and mulled wine on the mountain

Maybe it's the mountain air but the barbequed meat dished up in Uludağ restaurants tastes like no other. The "sucuk-ekmek" (garlic-flavored sausage and bread) is also exceptional; most of the shopkeepers claim that the sucuk's unique taste is due to the high-quality meat and the special blend of spices used in it. If the weather is cold, wash your meal down with some spicy, cinnamon-flavored mulled wine. It will hit you before you know it, so drivers beware!

Skiing is for everyone

If you are visiting Uludağ in winter, you probably want to go skiing. Even if you're an absolute beginner there's no need to worry; between five and 10 hours of tuition should set you up. There are 10 different slopes to suit all abilities. You can also enjoy a ride on one of the snowmobiles which are especially popular with the young. Equipment rental and private lessons are much cheaper than they used to be.

There are many accommodation options on Uludağ. If you avoid weekends and your holiday doesn't coincide with school holidays, you will benefit from cheaper rates. Alternatively, you can stay in Bursa and get to the mountain by minibus and cable-car.

WHERE TO **STAY?**

Ağaoğlu Resort
Phone: (0224) 285 20 01
www.agaoglumyresort.com.tr

Kervansaray
Phone: (0224) 285 21 87

Beceren
Phone: (0224) 285 21 11

Grand Yazıcı
Phone: (0224) 285 20 50

Club Voyage Alkoçlar
Phone: (0224) 285 23 22

World of Wonders
Phone: (0224) 285 22 88
www.wowhotels.com

Montebaia Hotel
Phone: (0224) 285 23 83
www.baiahotels.com
Best decorated hotel in Uludağ.

Karinna Hotel Convention & Spa
Phone: (0224) 285 23 60
www.karinnahotel.com
Provides five-star luxury, including spa facilities where you can get a good massage. The hotel offers free access to seven separate ski lifts on Uludağ's longest piste, Volfram Detachable. It is also popular for conventions, seminars, and corporate meetings.

HOW TO **TRAVEL?**

Regular dolmuş (shared taxi) from Bursa ferry passengers to the cable-car for Uludağ; look for those marked "Teleferik".

WHERE THE SNOWS LIE DEEP

018 Turkey's Alternative Ski Resorts

Saffet Emre TONGUÇ

Apart from the well-known resorts of Uludağ, Kartepe, Kartalkaya, Erciyes and Sarıkamış, Turkey also offers many less familiar options for ski lovers who prefer to escape the crowds.

Refik Ongan

One of the newest Davraz-Isparta

Just two hours away from Antalya, the Mount Davraz (2,637m) ski resort boasts two chairlifts, and ski runs suitable for both beginners and more experienced skiers. Straight skiing aside, you can also choose from a variety of other activities such as Nordic and Alpine skiing, snowboarding, mountaineering, botany, observation and trekking.

The Mount Davraz website (www.davraz.com) contains information – from hotel details to snow conditions - not just about Davraz but about other ski resorts as well.

Davraz currently has two hotels, one of them five-star; the 123-room Sirene Davraz Hotel is ideal for those who want to return to their hotel directly after skiing.

Otherwise, shuttle buses run from Davraz to Isparta, so that you can make use of the town center hotels as well.

Davraz is 26 kilometers from Isparta and 58 kilometers from Isparta airport. It is also close to the small lakeside town of Eğirdir.

Sirene Davraz Hotel
Phone: (0242) 710 08 00
Hotel Eğirdir
Phone: (0246) 311 39 61

A low-profile resort Bozdağ- İzmir

This ski resort is only 110km from the city, and mostly patronized by İzmir locals. The ski runs extend to 2150 meters. The northern slopes are most suitable for those interested in Alpine skiing. The Bozdağ Kayak Merkezi Oteli is the only accommodation at the resort. It has 20 rooms, 16 of them standard, and the remaining 4 suites. The rooms have satellite TV, central heating, telephones, and baths with showers. The staff can help guests find suitable skiing equipment.

Bozdağ Kayak Merkezi Oteli
Phone: (0232) 544 09 09
www.bozdagkayak.com

Before setting out for a ski resort, you can click on www.meteor.gov.tr to get more information on the weather and snow conditions.

Ski in the morning, sunbathe in the afternoon

Saklıkent - Antalya

Fifty kilometers from Antalya, Saklıkent has two hotels, one with 10, the other with 15 rooms; a new hotel with a capacity of 200 beds is still under construction. Because of its southerly position, the ski season here is relatively short and the amount of snow tends to be fairly low. Nonetheless, tourists, who are staying in Antalya need only travel for one hour to reach Saklıkent. What makes Saklıkent so special is that if there is enough snow in March, you can ski in the morning, and then enjoy a dip in the sea at Konyaaltı Beach in the afternoon. Mount Tahtalı (2300m), near Kemer to the west of Antalya, now has a cable car and a ski resort there is expected to take off in popularity in the coming years.

Saklıkent Ski Resort
Phone: (0242) 312 27 07
www.saklikent.com.tr

New kid on the block

Esentepe-Bolu

Bolu also has a newly developed ski resort. During the skiing season, Esentepe often boasts two meters of snow and the ski runs are usually open from December to March.

Esentepe Hotel
Phone: (0374) 311 40 80
www.hotelesentepe.com
Hotel Esentepe is a good place to stay.

One of Anatolia's most majestic mountains

Ilgaz - Kastamonu

Like Uludağ, Mount Ilgaz (2,850m) is located inside a national park. The ski resort, set beneath Karakeçilik Hill, is 40 kilometers from Kastamonu city center. It has a ski lift and a chair lift, as well as a baby lift for children. The ski runs, which are ideal for beginners and amateurs, run up to 2,000 meters, and the snow reaches a depth of up to two meters during the skiing season. Covered with all kinds of lovely trees including firs and beeches, Ilgaz also boasts many beautiful small creeks in the summer.
Ilgaz Mountain Resort has 440 beds and 88 apartments. Right next to the ski runs is the Dağbaşı Hotel. Le Chalet is a boutique hotel affiliated to Ankara University's Örsem Club; the rooms can accommodate up to six people. To reach Ilgaz, you take the motorway from İstanbul to Ankara, then take the Gerede exit and follow the Karabük road. After 30 kilometers, you turn on to the Samsun road for Ilgaz.

Ilgaz Mountain Resort
Phone: (0212) 217 13 10
Phone: (0366) 239 10 40
www.ilgazmountainresort.com
Ilgaz Dağbaşı Hotel
Phone: (0366) 239 10 10
Le Chalet Ilgaz
Phone: (0366) 239 10 04
Ilgaz Doruk Hotel
Phone: (0366) 416 12 10
Örsem Club
Phone: (0366) 239 10 61

And also…

Apart from these unexpected ski resorts, Turkey's mountainous terrain offers yet more obscure skiing possibilities including the slopes at Elmadağ, near Ankara; Yolaçtı, near Bingöl; Altınkalbur Dağları, near Bitlis; Sivrice-Hazarbaba, near Elazığ; Zigana, near Gümüşhane; Mount Bubi Ski Resort, near Ağrı; and Bolkar, near Erzincan. A new ski hotel opened at the bottom of Mount Nemrut in early 2007. It even has a pool which means that you can ski in the morning and jump into the pool in the afternoon. For the time being, these resorts mainly serve local snow enthusiasts, but as winter tourism develops and they become better known, they should start to attract skiers from all round the country.

101 OLIVE TREES
019 Trilye

Fatih TÜRKMENOĞLU

Also called Zeytinbağı, this lovely small town on the Sea of Marmara is better known as Trilye and looks as if a misplaced Aegean island somehow strayed into the outskirts of Mudanya. With its olive groves, narrow streets, and stone houses, it makes a perfect weekend destination. Here time stands still and the pages of the calendar forget to turn. Toss in a few olives, a dash of olive oil and lots of fish and Trilye is nothing short of a hedonist's heaven.

Zeytinbağı

In the Trilye town center olive trees line up along the roads with beautiful old houses scattered among them. Suddenly, you feel a breath of the Marmara blowing down your neck. Much of the town is a protected historic site, with traces of Greek, Byzantine and Ottoman architecture clearly visible as you wander around. It's a place best savored slowly and on foot. That way you will be able to appreciate the narrow streets, the stone buildings, and the dilapidated churches.

A beautiful example of the Neoclassical style, the Greek School was built in the early 1900s.

The fate of the churches

Until the Ottomans arrived, Greeks inhabited Trilye and busied themselves with fishing, wine-making and olive production (hence the town's modern name of "Zeytinbağı" meaning olive grove). Only three of the town's original seven churches still survive in recognizable form. The largest, once Hagios Stephanos, is currently in use as the Fatih Camii (Mosque). The Kemerli Church is thought to have had some of the earliest wall paintings in the world, but unfortunately it is now privately owned and has a family living in its courtyard. Hagios Yuannes has fared even worse and actually has people living inside it! The church of Hagios Ioannes Vassileios that used to stand in the main square was completely altered to serve as the dining hall of an orphanage.

Asude Akınlı

Even today the locals get by with a lot of olive production and a bit of viticulture, although the opening of a hotel suggests readiness to embrace tourism too. Many tourists from Greece already come here in the summer. An old grandpa summed it up like this: "They want to find out about the village of their ancestors, they want to smell their roots…"

Bread and olives

While in Trilye, you should certainly eat at least one fish supper, as well as sampling some of the tangy local olives and olive oil which go very well with the delicious sourdough bread produced by the bakeries.

HOW TO **TRAVEL?**

From İstanbul, you can either take the Eskihisar-Topçular ferry or the İDO sea-bus from Yenikapı to Güzelyalı to avoid going around the Gulf. These roads get very crowded over summer weekends. Minibuses run from Güzelyalı to Mudanya and Mudanya to Tirilye, which is only 10 km away.

WHERE TO **STAY?**

Hotel Tirilye
Phone: (0224) 563 22 20

Çınar Motel
Phone: (0224) 563 20 33

WHERE TO **EAT?**

Liman Restaurant.
Phone:(0224)5632410
www.trilyelimanrestaurant.com
The fish at the Liman Restaurant is renowned for its freshness. Waiters also bring olives flavored with thyme and paprika to the table. Experts say that the Trilye olives are particularly special, their unique taste is supposedly the result of the strong winds blowing in the area. Several local shops sell them as souvenirs.

Savarona Restaurant.
Phone: (0224) 563 26 08

020 STAYING IN A TRAIN STATION Mudanya

Fatih TÜRKMENOĞLU

Hugging the Gulf of Gemlik, the small town of Mudanya retains many of its beautiful old houses. Right on the waterfront, the Hotel Montania is housed in a particularly lovely building, which was once the train station. The coastal promenade gets busy on summer nights with enthusiastic locals taking the fresh sea air – it's great fun to join them.

Asude Akınlı

Over the centuries many different civilizations have left their mark on Mudanya, which started life as "Myrlea" in the 2nd century BC. The Macedonian King Philip V destroyed Myrlea and replaced it with a new town called "Apameia". Later, it took on the name Montania, which was eventually transformed into "Mudanya."

Mudanya was conquered by the Ottomans in 1321, during the reign of Orhan Bey. It was invaded by the Greek army in 1920 and occupied for two years. Every year on 12 September, the town celebrates its liberation with assorted festivities.

In the Mudanya back streets, you might stumble on a very old house with an inscription that dates it back to the 17th century.

Bursa's beautiful backyard

Mudanya lies on the Gulf of Gemlik, a part of the wider Marmara Sea. Although it boasts the inevitable modern housing complexes and tall apartment blocks, the town still retains enough beautiful old buildings, especially along the seafront, to justify a visit. The parks are also well cared for and there are several fish restaurants and cafés along the shore.

Many Bursa residents keep summer homes in Mudanya, so the population always soars in summer. Non-home-owners tend to come here in search of the traditional fish and rakı restaurants. The service at these restaurants is usually good and the prices very reasonable.

The local museum is housed in the building where the Armistice of Mudanya between Turkey, Italy,

Asude Akınlı

France, and Britain was signed in 1922, after the Turkish War of Independence. Several important documents and photographs are on display, and the building stands as testimony to one of the major turning points in modern Turkish history.

A station turned luxury hotel

After lying derelict for several years, a former station on the line from Mudanya to Bursa has been beautifully restored to house the Montania Hotel, with a restaurant on what was once the sea-facing platform; it's almost worth coming to Mudanya just to stay here. An article on the wall reminded me of what Ernest Hemingway wrote in 1922:

"The West and the East came face to face at the second-class coastal town of Mudanya on a crooked road covered with dust on the hot Marmara coast." I wish Hemingway could come and see this place again now.

He might want to rephrase his thoughts, perhaps along these lines: "...a first-class coastal town with olive trees, mountains, beautiful homes, parks, promenades and just a few too many concrete buildings..."

Asude Akınlı

HOW TO TRAVEL?

Mudanya is 32 kilometers from Bursa by car and minibus. There are İDO sea-buses from Yenikapı in İstanbul to nearby Güzelyalı. The ride lasts about one and a half hours. Coming by car, take the Yalova-Gemlik motorway and follow the signs.

WHERE TO EAT?

Erol Restaurant
Phone: (0224) 544 66 30
The seafood is delicious.

WHERE TO STAY?

Montania Hotel
Phone: (0224) 544 60 05
www.montaniahotel.com

WHAT TO DO?

Take a turn along the promenade in the early evening with the locals.

Watch the sunset from Yıldız Hill.

The old Greek settlements of Siye and Trilye are nearby. Make sure you see them both.

A CENTURIES-OLD HEALING CENTER

021 Gönen

Fatih TÜRKMENOĞLU

Gönen is likely to come as a complete surprise Its cobbled streets are immaculate, the locals are friendly, and the town's sense of tranquility has somehow survived the usual 21st-century hustle. Moreover, the thermal springs are some of the best in Turkey. Within easy access of İstanbul by seabus, it makes the perfect weekend getaway.

With its old houses and narrow streets, Gönen is one of those rare places in Turkey that still preserves its unique atmosphere.
Fatih Türkmenoğlu

Gönen is a small town in the Balıkesir province, with a population of 35,000. Some sources suggest that its name is derived from "germenon" which means "hot springs". However, its ancient names were first Asepsus (the "unpolluted"), then Artemea (a corruption of Artemis, the Greek goddess of fertility and hunt).

Gönen was the birthplace of the Turkish writer Ömer Seyfettin (1884-1920), who did a great deal to purge Turkish of Arabic and Persian words and phrases.

Thermal baths dating back to Byzantine times...

If Gönen would be famous for anything, it would have to be its hot springs. Apparently the temperature of the healing waters has remained the same throughout the centuries, at a constant 73°C (163°F).

Gönen is ideal for a weekend getaway.

The water is supposed to be good for rheumatism, neurological and orthopedic disorders, heart and circulatory system diseases, as well as for respiratory and gastro-intestinal illnesses – and, of course, for lifting the spirits! If you have a medical problem, experts recommend staying here for 21 days. However, you should always consult your doctor first.

There are three huge thermal hotels at Gönen: the Yıldız, the Yeşil and the Güneş. To find out more about them, click on www.gonenkaplicalari.com or phone (0266) 762 18 40.

Kelle cheese and Gönen lace

The narrow streets of Gönen are incredibly beautiful. The single-story wooden houses have stove-pipes sticking out of their windows and the residents often stand in front of the doors and greet passers-by. As you wander the streets you should look out for people selling the local kelle cheese and for women making lace, which they will be happy to sell to you. Look out in particular for Şaban Başak's old world grocery store for a real trip down Memory Lane.

Local women sell handicrafts on the streets of Gönen.
Fatih Türkmenoğlu

HOW TO **TRAVEL?**

Gönen is only 45 kilometers from Bandırma. The best way to get there is to take the İDO seabus from Yenikapı in İstanbul, and then hop on a bus; buses leave Bandırma for Gönen every hour.

If you're driving, the road is narrow, curvy and a bit rough, so try to leave before dark. It is especially easy to miss the junction off the main road where there is a nasty ramp.

WHAT **TO DO?**

Between Manyas and Bandırma lies a Kuş Cenneti (Bird Paradise) where you might be lucky enough to spot pelicans, spoonbills, cormorants or herons amongst the more than 250 species that visit the lake.

WHERE TO **STAY?**

MRG Hotel
Phone: (0286) 316 8800
Housed in a timber-framed, traditional-style building in Biga. Biga is a small inland town, where Alexander the Great achieved his first victory over the Persians in 334 BC.

At the village of Ekșidere, 13 km away, you can spend the night in an 80-room hotel and bathe in wonderfully refreshing water straight from a mountain spring.

WHERE CONTEMPORARY HISTORY COMES BACK TO LIFE

022 Çanakkale

Saffet Emre TONGUÇ

As one of the most important straits of water in the world, the Dardanelles changed history twice, first during the Trojan War, and later during the First World War. The first epic story was told by Homer, the blind poet of Smyrna. His masterpiece, *The Iliad*, in which he described the Trojan War, was passed down from generation to generation. The second epic tale was written by thousands of Turkish soldiers on 18 March 1915. Both Trojans and Turks died for their respective countries in and around what is now modern Çanakkale.

Necmettin Halil Onan's poem is inscribed on the hillside near Kilitbahir.

Saffet Emre Tonguç

The importance of the Çanakkale region is the direct result of its geo-political position. Without the İstanbul (Bosphorus) and Çanakkale (Dardanelles) straits, the Black Sea would be the world's largest lake. As it is, these two straits have managed to maintain their strategic significance throughout the centuries because they provided access to it.

> *Çanakkale's historic ceramics are so valuable that there is a special museum for them in Athens.*

Gallipoli (Gelibolu) means "Beautiful City" in Greek. The Gallipoli peninsula and the city of Çanakkale frame the two sides of the Dardanelles, which was named after a king of the same name who lived in the area. Astride the 70-meter-long strait are the Kilitbahir (Lock at Sea) Fortress, built by Sultan Mehmed II the Conqueror at the narrowest point, and the Çimenlik Castle, currently used as a museum. The Dardanelles succeeded in repulsing the Allied forces during the First World War, and it was on the Gallipoli Peninsula that one of the most outstanding leaders of the 20th century first revealed his military genius. As the commander of the 19th Reserve Division, Lieutenant Colonel Mustafa Kemal's star shone brightly after the Çanakkale Savaşı (Battle of Gallipoli) and the world learned that: "Çanakkale cannot be crossed!"

Some of the sites in the region have been named after the enemy forces who tried to capture Turkish soil. The cove where the Allied forces first landed is called Anzac Cove, and the cemeteries where foreign soldiers are buried bear names like Lone Pine, Courtney's Post, etc. Every year on 25 April thousands of descendants of the ANZAC soldiers visit Çanakkale and take part in a Dawn Service, singing peace songs arm in arm with new friends whose grandfathers fought against theirs. Atatürk's letter to the mothers of the foreign soldiers who lost their lives during the war, which was read by Secretary of State Şükrü Kaya to the first ANZAC group that came to visit the area in 1934, is now inscribed on the memorial at Anzac Cove:

"Those heroes that shed their blood and lost their lives… you are now lying in the soil of a friendly country. Therefore, rest in peace. There is no difference between the Johnnies and the Mehmets to us where they lie side by side here in this country of ours… You, the mothers, who sent their sons from far away countries, wipe away your tears. Your sons are now lying in our bosom and are in peace. After having lost their lives on this land they have become our sons as well."

Çanakkale Clock Tower

Saffet Emre Tonguç

World War I

The assassination, in Sarajevo, of the Austria-Hungarian crown prince Franz Ferdinand, who had been following an expansionist policy in the Balkans, was the spark that ignited the First World War. In August 1914, German forces occupied France and Belgium and created a front-line that extended from the borders of Switzerland to the English Channel. The Allied forces suffered repeated defeats at German hands. On 9 August, two German battleships, the Goeben and the Breslau, crossed the Dardanelles and arrived in İstanbul. After their names were changed to Yavuz and Midilli, they joined the Ottoman fleet and started dropping bombs on the Russian shore. Under pressure from the Ottomans on the Caucasian front-line, Russia sought help from the French and the British in January 1915. Hoping that the sight of the British fleet would cause panic, Winston Churchill, who was in charge of the British Naval Forces, decided to take over the Ottoman capital, İstanbul, after first securing the Dardanelles. Churchill's thinking was simple: Ottoman Sultan Mehmet Reşad would surrender as soon as he saw the enemy battleships in front of his palace. Then access from the Mediterranean to the Black Sea, into which poured the rivers of Russia and Eastern Europe, would be secured through the captured straits. The Suez Canal would also be secured and the success of the Allied forces would attract the Balkan countries to their side. Two birds killed with one stone! Well, things did not go exactly as planned…

A replica of the Nusrat mine ship

Saffet Emre Tonguç

Çanakkale Savaşı (The Gallipoli Campaign)

March 18th, 1915 is engraved in gold on the history of Turkey. On that day the mines laid by a tiny ship, the *Nusrat*, managed to destroy a third of the enemy fleet. As a result, the Allied forces had to change their plans. Seventy thousand soldiers, including 20,000 Australians, as well as soldiers from the French and British dominions who had been briefly trained in Egypt, landed on the Gallipoli peninsula under the command of General Ian Hamilton. The Australian and New Zealand soldiers had been persuaded to enlist with the promise that they would "see the world for the first time"; sadly for many, it turned out to be the last time too.

The British attacked from Seddülbahir, the southernmost point of the peninsula. Instead of landing at Anzac Bay The ANZACs (the acronym stands for Australia and New Zealand Army Corps) mistakenly came ashore at Arıburnu at dawn on 25 April. Expecting flat terrain, they found themselves staring at a steep hillside instead. This fatal mistake gave the Turkish soldiers a great advantage. When the thousands of ANZACs landed on the Gallipoli Peninsula that morning, they only saw 160 Turks at first. But, encouraged by Mustafa Kemal's famous words, "I am not commanding you to attack, I am commanding you to die", the Turkish troops resisted the ANZACs and managed to attract reinforcements from other fronts. By the end of the first day, the ANZACs had suffered 2,000 casualties.

Over the following months, they settled in and prepared for the real fight. On 19 May, 42,000 Turkish soldiers launched an attack, but the enemy was equipped with powerful weapons; in a single day, 3,000 Turkish soldiers were killed and 10,000 were injured. There were, however, some interesting developments afterwards. In some areas, the opposing trenches were only a few meters apart. This proximity led to a growing affinity between the soldiers on both sides who started exchanging cigarettes and photographs. The ANZACs would offer the Turkish soldiers (whom they affectionately called "Johnny Mehmetçik") canned food in return for tobacco. But the summer heat had a devastating effect on the soldiers. Living in unhygienic conditions under the blazing sun led to many diseases from dysentery, to diarrhea, and from typhoid fever to cholera. Morale was low, and hope almost non-existent. The war gained new momentum when more British troops were sent to the area in August. But by November, disease and an icy winter had started to take their toll.

Between 8 and 20 December, nearly 90,000 Allied soldiers were rescued from the area through a top-secret operation and without further casualties. Those ANZACs who managed to survive celebrated Christmas on Limnos island before returning first to Egypt and then to their own countries.

CONTACT PHONES

Çanakkale Province, Directorate of Culture and Tourism
Phone: (0286) 217 50 12

Tourism Police
Phone: (0286) 217 52 60

Çanakkale State Hospital
Phone: (0286) 217 10 98

Çanakkale Maritime Lines
Phone: (0286) 217 18 15

A special park was created in Tarsus for the Nusrat battleship, which was saved from being transformed into razor blades at the last minute!
Saffet Emre Tonguç

HOW TO **TRAVEL?**

Çanakkale is equidistant from İstanbul and Izmir. It is 350km from either city. From Istanbul, you reach the war cemeteries via Tekirdağ, Keşan and Gelibolu; you will see the entrance to the National Park just before you arrive in Eceabat. The Çanakkale Memorial is in the southern part of the peninsula, beyond Eceabat and Kilitbahir. The cemeteries are accessible via the road next to Kabatepe Museum. Coming from Izmir, you will see signs to the ancient city of Troy 30 kilometers before you reach Çanakkale. Hourly ferries run from Çanakkale to Eceabat on the Gallipoli Peninsula. If you miss the ferry, there are also smaller boats to Kilitbahir from the pier nearby.
If you would like to visit the area with a professional guide, contact Serhan Güngör, a graduate of Ankara's Middle East Technical University's department of Political Science. Güngör offers war-themed tours in Turkish and English and mixes in his own military experience.
Phone: (0532) 787 29 16
www.serhangungor.com

Fez Travel
Phone: (0212) 516 90 24
www.feztravel.com
For younger people, who wish to visit the area at an affordable price, Fez organizes tours throughout the year, and its clients often include descendants of the ANZACs. Tours leave early in the morning from İstanbul and visit the Gallipoli Peninsula and Troy. Rates include lunch and overnight accommodation. In the summer, they also offer a fixed-price hop-on, hop-off bus service around Turkey.

WHERE TO **EAT?**

Çanakkale Balık
Phone: (0286) 218 04 42.
Çanakkale Balık next to the Kolin Hotel is one of the better choices for delicious seafood.

Yalova Restoran
Phone: (0286) 217 10 45
www.yalovarest.com
Right in the town center, this restaurant boasts a good view of the Dardanelles, as well as delicious seafood and mezes (appetizers).

View of the Gallipoli coastline.
Bünyad Dinç

WHERE TO **STAY?**

Kolin Hotel
Phone: (0286) 218 08 08
www.kolinhotel.com
Right on the waterfront, the Kolin Hotel is the only five-star hotel and offers the best facilities in the area.

İda Kale Resort
Phone: (0286) 232 83 32
Lovely beach and pleasingly decorated rooms. Most guests enjoy the pool and the food. Located in Güzelyalı, a short dolmuş ride from Çanakkale.

Çanak Hotel
Phone: (0286) 214 15 84
If you are looking for a place in the town center, this is a decent option. There is a nice view from the roof, as well as live music in the evening.

Kervansary Hotel
Phone: (0286) 217 81 92
Attractively-decorated rooms in a restored pasha's house dating back to 1903 close to the clock tower and ferry terminal.

Hotel Artur
Phone: (0286) 213 20 00
A pleasant modern hotel.

Tusan Otel
Phone: (0286)
Straightforward rooms in a complex set in a landscaped garden with steps down to the sea. Located in Güzelyalı, a short dolmuş ride from Çanakkale.

THE ANZACs
AND THE 25 APRIL DAWN SERVICE
023 Gallipoli

Saffet Emre TONGUÇ

The Turks call it Çanakkale, the French the Dardanelles, and the British and Australians Gallipoli. Today, the site of the 1915 Gallipoli Campaign is a 33,000-hectare national park visited by thousands of people every year.

The Statue of Atatürk at Conk Bayırı
Saffet Emre Tonguç

The Gallipoli Campaign was a milestone in history for both Turkey and Australia, which is why thousands of "Aussies" (Australians), and "Kiwis" (New Zealanders) come here every year to take part in the 25 April memorial service. After the dawn service, the Australians commemorate their war dead at Lone Pine (Kanlı Sırt) Cemetery while the New Zealanders do the same at Chunuk Bair (Conk Bayırı). A service for the Turkish dead is also held at the Çanakkale War Cemetery. During this unfortunate and bloody First World War campaign, 500,000 soldiers of the Allied forces (Australian, British, French, Indian, and New Zealand) fought against an equal number of Turkish soldiers, who bravely defended their country. In the course of the eight-month-long war, there were 130,000 casualties, 86,000 of them Turkish.

A WOMAN IN LOVE WITH TURKEY

Grethe Knudsen is a successful author who first visited Turkey in 1988 and was very much taken with the country. Despite being a foreigner, she turns out to know Turkey better than most natives! Grethe is a voluntary ambassador for Turkey in her native Australia, and brings lots of Australians to Turkey each year by assuring them that they must see Gallipoli. After the 1999 earthquake, she held an auction and donated a generous sum to the victims. Her love for Turkey also prompted her to write her dissertation on the Australians who came here to fight in the war. Grethe regards the campaign as marking an important turning point that helped create an affinity between the two nations. Her latest novel takes place in Turkey, and is centered on the daughter of the celebrated philosopher Aristotle, who lived in Assos for almost three years. Grethe Knudsen's husband Knud is an expert on Atatürk.

Arıburnu Cemetery

WAR CEMETERIES

At the entrance to the Gallipoli peninsula and the war cemeteries lies Kabatepe Museum, which boasts a large collection of documents, photographs, and other material on the war. The letters to the families of the soldiers are particularly heart-breaking.

Arıburnu and Anzac Cove are the most popular destinations on the peninsula. More than half of the 31 war cemeteries maintained by the Commonwealth War Graves Commission are located near Anzac Cove; the Commission has been looking after them for 85 years. One of the most important cemeteries en route to Chunuk Bair (Conk Bayırı) is Lone Pine; the solitary pine tree in the middle of this predominantly Australian cemetery was grown from the seed of a tree that stood here during the war. You can also see Turkish trenches and tunnels in this area.

© Saffet Emre Tonguç

Lone Pine Cemetery

Further away is the 57th Regiment Cemetery and Memorial. At the entrance to the Cemetery stands the statue of veteran Hüseyin Kaçmaz who died in 1994, at the age of 108. The colossal Mehmetçik Memorial, unveiled in 1992, commemorates the Mehmetçik (a Turkish word, like "Johnny", meaning simply "soldier"). Chunuk Bair (Conk Bayırı), at the top of the hill, was the main target of the ANZACs during the war and was briefly captured by New Zealanders in August 1915; the inscription on the New Zealand National Monument reads: "From the Uttermost Ends of the Earth". The statue of Atatürk in the same location bears an inscription that tells how the great Turkish leader had a close shave with death when a piece of shrapnel hit his pocket watch.

57th Regiment Memorial

Kilitbahir Castle

WHERE TO **EAT?**

There is a distinct shortage of restrooms and restaurants in the area of the battlefields. It might be wise to bring a picnic.

İlhan Restaurant, Gelibolu
Phone: (0286) 566 04 42
This excellent harbor fish restaurant is in the nearby town of Gelibolu, where you'll find the small Piri Reis Museum and the ferry for Lapseki.

Maydos Café, Kilitbahir
Phone: (0286) 213 59 70
Opposite Kilitbahir landing stage.

WHERE TO **STAY?**

Gallipoli Hotel
Phone: (0286) 576 81 00
www.gallipolihotel.com
This waterfront hotel is 13 kilometers from Eceabat.

Gallipoli Houses
Phone: (0286) 814 2650
www.gallipoli.com.tr
Run by a Belgian-Turkish couple, these brand-new cottages are in a quiet location right on the historic peninsula.

Hotel Kum
Phone: (0286) 814 14 66
A pleasant hotel on a sandy beach, on the west side of the peninsula.

HISTORY'S MOST FAMOUS WAR

024 Troy

Saffet Emre TONGUÇ

To most people's surprise, many of the events in Greek mythology actually took place in the lands of Anatolia. There are at least 10 supposed Mount Olympuses in Turkey; Uludağ in Bursa, and Tahtalı in Antalya are just two examples. Almost everyone will have heard of the Trojan War, which began as a myth and evolved into reality. The tragic story of the war is taught in most history classes, alongside the story of Helen's legendary beauty. Yet many people are probably unaware that the war actually happened on Turkish soil!

The Odeon is one of the few structures at Troy that is still intact.
Saffet Emre Tonguç

Let's start by immersing ourselves in the tales of Homer. When Paris, the son of King Priam (also known as Ilion) of Troy was born, the fortune tellers told the king that his son would bring about the city's downfall. As a result, the infant Paris was left to perish on Mount Ida. There he was suckled by a she-bear and was eventually discovered and brought back to the city to be raised by the same man, who had been ordered to kill him on the mountain. Legend has it that Zeus later asked Paris to pick the fairest of three goddesses in history's first known beauty pageant. Aphrodite, Hera and Athena all offered power and riches to Paris, who in the end selected Aphrodite, the goddess of love. In return she promised him Helen, the most beautiful woman in the world.

Nine different cities were established at Troy over a period of 5,000 years.

In an allusion to the story of the Trojan War, the famous English expression "Beware of the Greeks bearing gifts" basically means "don't trust your enemies".

Saffet Emre Tonguç

The horse used in the movie *Troy*, featuring Brad Pitt and Orlando Bloom, now sits on the Çanakkale waterfront.
Saffet Emre Tonguç

Unfortunately, Helen was the wife of the Spartan king Menelaus. To get round this inconvenience, Helen was kidnapped (or fell in love with Paris and left willingly) and brought to Troy, whereupon the king set sail for Troy to save his wife and his honor. The story goes on to list Agamemnon, Achilles, Odysseus, Patroclus and Nestor as lined up to fight on the Greek side, while Priam and his sons Hector and Paris were on the Trojan side.

The war lasted for 10 years with no victories to speak of. In the end, the Greeks resorted to a trick. They pretended to withdraw but, before leaving, they left a wooden horse as a gift at the gates of Troy. Tired and drunk in the aftermath of the fighting, the Trojans wheeled the horse inside the city without realizing that it was packed with Greek soldiers. By this subterfuge the Greeks managed to beat the Trojans and bring the war to an end.

In another version of the story, Poseidon, the god of the sea and earthquakes, sparked off a tremor, which brought the city walls tumbling down. When the Greeks finally entered Troy through the shattered walls, they erected a monumental wooden horse to give thanks to Poseidon.

Nine different Troys

The real Troy turns out to be an ancient settlement where a number of cities were built right on top of one another over the centuries. In the course of 5,000 years, nine different cities were established here. The Trojan War of c. 1250 BC is thought to have taken place during the lifetime of the sixth city. Over the centuries, Troy has welcomed many great leaders including Alexander the Great. The Roman emperors believed that their ancestors fled to Rome and established the empire there after the Trojan War, so they always made a point of stopping in Troy during their visits to Asia Minor. Emperor Constantine even considered using Troy as a capital instead of İstanbul. After conquering İstanbul, the Ottoman Sultan Mehmed II arrived to take Troy and is said to have declared that he was avenging the Greeks even after all those centuries. But, then Troy was forgotten and people regarded the story of the war as no more than a colorful legend until a man named Schliemann came along…

The first beauty pageant was held on Mount Ida, between goddesses Aphrodite, Athena and Hera

WHERE TO **EAT?**

Priamos Restaurant
Phone: (0286) 283 00 44
At the entrance to Troy. It also offers a bookstore.

TROJAN RUINS AND EXCAVATIONS

The legend of Troy is enchanting, but if you visit the site, especially after seeing the ruins of Ephesus and Pergamum, you could be a little disappointed. Realizing this, the Ministry of Tourism erected a wooden horse at the entrance to the city in the 1970s, thinking that people could at least photograph that! Well, the horse used in the movie *Troy* is much nicer...

This bit of trivia aside, Troy was added to UNESCO's list of World Heritage Sites in 1996. All you have to do is use your imagination to appreciate that what you are looking at has been here for thousands of years. Archaeologists from Tübingen University have been excavating the city since 1988, but the first person to discover the city and start digging here was the famous German archaeologist Heinrich Schliemann, who made his fortune during the California Gold Rush. A treasure-hunter by instinct, Schliemann assumed that what Homer wrote was actually true, so he traveled to what is now Turkey, asked permission from Sultan Abdülaziz and began excavating the site (although destroying it might be a better description). He had only one goal: to find the treasure he assumed lay buried at the site. So instead of conducting horizontal excavations, he dug straight down to what he assumed to be his target. The day he finally hit gold, he allegedly let his workers go and fled, with his wife Sophia, first to Greece and then to other countries to try and sell it. But a sense of nationalism must finally have outweighed his greed, because in the end he donated what remained unsold to Germany.

The treasure, which was lost during the Second World War, miraculously resurfaced in Russia in 1993; it is currently on display in the Pushkin Museum.

Trojan Horse at Troy

Mehmet Çabuk

So famous is the treasure of Troy, that ownership of it almost caused a diplomatic incident between Turkey, Germany and Russia! But Troy was so prosperous that excavated objects from the site are currently on display in 50 different museums around the world.

As you circle the walls of Troy, you come across structures from a variety of different periods from the Bronze Age right through to Greek and Roman times. Look out for the long 5,000-year old houses that Schliemann first excavated, as well as for the 4,500-year-old ramps into the city. The seashells you will see poking out from the ground tell you that in ancient times the city was much closer to the sea than it is now and probably controlled access to the Dardanelles. Look out, too, for the altar where people would have sacrificed animals to the gods before starting a military expedition. The diminutive size of the Trojan Odeon (small theater) suggests that the city's population was quite small.

THE UNSPOILT WINDY ISLE

025 Gökçeada

Fatih TÜRKMENOĞLU

Gökçeada is the larger of the two inhabited Aegean islands belonging to Turkey. It's a place of rugged scenery, famous for its high winds, with several interesting old hill villages tucked away out of sight so pirates wouldn't find them. Don't be fooled by the emptiness you see when you first get off the boat - the center of the island is 5 kilometers away!

Kaleköy offers picturesque landscapes for photography enthusiasts.

Gökçeada is a large island in the north-east Aegean, accessible by ferry from Çanakkale and Kabatepe. It's still a fairly wild and remote place, graphically described as "craggy" by Homer. The liveliest spot on the island is Kaleköy, a small beach resort with a number of restaurants and cafés. More interesting are Tepeköy, Zeytinliköy and Dereköy, small villages running down the spine of the island which were built high up in the hills so that marauding pirates wouldn't spot them; Tepeköy is the liveliest of the three; Dereköy is completely abandoned. There are also great views from Eskibademli.

Since the opening of an arts and crafts school affiliated to 18 Mart University in Çanakkale, the island seems to have been given a much-needed new lease of life.

With its vineyards, olive groves and beaches, Gökçeada is both beautiful and sad...

The island formerly known as Imroz

Settlement on Gökçeada is thought to date back to prehistoric times. Imroz (or Imbros), the old name for the island, may have been derived from the word "Ambrosia," meaning "the food of the gods." The island was conquered by the Ottomans in 1456, during the reign of Sultan Mehmed II. Although it remained under Greek rule during the Balkan Wars, it was returned to Turkey after the signing of the Treaty of Lausanne in 1923. Exceptionally, the Greeks were allowed to stay in their ancestral homes, although most of them left in the 1960s when the fraught atmosphere in Cyprus spilled over into Turkey.

Most locals earn a living from cultivating olive groves and vineyards; the wines of Bozcaada may be better known, but those of Gökçeada are beginning to make a name for themselves too. The State Production Farm, established on the island in 1967, created a major source of income for the locals.

Beaches and hill villages

Tourism to Gökçeada is still in its infancy, which is both an advantage and a disadvantage. The food at the town-center restaurants is never going to win any prizes. On the other hand, each bay is more beautiful than the next.

Abandoned in 1964, Dereköy (formerly Pirpos) is a must-see ghost-town, where every crumbling wall seems to have a tale to tell. Aydıncık (Kefalos) offers the most beautiful beach on the island. You can reach most of the villages by (infrequent) minibus or taxi, although the drivers seem to delight in performing acrobatics on the curvy roads.

A few remaining Greeks

A few Greeks still live in the villages of Gökçeada which means you get a chance to experience the local Greek culture. In the tavernas, men and women sit side by side at the tables and rakı glasses are immediately filled and the mezes brought over, but the stories told tend to be sad and there is always an air of melancholy.

You can have a cup of coffee at "Madam'ın Dibek Kahvesi" in the hill village of Zeytinliköy, where most of the houses have been restored and where you can stroll round cobbled streets and inspect ancient fountains and churches. The usual ground coffee is beautifully presented, and the atmosphere is lovely.

Pause for coffee at "Madam'ın Dibek Kahvesi" in Zeytinliköy.

Every year, on 15th of August the death of the Virgin Mary is commemorated with the "Feast of the Panayia". The day is celebrated in different ways all over the island, and former islanders flock home to take part in festivities that last for three days and three nights. This is by far the most colorful time to visit Gökçeada.

HOW TO **TRAVEL?**

Ferries to Gökçeada leave from Çanakkale and Kabatepe, although in winter services can be disrupted for days on end. The boats dock in Kaleköy Port; Çınarlı, the center of the island, is five kilometers away by dolmuş.

WHERE TO **STAY?**

Most Gökçeada accommodations are closed in winter.

Barba Yorgo, Tepeköy
Phone: (0286) 887 35 92
www.barbayorgo.com
Hotel with a Greek taverna that serves great food and drinks. Baba Yorgo ("Father George") more or less put Gökçeada on the tourist map.

Zeydali Hotel, Zeytinliköy
Phone: (0286) 887 32 33
www.zeydalihotel.com
A stylish hotel with its own restaurant in a sleepy hill village.

Aydıncık Beach

ISLAND OF WIND AND WINE
026 Bozcaada

Fatih TÜRKMENOĞLU

Chances are that you'll fall in love with Bozcaada as soon as you sail in and set eyes on the massive castle which dominates its pretty fishing harbor. Set back from the shore is the unspoilt Greek town also called Bozcaada, its narrow streets lined with beautiful stone houses. Boutique wineries, soft sandy beaches, fish restaurants and excellent small cafes - who could possibly ask for more?

Lovely old houses back onto Bozcaada harbor.

Saffet Emre Tonguç

Formerly called Tenedos, Bozcaada has been known for its grapes and wines since antiquity. This well-deserved reputation still holds today; most of the centre of the island is covered with vineyards. In his travel book, famous 17th-century traveler Evliya Çelebi describes Bozcaada as growing "the best 'çavuş' grapes in the world", but if you visit one of the small wineries that offer wine-tasting today, you will soon discover that many other kinds of grapes grow here as well.

Until the 1960s Bozcaada was mainly occupied by Greeks and today the main reason to

Bozcaada has beautiful beaches.

come here is to roam around the narrow streets of the lovely old Greek town which has somehow managed to hold on to most of its elegant town-houses. There are one or two specific sites to visit - the Köprülü Mehmet Paşa and Alaybey mosques, for example – but really this is a place for just drifting aimlessly, with most roads bringing you back eventually to the jewel-like harbor with the castle brooding over it at one end.

Bozcaada is ideal for diving.

A castle half as old as time

There is thought to have been a castle overlooking the harbor since the time of the Phoenicians. However, the present model is mainly a mixture of Venetian, Genoese and Ottoman work. There is a small museum inside the castle and the amphorae on display are quite interesting. The building looks simply superb when floodlit at night.

Beautiful beaches

It's not hard to get about Bozcaada because of its small size. This means that the lovely beaches on the south side of the island are only a taxi ride away. The sand on Ayazma Beach is said to have healing qualities; it certainly helps heal the soul! If you keep going to Cape Mermer you will find a beautiful and much calmer beach littered with the marble blocks that gave it its name. It's also worth visiting Akvaryum (Aquarium) Cove where walls of rock embrace a small harbor.

Floodlighting was installed in the castle in recent years. Now it looks beautiful by day and night.

Saffet Emre Tonguç

Recently, new people have started moving to Bozcaada. Most of them are intellectuals, artists and retirees, who are fleeing the stress of the big city.

Saffet Emre Tonguç

View from Bozcaada Castle.
Saffet Emre Tonguç

HOW TO TRAVEL?

First you must take the ferry to Çanakkale from Lapseki or Eceabat; there are also "dolmuş" (first come first serve) motorboats from Gelibolu, which save you from having to wait in line. From Çanakkale you must drive to Ezine (pausing to buy some of its famous feta cheese), then to Geyikli, and finally to Yükyeri İskelesi (Harbor) where you find the Bozcaada ferry.

Once on the island, the roads are good, so if you come by car, you will be able to get around easily. The terrain is also perfect for biking; if you pack your bike in the car, you certainly won't regret it.

WHERE TO EAT?

Lots and lots of fish and seafood. The fried calamari is delicious but do also try the "sardine köfte" or the köfte called "kulfada" which is made from a shellfish that lives on the rocks; it is usually served as a "meze" (appetizer). One of the best fish restaurants in the harbor is Koreli.

In high summer, Bozcaada prices could give the high-end restaurants in İstanbul a run for their money. For something cheaper try Sandal Café, the Café At Lisa's, or Café Tena.

WHERE TO STAY?

Over the last 10 years, lots of hotels have opened in Bozcaada, some of them very beautifully decorated. Finding somewhere to stay is unlikely to be a problem, but if you are planning to visit in July and August, especially over a weekend, it's best to reserve a room in advance.

Rengigül Konukevi (Guest House)
Phone: (0286) 697 8171.
If you have ever wondered how an artist's personality would be reflected in his/her own surroundings, head straight for Rengigül in Bozcaada Town to discover one answer. After living in Germany for many years, owner Özcan Germiyanoğlu restored a 19th-century Greek house on the island and began welcoming guests. All the rooms are individually decorated; you feel as if you are a guest in a friend's house. The garden is splendid and the breakfast spread a veritable banquet. Don't forget to check out the exhibitions in the nearby art gallery either.

Kaikias Hotel Bozcaada
Phone: (0286) 697 02 50
www.kaikias.com
In Greek mythology, Kaikias was the god of the northeast wind ("poyraz" in Turkish). Only a few minutes away from the fish restaurants in the harbor and Bozcaada Castle, this lovely hotel has spacious, elegantly-decorated rooms. Its beds are incredibly comfortable and the baths are perfectly sized for lengthy relaxation. The splendid breakfast is served in a separate room overlooking the sea. The hotel boasts books dating back to the 1750s, historic icons, and relics taken from an old ship called the Venetian Star. You can even join readings of the *Iliad* with Haluk Şahin - my tip for poetic souls.

Akvaryum Pansiyon
Phone: (0532) 746 46 18
Complete solitude without even any electricity in remote Akvaryum Cove.

Ege Hotel Phone: (0286) 697 81 89.
Housed in the old Greek school.

Aksoy Hotel Phone: (0286) 697 84 84
Güler Hotel Phone: (0286) 697 88 99
Thenes Hotel Phone: (0286) 697 88 86
Tuna & Deniz Pansiyon Phone: (0286) 697 82 62
Hotel Tena Phone: (0286) 697 88 80
Ataol Farm Phone: (0286) 697 03 84

Click on www.bozcaada.biz to explore the alternative of staying in a privately-owned old stone house.

WHAT TO DO?

Long walks in the coves, especially early in the morning and before sunset, are very romantic. Take your beloved with you!

Tour the island on a bike. You can rent wheels from Tenedos Bisiklet to work out those lazy leg muscles.

The island is perfect for scuba diving and has several diving schools.

Take a boat tour. The captains hand out a sea fruit they call "fusk". Don't be afraid to try it; it is supposed to be good for goitre.

Sample the local wines. Prices are reasonable and if the season is right, it's fun to visit the producers.

For nightlife, try the Salhane Bar, Polente Café, Bar Ali Café, Fuska Café Bar or the Beach Club.

27 MUST-SEE PLACES
IN THE AEGEAN REGION

THE AEGEAN REGION

THE PHILOSOPHER ARISTOTLE and Assos

027

Saffet Emre TONGUÇ

Assos is a perfectly beautiful harbor with a line-up of hotels and restaurants in old Greek houses. Ruins of the ancient settlement straggle up the hill to the equally exquisite village of Behramkale, which is topped with the remains of a temple to Athena. As the sun is about to set on the village, the rays flicker over the island of Lesbos (Midilli) where the poet Sappho once lived. Having once enchanted Aristotle, the celebrated philosopher of Antiquity who spent three years here, beautiful Assos will surely do the same for you too.

Seljuk Bridge
Saffet Emre Tonguç

First off, let's clear up a bit of geographical confusion. Although "Assos" is the name people generally use when referring to this part of Turkey, the settlement falls into two quite distinct parts: real Assos, the tiny resort set around the harbor, and Behramkale, the rather larger village at the top of the hill. As you travel towards Assos from Çanakkale, you will know you have arrived, when you pass the graceful arched Selçuklu Köprüsü (Seljuk Bridge) on the outskirts. Shortly afterwards the road forks: one road heads up to Behramkale, the other down to Assos.

The 24-kilometer coastal road between Assos and Küçükkuyu is very beautiful.

Athena, Aristotle and St Paul

It's a difficult climb up to the temple at the very top of Behramkale, but once there you will be reminded of the stories of Athena, the Greek goddess of wisdom, who gave this beautiful temple- as well as the city of Athens - her name. Athena, who set traps for the Trojan soldiers and supported the Greeks in the Trojan War, was also one of the three candidates in history's first beauty pageant from which seductive Aphrodite emerged the winner.

Like many of the cities in western Anatolia, Assos (which means "first" in Greek) passed through periods of Lydian, Persian, Hellenistic, Pergamene, Roman, Byzantine and Ottoman control before evolving into the place that it is today. Hermias, one of Plato's students, ruled Assos in the 4th century BC, and he encouraged many scientists and philosophers to settle in the city. Among them was Aristotle, who was married to Hermias's niece. In his quest to spread Christianity across Anatolia, Saint Paul also set sail from Assos.

Beautiful Behramkale

As you are descending from the Temple of Athena, take a look at the 14th-century Murat Hüdavendigar Mosque. Along the road, villagers will try to sell you handicrafts or produce from their gardens. Take a breather in one of the cafés in the upper part of the village; places like this are often helpful for shedding light on the sites you have visited and the streets you have walked along. After sipping your tavşankanı tea (in Turkish, well-brewed tea is referred to literally as "rabbit's blood"), you will feel refreshed and ready for the walk down to the harbor.

And even more beautiful Assos...

From Behramkale the road zigzags down to the harbor, offering ever more breathtaking views of the sea. For part of the way you will be walking alongside a stretch of the old city walls of Assos. A gate also opens onto the remains of an ancient theater.

At the end of the road you'll be met by architectural perfection: half-a-dozen exquisite stone buildings lining a cobbled harbor with nothing in front of them to mar the view. What could possibly be finer than this?

The Temple of Athena, perched high above legendarily beautiful Assos harbor, was the first Doric-style temple in Anatolia.

Saffet Emre Tonguç

HOW TO **TRAVEL?**

Assos is 270km from İzmir, 300km from Bursa and 400km from Istanbul.
Buses run regularly from Çanakkale to Ayvacık.
From Ayvacık, you can take a minibus to Assos, which is only 25 kilometers further on.
With a car, you should use the İDO Yenikapı to Bandırma sea-bus to cut down on the driving.

WHERE TO **STAY?**

Kaldera Hotel
Phone: (0286) 723 44 20
www.kaldera.org
Super stylish boutique hotel in Bektaş Köyü on the road to Sivrice.

Biber Evi
Phone: (0286) 721 74 10
www.biberevi.com
Lütfi Oğuzcan, the owner of this stone building in Behramkale, which dates back at least 150 years, is a wonderful cook, familiar with both Turkish and world cuisine.

Kervansaray Hotel
Phone: (0286) 721 70 93
www.assoskervansaray.com

Assos Group Hotels
Phone: (0286) 721 74 35
www.assoshotel.com
Like the Kervansaray Hotel located on the waterfront in Assos harbor.

Lesbos Island from the acropolis of Assos

Mehmet Çabuk

A BREATHE OF FRESH AIR

028 Kazdağı (Mount Ida)

Fatih TÜRKMENOĞLU

With its lush greenery, cool waterfalls, hidden valleys and graceful old stone bridges, Kazdağı (Kaz Mountain; Mt Ida) offers some of the most beautiful scenery in Turkey. On a map it looks far from Istanbul, but in fact it's easily accessible for a long weekend, courtesy of the sea-buses across the Sea of Marmara. The mountainside makes a refreshing break from all that urban hassle.

With its fresh air, waterfalls, and creeks, Mount Ida is one of the most beautiful corners of Turkey.

Bünyad Dinç

Called Mount Ida in ancient times, Kazdağı is the highest peak of the Kazdağları range at 1774 meters. This is real trekking country, and you should come equipped with clothes and shoes suitable for hiking. It gets cooler in the evenings, so be sure to bring a sweater or a jacket too.

The most beautiful villages in the Kazdağı area are probably Yeşilyurt and Adatepe, both of them full of picturesque stone houses and cobbled streets offering accommodation in characterful boutique hotels.

Centuries ago, this part of the country was settled by Türkmen people who had originally come from Central Asia. According to the stories, Sultan Mehmed II ("the Conqueror") needed wood-carvers to work on the ships that he intended to use to capture Constantinople (Istanbul). To help him, he brought a group of Türkmens down from the Taurus Mountains and here they decided to stay. A small museum at Tahtakuşlar describes their lifestyle and customs.

On a visit to the Kazdağı region you can learn what a pivotal role olive oil has played in local life over the centuries.

Sarıkız and the dozen geese

The Türkmen regard the goose ("kaz" in Turkish) as sacred. Local legend tells the story of a widowed shepherd called Baba Çılbık who spent every spring and summer on the mountainside with his daughter, called Sarıkız ("blondie"). Fearing that she would become bored, he bought her a dozen geese as pets. Unfortunately the geese were the ones to grow bored. After they fled to the fields of Bayramiç. Baba Çılbık made his daughter build a pen of stones to keep them in. Inevitably his daughter grew to be a beautiful young woman. While her father was away on pilgrimage to Mecca, she was pursued by ardent suitors. Sarıkız rejected them all and was still single when her father died on the peak, later named Babadağı after him. His grief-stricken daughter retreated to the pen with her geese whereupon a thick white cloud descended and they were never seen again. The Türkmen then renamed the summit of Mt Ida, Kazdağı (Goose Mountain).

Mt Ida and a fateful decision

According to Greek mythology, when an oracle warned King Priam of Troy that his son would be responsible for his downfall, he had the boy, Paris, abandoned on the slopes of Mt Ida. There he was suckled by a she-bear until his father relented. Later, it was on the same mountainside that Paris judged Aphrodite, the goddess of love, the most beautiful of three goddesses. This epoch-making decision led directly to the start of the Trojan War. The ruins of Troy lie around the coast to the north of Assos.

In another piece of Mt Ida-related Greek mythology, it was believed that the mother goddess Rhea and her sister Ida brought up Zeus, the king of the gods, here. Later, he and the other Olympian gods gathered on Mt Ida to watch the progress of the Trojan War rather like modern football spectators watching a match, except that these spectators had the power to determine its outcome.

Finally, Mt Ida was also said to have been the scene of the rape of the beautiful young Trojan prince Ganymede by Zeus who had disguised himself as an eagle to carry out the dastardly deed. Perhaps repenting of his misbehavior, Zeus later made Ganymede the cup-bearer to the gods.

Kazdağı was the Mount Ida of ancient mythology. In Homer's *Iliad*, Ida was mentioned as "a mountain with many springs and wild beasts". Even today there are many wild animals living in the mountains although you're unlikely to see any of them.

WHERE TO **STAY?**

İliada Hotel
Phone: (0286) 484 77 78
Up high on Mt Ida, the İliada is a remote hunters' and walkers' paradise with a vast garden that is vaguely reminiscent of the UK.

Zeytinbağı Hotel, Çamlıbel Köyü
Phone: (0266)387 37 61-62
www.zeytinbagi.com
Zeytinbağı (The Olive Grove) is one of the nicest places to stay in the area. Owned by famous movie star Tuncel Kurtiz and his wife Menend, it's a place where you can savor locally-grown organic produce as well as take part in a cooking class or join a guided walk. If he's in the mood, Tuncel Kurtiz will treat you to his rendition of the legendary Kazdağları folk tune: "Sarıkız Efsanesi".

Manici Kasrı, Yeşilyurt
Phone: (0286) 752 17 31
www.manicikasri.com
This wonderful 10-roomed hotel takes its name from that of the artist who painted the walls. It's tucked away in a valley overlooking a river and stands of plane trees.

Çeşmeli Konağı, Altınoluk
Phone: (0266) 396 68 48
www.cesmelikonak.com
The road from Küçükkuyu to Altınoluk is completely overrun with summerhouses but if you turn inland to Köyiçi (the inner village), you will find a lovely and completely unexpected Ottoman konak (mansion) standing right at the top of the village. The bedrooms are large, the living room spacious, and the view is magnificent. The rooms on the top floor have exquisite wooden ceilings. You will feel as if you are floating amid the clouds.

İdaköy Çiftlik Evi (Farmhouse)
Phone: (0266) 387 34 02
Pleasant rural accommodation run by a retired philosophy teacher and lawyer, who have written a guidebook to the Kazdağı area that outlines many local walks and details the flora and fauna.

WHAT **TO DO?**

The best way to explore Kazdağı is on foot. Of course you can go off on your own but if you'd rather have things organized for you the five-kilometre-long "Aydındere Tour" begins at 9:30am and ends at 5pm. To find out more, contact Mare Monte Tour Phone: (0266) 396 17 30

Don't miss the Etnoğrafya Galerisi (Ethnography Gallery), in Tahtakuşlar Köyü. A small museum founded by retired teacher Alibey Kutar, it offers a wonderful opportunity to get to know the fast-vanishing local Türkmen culture. It's two kilometers inland from the bay of Edremit, between Küçükkuyu and Altınoluk.

Beyond Akçay, keep driving towards Zeytinli. Signs marked "Sütüven Şelalesi" will lead you to Beyoba village and the 17-meter-high waterfall, which is breathtakingly beautiful.

Visit the lovely, but largely ignored 19th-century Abdullah Efendi Konağı in Altınoluk Köyiçi

IN THE HEART OF OLIVE COUNTRY
029 Adatepe

Fatih TÜRKMENOĞLU

Adatepe is an exquisite village of honey-colored stone houses just four kilometers inland from the resort sprawl of the Bay of Edremit. It offers some great hotels and absolute tranquility - and the beaches are only a short drive away.

Adatepe is a place to come to soak up fresh air, atmosphere and history.
Bünyad Dinç

The area around Adatepe has been inhabited since antiquity; settlers followed the local tradition of never settling right by the sea because it was always easier to defend an inland settlement. The town crops up in Homer's *Iliad* as Gargarus when Zeus pours praise its food: "There is a place between the blue of the Aegean and Mount Ida; I have never found anywhere else the taste of those olives sprinkled with oregano", words that still ring true today in an area renowned for its olive groves.

Taşmektep in Adatepe organizes art and philosophy seminars.

In Adatepe itself the mosque, which is said to have been built by the wife of Zağanos Paşa, and the Hacı Mehmet Ağa Konağı (mansion) are both well worth visiting. What was once a dying village has undergone a recent revival as city-born intellectuals moved in, and the derelict school building has been converted into the Taşmektep (Stone School), which offers philosophy courses and brings together thinkers and writers. Alongside the refugees from İstanbul, a few French and Japanese people have also bought houses here over the last few years.
There is no grocery shop or hair-dressing salon in Adatepe. Instead, people get together to chew the fat in the teahouse in the main square.
Adatepe makes the perfect getaway from any crowded, traffic-polluted, high-octane metropolis. At night there is not a sound to be heard, only the gentle sway of the leaves.

Olives everywhere

Adatepe lies at the heart of olive-growing country, and you'll see gnarled old trees alongside newly-planted saplings everywhere you look. A few kilometers away, right on the roadside in Küçükköy, stands the Adatepe Zeytinyağı (Olive Oil) Museum where you can learn

about the process of making olive oil in what was once an old olive-oil factory. The on-site shop stocks many olive-oil products including olive-oil scented soap, which makes a popular souvenir.
Near the center of the village, the Hüseyin Meral Zeytinyağı ve Sanat Evi (Olive Oil and Art House;
Phone: (0286) 752 66 10, www.huseyinmeral.com) was set up to teach people about the healing powers of olive oil. With only half a liter of oil extracted from 100 kilograms of olives, the owners produce a kind of olive oil that is unique to Turkey. First they crush the olives in a stone mill. Then they store them for three months in a dark, well-ventilated room where the oil starts to release itself naturally. This special kind of olive oil is called olive milk. Saturated in Vitamin E, it is said to be especially good for babies and the elderly. It is absolutely delicious! The owner of the Art House, Mrs. Asuman, also serves a very refreshing "Melissa" (lemon balm) tea.

The Altar of Zeus

According to Ancient Greek mythology, this is where the three goddesses Hera, Athena and Aphrodite competed for a golden apple which was to be awarded to the fairest of them in history's first beauty pageant. Hoping to avoid retribution for an unpopular decision, Zeus asked the Trojan prince Paris to decide. Paris chose Aphrodite because she promised him Helen, the most beautiful woman in the world, as his wife. Then came the Trojan War...

Rıfat Yüzbaşıoğlu

HOW TO **TRAVEL?**

Adatepe is 450 kilometers from Istanbul (230km from Bandırma for people using the sea-bus across the Sea of Marmara). Alternatively you can drive here via Tekirdağ, Keşan, Çanakkale and Ayvacık, a scenic route that takes at least six hours. To get here by bus is time-consuming and involves several changes of vehicles along the way.

WHERE TO **STAY?**

Zeus Han
Phone: (0286) 752 54 04
Only six rooms.

Hünnap Han
Phone: (0286) 752 65 81
Beautifully converted Ottoman farmhouse with attractive garden.

Ayşe Pansiyon
Phone: (0286) 752 66 15

WHAT **TO DO?**

Visit the beautiful harbor of Assos which is only 24 kilometers away and perfect for a day trip.

Go swimming with holidaying Turks at Küçükkuyu or Altınoluk.

Climb the hills to look at the breath-taking forest scenery. The Adatepe of the past, in which Greeks and Turks lived contentedly side by side, will unfold itself before your eyes.

A "QUINCE ORCHARD" FULL OF OLD OTTOMAN HOUSES

030 Ayvalık

Fatih TÜRKMENOĞLU

Ayvalık is a small town on the south side of the Gulf of Edremit whose back streets are full of beautiful old Ottoman Greek houses, some of them converted into exquisite small pensions. There is a long strip of sandy beach at nearby Sarımsaklı, and the off-shore island of Cunda heaves with lovely fish restaurants. Daily ferries connect Ayvalık with the Greek island of Lesbos.

A lovely small town on the Bay of Edremit, Ayvalık was known as Kydonia in ancient times.

Ayvalık ("Quince Orchard") is a thoroughly enjoyable small coastal town which hides much of its charm in back streets that are lined with old Ottoman Greek houses, some of them virtually derelict, others being brought back to life as new homes, pensions and shops.

A long coastal promenade is lined with fish restaurants, a fish market and a marina; it's a great place to stroll up and down with the locals.

To appreciate Ayvalık to the full it pays to know something about its recent history. Until 1923, this was a town with a large "Greek" population, but after the Turkish War of Independence ended with the Treaty of Lausanne these "Greeks" were forced to leave Turkey, their place taken by "Turks" from Greece. Most of these Turks arrived from Crete (Griti in Turkish) and Lesbos (Midilli in Turkish). Those who came from Lesbos were dubbed "the Islanders", while those from Crete were called "Gritikos." The richer incomers settled in Çamlık, just down the road, where there are still some extraordinarily lovely turn-of-the-20th-century houses.

The Ayvalık back streets also house two huge churches that have been converted into mosques: Agios Yannis (Saatlı Cami) and Agios Yorgis (Çınarlı Cami).

As you explore Ayvalık and Cunda, you will feel as if you are traveling back in time for more than 100 years.

The island with two names

Cunda, or Alibey Adası as it was named after the 1980 coup, is connected to Ayvalık via a narrow causeway. You can get there by bus or boat or walk the eight kilometers before lunch or dinner.

Just like Ayvalık, the back streets of Cunda are full of crumbling Ottoman Greek houses, which cluster around the remains of the huge Taxiyarhis church. The waterfront is lined with restaurants and cafes, including the lovely Taş Kahve (Stone Coffee-house), a high-ceilinged space where the old men of the village gather to sip tea beneath the nests of swallows who prefer an indoor home to the great outdoors.

Coming to market

Thursday is market day in Ayvalık and people pour into town clutching empty baskets. The town is quite literally ransacked; by the end of the day there is no food in the restaurants and no merchandise left in the shops. Try to avoid starting your vacation on a Thursday, especially if you're hoping to park in the town center.

A beach called garlic

Sarımsaklı beach probably acquired its startling name (literally "with garlic") from the wild garlic that used to grow around here. But that's not much of a story, is it? So instead the locals tell the tale of a youth with a blonde girlfriend whose father hid her away to prevent them marrying. The youth then roamed the district wailing "Sarım saklı, o nerede?" (where is my hidden blonde-haired girlfriend?"). Hence the name!

HOW TO **TRAVEL?**

The best way to get to Ayvalık from Istanbul is to take the İDO Yenikapı-Bandırma sea-bus; Ayvalık is 223km from Bandırma. If you prefer to drive around the Gulf of Edremit, it will be 520km from Istanbul to Ayvalık. Coming from Ankara, it is about 675km via Eskişehir. Several bus companies offer services to Ayvalık from Istanbul. Atlasjet has also started flying to Edremit airport which is 40 minutes drive from Ayvalık.

WHERE TO **STAY?**

Yalı Pansiyon
Phone: (0266) 312 24 23, www.yali-pansiyon.com
One of the most beautiful places to stay is the historic Yalı Pansiyon right on the waterfront. The Yalı served as the Italian Consulate in Ottoman times. Later, it became the home of a Greek general. In 1977, Çetin Akkoç bought the property and began running it as a small pension. Nothing can compare with the pleasure of a prolonged breakfast of home-made grape and sour-cherry marmalade in the garden of this pension. Instead of air-conditioning and private bathrooms, there is the company of retired sergeant Çetin Amca (Uncle) and his wife Mediha Teyze (Aunt). What more could you possibly ask for?

Taksiyarhis Pansiyon
Phone: (0266) 312 14 94
Lovely pension spread across two old Greek houses in the town center.

Haliç Park Hotel
Phone: (0266) 331 52 21
Spacious hotel two kilometers outside town at the start of the road to Cunda.

Chez Beliz Pansiyon
Phone: (0266) 312 48 97
Bags of character. Owner Mrs. Beliz is a retired actress, who livens up every corner of her pension.

Bonjour Pansiyon
Phone: (0266) 312 80 85
Another beautifully decorated old Greek house which used to belong to a French priest who served as ambassador to a sultan.

Cundahan Konukevi
Phone: (0266) 327 16 81
Cozy, small hotel with handkerchief-sized pool on Cunda island.

Ortunç Hotel
Phone: (0266) 327 11 20
An Ayvalık classic on Cunda, it has a Blue Flag beach which means that the water is guaranteed to be clean.

WHAT TO **EAT?**

Dishes cooked in olive oil ("zeytinyağlı" dishes) dominate Ayvalık menus just as the factories of the old olive-oil factories dominate the skyline.

Do try the red mulberry and mastic ice cream. You can find it all over town but the best is served by the ice-cream vendor on the waterfront, right in front of the fishermen.

On a tight budget, you can eat so-called Ayvalık Toast at "Avşar", although what distinguishes this particular toast sandwich from any other is a mystery known only to the locals. The owner is an incorrigible fan of Hülya Avşar (a Turkish TV and cinema mega-star).

One speciality of Cunda worth looking out for is midye tava, mussels fried in garlic, white wine and olive oil. There are two particular species – kidonya and akivadis – that are especially flavorsome.

WHERE TO **EAT?**

Çorbacı Mehmet Usta
Phone: (0266) 312 66 56
A particular favorite, right behind the Belediye (Municipality), which serves excellent kabak çiçeği dolması (stuffed squash flowers), as well as chickpeas and baked beans cooked in olive oil.

Ayvalık Balıkçısı (Zaro Balıkçısı)
Phone: (0266) 312 45 83
This is the best place to come for seafood; try the ink-fish stew, fried mussels, sardines or papalina (a whitebait-like fish commonly found off the Ayvalık coast). Sprinkled with olive oil and lemon juice, the glasswort salad is delicious. They also serve a dessert called Helvani, or irmik helvası (semolina dessert), which will leave you licking your lips for more. Zaro Balıkçısı is a very unpretentious place right in the middle of town, at the heart of Ayvalık vegetable market.

Ayvalık Şehir Külübü
Phone: (0266) 312 1088
The mezes (appetizers) served at the City Club are delicious and the prices reasonable.

Deniz Restaurant
Phone: (0266) 327 16 85
The mezes and fish served at this Cunda restaurant are always very good.

Yeni Güler Pastanesi (Patisserie)
For dessert, try mastic and olive oil cookies; they use lye instead of baking soda and grape extract instead of sugar to make these tasty treats. The lor tatlısı (a dessert made from curd cheese) is also a killer.

THE CITY THAT GAVE ITS NAME TO PAPER

031 Bergama (Pergamum)

Saffet Emre TONGUÇ

Bergama, the ancient Pergamum, was once such a powerful place that it rivaled Athens in importance. Just above the dusty present-day town, the great Acropolis has a stunning location; graced with many splendid public buildings, it served as the home of the Bergamese royal family for centuries. Come here, too, to visit the ancient Asclepion and one of Turkey's best archeology museums, and to take a trip out to the ancient spa resort of Allianoi.

The steepest of its kind in Anatolia, the theater has 80 rows of seats which could accommodate 10,000 spectators.

Saffet Emre Tonguç

Bergama has a very special place in history, because it once housed one of the two largest libraries of the ancient world. The Library of Alexandria held 500,000 volumes, whereas its arch-rival, the Library of Bergama, had just 200,000. Fearing that the Bergama library would come to exceed theirs in size, the Egyptians brought the export of papyrus to a halt. An enraged King Eumenes II (r. 197-160 BC) gathered his scientists in Bergama, and ordered them to invent something that would replace papyrus. Thus, it was that under the patronage of Eumenes II, dried animal skin, commonly known as parchment, was invented. Papyrus came in a scroll, and it was difficult to unroll it and roll it back up again every time it was used. However, parchment sheets, which could be piled on top of one another, made binding a book a lot easier.

If you wonder what became of all those books, it is said that Marcus Anthony bequeathed them to his wife, Cleopatra, as a wedding gift, whereupon they were removed to Alexandria. Later, the Alexandria library burnt down and all those masterpieces that would have shed light on the ancient world were turned to ash.

The Zeus (Pergamon) Altar was one of the finest structures on the Acropolis. Erected by King Eumenes II to commemorate the victory of his predecessor Attalus I over the Celts, it was later shipped to Berlin, where it remains one of the highlights of the Pergamon Museum.

As one of the most important towns in Anatolia, Bergama boasted an imposing temple, the Kızıl Avlu (Red Courtyard), which was dedicated to the gods and

Trajan Temple

The Zeus Altar in Berlin's Pergamon Museum.
Saffet Emre Tonguç

goddesses of Ancient Egypt. In the Bible, St John of Patmos identified this as one of the seven churches of the Apocalypse and as the seat of the devil. Its ruins are still worth a quick look today.

Early medicine men

Bergama's ancient Asclepieion was one of the three main healing centers of Antiquity. The other two were on the island of Kos, and on the Greek mainland at Epidaurus, where the structure dedicated to Asclepius, Apollo's son and the god of medicine, carries a telling inscription: "Death may not enter." In this historic place all sorts of ailments were treated with methods ranging from psychology to mud baths, and from herbal treatments to the sprinkling of holy water. Centuries later, the symbol of the snake twined round the "Rod of Asclepius" is still used in medicine. A patient healed in a hospital is likened to a snake, which in shedding its skin, starts a new life after being "reborn."

Carl Humann, who came to Bergama to help build the railroad in the 1870s, shipped the Zeus (Pergamon) Altar off to Germany.

Galen, one of the leading physicians of the ancient world, whose writings were used in the medical world until the 16th century, also lived in 2nd-century Bergama.

WHERE TO **EAT?**

Asklepion Restaurant
Phone: (0232) 632 20 06
The home-cooked meals are mouth-watering. Make sure to leave room for some köfte (meatballs).

ALLIANOI

While in Bergama, be sure to visit nearby Allianoi. Excavations there have revealed that, although Allianoi was founded during the Hellenistic period, the main construction of the city took place in the 2nd century in the time of the Roman Empire. Byzantine churches and chapels were later added to the bridges and streets built then.

What makes Allianoi so special, is the thermal bath complex, which the Romans built over a huge area of 9,700 square meters. Consisting of a caldarium (hot), tepidarium (luke warm) and frigidarium (cold) and dressing rooms, the complex made use of waters certified as healing by modern chemical analysis. Among the excavated artifacts was the lovely 1,800-year-old statue of a nymph that now graces Bergama Museum. Allianoi has the only functioning spa in tne world from Antiquity, where you can see pools with hot thermal water. Try to visit site as soon as possible, because it could vanish beneath the waters of a dam any day now.

A POTTERY-LOVER'S PARADISE

032 Kütahya

Fatih TÜRKMENOĞLU

The art of tile-making has existed in Kütahya since the 14th century but reached its peak in the 17th and 18th centuries. Today the tile-makers are still hard at work, alongside a growing number of potters. The picturesque old Ottoman quarter of Germiyan is being restored and is well worth exploring. Not far away, the ruins of ancient Aizonai also repay a visit.

There are several beautiful archeological sites near Kütahya.

Starting life as it meant to go on, Kütahya was originally called Ceramorium which meant "The City of Ceramics". During the Byzantine era, its name was changed to Cotyaeum ("the City of the Goddess Coys"). Only when it was captured by the Turks in 1078 did it finally become Kütahya.

The best place to start exploring Kütahya is the Byzantine fortress which bestrides Hıdırlık Tepesi (Hill) and offers great views. Afterwards you can take a turn down Germiyan Street and admire the old Ottoman houses, fine mosques and tiled fountains. The house where Lajos Kossuth (1802-94), the Hungarian freedom fighter, lived for a year is now a dusty but interesting museum on the hillside. The Kurşunlu Cami (Mosque), Dönenler Cami, Çinili Cami, Lala Hüseyin Paşa Cami and Ulu Cami should all be on your list of must-sees as should the Vecidiye Medresesi (Seminary) which is currently serving as Kütahya's archeology museum. Nearby, in the İmaret Cami, is a small tile museum which showcases not just Kütahya but also İznik tiles. The area around the museums is old Kütahya at its creakiest and most interesting, a far cry from the mainly modern town center.

Travelers may like to note the statue of 17th-century travel writer Evliya Çelebi (1611-82) who was born here.

Purchase one of Sıtkı Usta's beatiful blue birds. It will make a lovely souvenir of Kütahya

Tile shops

According to legend there once lived an old woman who made beautiful pottery and whose works were famous all across the region. Other potters, determined to find out her secrets, had her followed. Eventually, they discovered that she was traveling to Kütahya and filling her bag with earth to bring back with her, whereupon they all rushed to Kütahya and settled in to continue their craft, thereby starting a tradition that has endured for centuries.

Kütahya's çini (tile-making) industry dates back to the 14th century. It received a boost in the 17th century when many tile-makers left İznik and resettled here, and continued to flourish right through until the First World War, after which it went into such a sharp decline that, at one point there was only one workshop left. Since then, however, it has made an equally dramatic recovery, and today, you can hardly move in the town for pottery and tile workshops.

It will take ceramic enthusiasts a few days of touring to sate their pottery lust. For even more overkill on the tile front you could always try visiting during the annual Dumlupınar trade fair when all things çini go on display.

Thermal waters

Near Kütahya are the Yoncalı, Ilıcaköy and Kaynarca Kaplıcaları (hot springs) which are said to have health-giving qualities. Experts recommend that you should stay at the spas for at least seven and preferably 21 days to take full advantage of their water.

The ancient city of Aizonai

Refik Ongan

HOW TO **TRAVEL?**

Kütahya is 360km from Istanbul and 310km from Ankara. The best way to get there is to follow the Bozüyük signs from Bursa. There are plenty of bus services to Kütahya, which is also reachable by train.

Victory medals from the Roman period.

WHERE TO **STAY?**

In addition to the normal city-center hotels, there are a few local thermal hotels where you can round off a day of sightseeing with a spa treatment.

Gül Palas Hotel
Phone: (0274) 216 23 25
Pleasant town-center hotel with attractive bathrooms.

Yoncalı Termal Hotel
Phone: (0274) 249 42 12
Four-star thermal resort hotel

Hotel Erbaylar
Phone: (0274) 223 69 60
One of the best town-center hotels.

Other possibilities include the Tütav Termal Hotel, Hotas Hotel and Gönen Hotel. The restored Germiyan Konağı makes a good place to dine.

WHAT **TO DO?**

Visit the ruins of ancient Aizanoi scattered in and around the modern village of Çavdarhisar, just 60 kilometers from Kütahya. The Temple of Zeus, commissioned by the Roman Emperor Hadrian (r. 117-138), remains largely intact and is very impressive, as are the remains of the theater and stadium. In the village look out for a circular market building which has the prices of different goods inscribed on the walls in Roman numerals; apparently a strong slave cost two horses.

Kütahya is one possible base for driving through the remote and lovely Phrygian Valley (Frig Vadisi) which is full of reminders of the lost Phrygian civilization. It's at its prettiest in late May/early June when the poppies are in bloom.

WHERE TO **EAT?**

Döner Gazino
Phone: (0274) 226 2176
The food may not always be top-notch but the views are magnificent from this sporadically revolving restaurant inside the remains of the fortress.

HOME TO THE LAST MEDITERRANEAN MONK SEALS

033 Foça

Fatih TÜRKMENOĞLU

Foça is a delightful small resort set around two bays just north of İzmir. Lovely old houses line the harbor and ancient ruins lurk down the back streets. At night it's fun to eat fish with the locals in the quayside restaurants. During the day you can swim, sunbathe or take a drive to nearby Yeni Foça which is full of old Ottoman Greek houses.

Foça, the ancient Phocaea, is an Ionian city, which took its name from that of the Mediterranean monk seal (phoca vitulina).

Nil Yüzbaşıoğlu

"The Phocaeans; they founded their city under the most beautiful sky and in the most beautiful climate we know in the world," wrote Herodotus of Halicarnassus, the "father" of history. Once you arrive in Foça, and see the sea, feel the evening breeze in your hair and glimpse the star-filled sky, it will be hard not to agree with him.

One of the 12 historic Ionian cities, Foça (also known as Eski, or Old Foça) was founded by the Phocaeans and was called Phocaea after the islands in the bay, which were thought to resemble the local monk seals (phoca vitulina). Immigrants from Erythrae and Teos also settled in this area which, in time, became powerful enough to send colonists to found cities such as Ampurias in Spain, and Marseille, Antibes and Nice in France (not to mention Samsun on the Black Sea). The rooster, which has been the symbol of the city since time immemorial, traveled all the way to Marseille and Nice with the sailors. At first just the symbol of these new colonies, it eventually became an icon for la toute France, a valued gift from the Phocaeans.

Old Foça is one of the least spoilt towns of the Aegean. The climate, scenery and cuisine are all wonderful.

Having served as the seat of an early Christian bishopric, Foça was conquered by the Ottomans in 1455 whereupon Sultan Mehmed the Conqueror had a mosque built in the town center.

Foça is easy to explore on foot. Look around in particular for the remains of a fortress called Beşkapılar (Five Gates) and for the ruins of the old city walls which sit right on the beach with the remnants of an ancient theater inside them. A town archeology museum is in the process of being set up.

Seal-spotting

You are unlikely to get bored in Foça. In one sense, it's a typical small seaside resort but in another, it's a sizeable town with

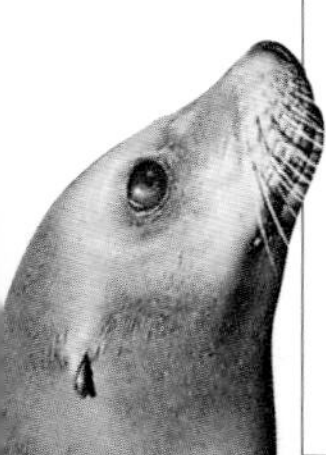

everything from its own courthouse to doctors and banks.

Boat trips out to the off-shore islands are very enjoyable; İncir Adası (Fig Island) is especially beautiful. The same boat trips pass the Siren Rocks; legend has it that the sirens - who had the bodies of birds and the heads of women - would enchant sailors with their singing, thus causing them to crash into the rocks. The lucky few passengers might get a glimpse of a rare Mediterranean monk seal – there are believed to be only about 400 left in the world, so don't hold your breath.

A magnetic black stone

Stories have it that somewhere in Foça there is a rock called the Karataş (Black Stone). Anyone who goes near it and is pulled into its orbit will return to Foça over and over again - which is hardly something to complain about because the town always has something new to offer its visitors, be it a recently renovated house, a new café or different flowers in bloom.

Boat trips out to the islands and the Rocks of Siren are very enjoyable.
Bünyad Dinç

HOW TO **TRAVEL?**

Foça is 65km from İzmir town center, between Menemen and the Gulf of Çandarlı; if you take the highway, the signs will point you in the right direction. If you prefer to catch a bus from İzmir, there is plenty of transport heading for Eski Foça.

WHERE TO **EAT?**

Don't go home without trying the local fish - shrimp, crab, octopus salad, fried mussels - accompanied by lots of fresh salad. The locals make a kind of arugula (rocket) salad with lots of garlic, lemon, extra virgin olive oil, and salt; it tastes extraordinary.

Deniz Restaurant
Phone: (0232) 812 20 39
Serves a range of delectable "zeytinyağlılar" (olive-oil dishes).

Nil Tuzcuoğlu

WHERE TO **STAY?**

Foçaantique Hotel, Eski Foça
Phone: (0232) 812 43 13
www.focantiquehotel.com
At the end of the Foça promenade, this is an extremely charming 12-room hotel. It was created out of an old stone house, a mix of Greek and Ottoman architecture from the 1890s, and has its own private hamam (bath). The bedrooms are all completely different and very colorful; their bathrooms are an imaginative tour de force. The owners, İnci and Alemdar Alemdaroğlu were professional guides who have thrown their hearts and souls into their hotel. The breakfast buffet is a veritable feast. At night, they serve dinner to non-residents as well.

İyon Pansiyon, Eski Foça
Phone: (0232) 812 14 15
www.iyonpansiyon.com
Run by retired teachers, this 10-roomed pension is in an old house from the 1870s. No breakfast is served but the rooms have refrigerators, TVs, and bathrooms. Dinner is prepared in the common kitchen and tables can be set up in the central garden.

Hotel Naz, Yeni Foça
Phone: (0232) 814 66 19
Large rooms in a sea-facing hotel with a garden restaurant.

WHAT **TO DO?**

Drive the 23km from Eski Foça to Yeni Foça along a very beautiful coast road. Yeni Foça used to be a sleepy backwater full of lovely old Ottoman Greek townhouses. Recently, it has been discovered by second-homers, who are fast restoring the houses in a wide variety of styles.

The Foça mausoleum, a rare reminder of the Phocaeans, is seven kilometers out of town on the road towards İzmir. It is thought to have been built c. 500 BC.

THE TOWN WITH A MASTIC FLAVOR

034 Çeşme

Fatih TÜRKMENOĞLU

Çeşme is a small seaside resort on the peninsula immediately west of İzmir. Dominated by a massive castle, it offers easy access to several lovely sandy beaches and to the wind-surfing possibilities at nearby Alaçatı. Daily ferries connect Çeşme with the Greek island of Chios.

Çeşme Square
Saffet Emre Tonguç

One of the 12 cities of Ionia, Çeşme ("Drinking Fountain") used to be called Kyssus. The Ottomans captured it from the Aydınoğlu emirate and used it as a naval base. In 1770, the Russians launched an attack on the town; the ships wrecked in the encounter are still being excavated by archaeologists.

After Çanakkale, Çeşme is Turkey's most western point and it has one of the loveliest climates in the country, with almost no humidity and frequent cool breezes. The town was always an important port and even now many cruise ships call in here. What with the nightlife, the sports and the many restaurants, you will be amazed at how quickly the days slip by. Çeşme is one of the few places in the world, where mastic gum trees grow.

Çeşme Castle
Saffet Emre Tonguç

Changing places

Before Turks took their place in 1923, Çeşme was inhabited by Greeks from the island of Chios and was called Perama which means "passageway". The town quietened down considerably after the population exchange, but was rediscovered in the 1990s. It has a lovely waterfront promenade for evening strolls, as well as a pedestrianized main street lined with old houses that have been restored and converted into little shops. What was the Ayios Haralambos church, midway along the street, is now a cultural center – it's worth dropping in to find out what's showing.

The citadel

The most impressive structure in the town center is the citadel built by the Genoese and renovated by Sultan Mehmet the Conqueror's son, Bayezid. In front of it stands a statue of Cezayirli Gazi Hasan Paşa (1714-90), who was sold as a slave but went on became a vizier to the Sultan. The Citadel houses a small, indifferent museum but the views from the ramparts are spectacular.

Çeşme lies to the west of İzmir, just 75km from the city center. It might as well inhabit a completely different world.

Saffet Emre Tonguç

HOW TO **TRAVEL?**

It's one hour to Çeşme along the highway from İzmir's Adnan Menderes Airport. Central İzmir is only 40 minutes away, accessible by regular bus. Kuşadası is just two hours away.

WHERE TO **STAY?**

Most boutique hotels are in nearby Alaçatı on the Çeşme peninsula.

Rıdvan Antik Hotel
Phone: (0232) 712 97 72
Small hotel in an old Greek house.

Sisus Hotel
Phone: (0232) 724 03 30
www.sisushotel.com

Altınyunus Hotel
Phone: (0232) 723 12 50
www.altinyunus.com.tr

Grand Ontur Hotel
Phone: (0232) 724 00 11
www.onturcesme.com

Pırıl Hotel
Phone: (0232) 712 75 74
www.pirilotel.com.tr

Kervansaray Hotel
Phone: (0232) 712 71 77
Rooms in an Ottoman caravanserai dating back to 1528 and the reign of Sultan Suleyman the Magnificent. Achingly authentic although it is crying out for better maintenance.

Club Ilıca Hotel
Phone: (0232) 723 26 36
www.ilicahotel.com.tr

Sheraton Hotel Çeşme, Ilıca
Phone: (0232) 723 12 40
www.sheratoncesme.com

Kum Motel
Phone: (0232) 722 22 95
Lovely set of wooden bungalows and a restaurant overlooking two secluded bays in Çiftlik Köyü. Sea lilies bloom here in August and September.

WHERE TO **EAT?**

Sample some mastic marmalade or ice-cream, two local delicacies on sale in the town center.

Try one of the kumru sandwiches for which Çeşme is known. Made from bread with sesame seeds, they make the perfect snack to round off a long night of partying!

For chic dining, head out to nearby Alaçatı which boasts several gourmet restaurants with delectable decoration

Dalyan Körfez Restaurant
Phone: (0232) 724 79 47
www.dalyankorfezrestoran.com
Lengthy menu at a classic fish restaurant. Come in early evening for fantastic views.

Altınkapı
Phone: (0232) 723 18 41
This kebab joint dates back years. Worth visiting to sample the house specialty, Altınkapı kebab.

Gözde
Phone: (0232) 723 34 14
Great fish restaurant in nearby Ilıca.

La Passione
Phone: (0232) 712 01 82
Offers French and Italian cuisine, and post-prandial music.

Rıhtım
Phone: (0232) 712 74 33
Meat and seafood right beside the water.

WHAT **TO DO?**

Enjoy a boat trip to visit "Eşek Adası" (Donkey Island), where – surprise! surprise! - only donkeys live.

Ilıca is only 10km away. The beaches are beautiful and the sand practically white. Wilder beaches not overlooked by a Sheraton can be found at Altınkum ("Golden Sand"), a short bus ride out of Çeşme.

Ildırı, on the road to Karaburun, is a pretty village on the site of the ancient Erythrae where you can see the remains of a Greco-Roman theater, aqueduct, mosaic floor and temple of Athena. The Karaburun peninsula is known for its narcissi, which perfume the air in early summer.

Çeşme is close to the Greek island of Chios, where you can spend a few days and bring back some delicious mastic liqueur as a souvenir.

Ertürk Turizm
Phone: (0232) 712 67 68
www.erturk.com.tr

Aramis Kalay

AND THE BEACHES...

Çeşme has several beautiful beach clubs where you can sunbathe and swim during the day, then dine and dance until the wee hours of the morning.

Just 10 kilometers away from Çeşme, **Altınkum** is a fantastic beach where the sea is like an aquarium. For the time being, it rivals the Caribbean for splendor, but the Ministry of Tourism is planning to build resorts with thousands of beds here, so make haste to enjoy this paradise before it is turned into hell! Nearby **Kum Beach** is one of Çeşme's most popular beaches. Throne-like sun loungers line a two-mile-long beach. You feel like a king on his own private beach!
Phone:(0232) 722 22 95
www.kumbeach.com

One of the first things that springs to mind when thinking of Çeşme is the many beach clubs...

Named after St George, **Aya Yorgi** is a post-'80s classic. The water is crystal clear and several beach clubs line up along the sand:
Granada (0232) 724 03 55
Sole Mare (0232) 712 20 57
Shayna (0232) 712 11 22
Paparazzi (0232) 712 67 67

Paparazzi was one of the first of its kind and serves delicious pizzas. Shayna houses the Italian restaurant Alliance; also a club at night, it welcomes guest DJs. Sole Mare is the main hangout for the young, but the bouncers at the door pretty much run the place - if you're nice to them, they will probably let you in! Granada Café de Paris makes a good alternative for dinner.

Over in Paşalimanı, **Fontana** is one of the best local beaches. Don't miss the popular weekend parties. Turkish pop stars often give night-time concerts here.
Phone: (0232) 717 08 60

Aqua, near **Fontana**, is a secret oasis with an indoor thermal pool where you can sip your cocktail while enjoying the delectable warm water. You can also get a massage here and, afterwards, choose from a selection of delicious pastas.
Phone: (0232) 717 02 62

A USEFUL TIP

Çeşme has a large port to cope with ferries departing for Italy. If you are traveling to Turkey by car, getting on/off at Çeşme can save you a lot of driving.
www.marmaralines.com

Kum Beach
Saffet Emre Tonguç

A STORY OF CHANGE
035 Alaçatı

Saffet Emre TONGUÇ

Wonderful things are happening in Turkey. A group of entrepreneurs from Istanbul and İzmir have turned Alaçatı, an erstwhile crumbling, forgotten village, into a wonderful vacation spot with the support of the municipality. As you walk through the streets of Alaçatı, you will be amazed at the transformation.

Alaçatı: Windsurf Heaven
Saffet Emre Tonguç

Alaçatı is one of those rare Turkish towns that has managed to preserve its historic texture virtually intact. Realizing the potential benefits, the locals of Alaçatı have embraced the restoration of their town; the mayor refused to allow the construction of concrete high-rises, and so Alaçatı was saved from the kind of contractors, who care only about throwing up identical buildings everywhere.

The cobblestoned streets and stone buildings with elegant bay windows, the chic restaurants and unconventional hotels, the cafés and windmills, and the public square surrounding the mosque will cast a spell over you as soon as you arrive. Most of all, the 150-year-old stone houses built by the Greek stonemasons are awe-inspiring. Beauty almost oozes out of them, especially in the evenings.

As far as possible, most of the

Alaçatı houses
Saffet Emre Tonguç

houses have been restored to their former glory, but there is a wonderful blend of the trendy and the traditional side by side here: an up-to-the-minute boutique rubbing shoulders with an old butcher's shop, for example.

In summer the narrow streets are awash with bougainvillea, geraniums, and honeysuckle, making them even more delightful, even though the crowds of visitors can make walking along them a chore.

Değirmen Hotel
Saffet Emre Tonguç

Looking back in time

Ancient sources refer to this part of the coast as Ionia. The Persians, who could barely pronounce the name, called the natives simply "Yunan" (the word for Greek in Turkish), a word which was eventually incorporated into Turkish as well.

Alaçatı first crops up in history as a settlement within the borders of Ionian Erythrae. Its name is assumed to be derived from "Alaca at" (motley horse) or "Alacık" (tents). It seems to have been a coastal settlement until the sea retreated, leaving only marshland. Once the marsh dried out, wine-making and tobacco production became important sources of income. After the population exchange between Turkey and Greece in the 1920s, the Greeks had to leave Alaçatı, their place taken by Turks from Thessalonica, Crete and Kos.

Bodrum has an increasingly popular rival for the role of Turkey's most revered summer vacation spot these days. Alaçatı has set a fine example of how the preservation of cultural heritage can help create a popular new destination. If only the town could extend its short summer tourist season both Turks and foreign tourists would stand to benefit.

Port Alaçatı
An establishment with a lot to offer in terms of architectural originality, it is part Fort Lauderdale, part Port Grimaud. You can dock your boat at the front and park your car at the back!
Saffet Emre Tonguç

From cobblestoned streets to bay windows, from chic hotels to cozy little squares, this is Alaçatı.

Saffet Emre Tonguç

HOW TO **TRAVEL?**

If you take the İDO sea-bus from Istanbul (Yenikapı), you will need to drive for another 340 kilometers after Bandırma. If you are coming from İzmir (70km), most Çeşme buses leave from the small Üçkuyular bus terminal and pass through Alaçatı.

Çeşme Seyahat.
Phone: (0232) 716 82 99
If you are driving, take the Çeşme highway direct from İzmir.

WHAT **TO DO?**

At the local bazaar on Saturdays you can find almost anything from fresh produce to textiles. At weekends, there is also an antiques bazaar.

For those looking for something more than touristy souvenirs, there are interesting surprises at shops like Ayşe'nin Dolabı, Mon Jardin, Light House and K&S Takı, where you can find original jewelry and other articles. The small art galleries are the icing on the cake.

The Belediye (Municipality) organizes classical music concerts in the summer.

With an average 300 windy days a year, Alaçatı is one of the best places in the world for windsurfing and offers some excellent windsurfing schools.

ASPC
Phone: (0232) 716 66 11

Alaçatı Windsurf School
Phone: (0232) 716 05 11

Orsa
Phone: (0532) 655 20 10
Dine at one of Orsa's tables set in the sea and sip your wine in one of the hammocks.

Get further information on the town by clicking on www.alacati-rehberi.com.

WHERE TO **STAY?**

Taş Hotel
Phone: (0232) 716 77 72
www.tasotel.com
Zeynep Öziş was a key figure in making Alaçatı what it is today. Her hotel is magnificent. There are eight rooms in the beautifully restored historic structure and an inviting pool in the garden.

Sakızlıhan
Phone: (0232) 716 61 08
www.sakizlihan.com
In the garden of this lovely stone structure stands a beautiful terebinth (turpentine tree), grown only on the island of Chios (Sakız) and in Alaçatı.

Lale Lodge
Phone: (0232) 716 79 99
www.lalelodge.com
The Lale family, owners of this eight-room establishment, like to say "as you dance with the wind, so you will ease your soul". Some of the rooms have large Jacuzzis and candles, the key, perhaps, to a romantic holiday.

Değirmen Hotel
Phone: (0232) 716 67 14
www.alacatidegirmen.com
Built to look like a local windmill, this hotel has waterbeds in some of the rooms.

Ümit Ev Hotel
Phone: (0232) 716 81 33
www.umitevotel.com
A cozy, affordable alternative. You can enjoy your breakfast beneath the grapevines and fig trees here.

Sailors Hotel
Phone: (0232) 716 87 65
www.sailorsotel.com
A five-room hotel in the village center. Its café, called Orta (meaning "the middle" in Turkish), is a great favorite.

O Ev Hotel
Phone: (0232) 716 61 50
www.o-ev.com
A former olive-oil depot is now a super-chic boutique hotel and gourmet restaurant with a lovely garden.

One Resort Ephesus
Phone: (0232) 716 97 77
www.onehotelsandresorts.com
If you prefer an all-inclusive package arrangement, this resort is a good choice. The former "Süzer" hotel boasts an excellent restaurant.

WHERE TO **EAT?**

Mavi Bistro
Phone: (0232) 716 04 20
www.mavibistro.com
Hidden in a back street this simply-decorated joint offers good service.

Agrilia
Phone: (0232) 716 85 94
Grape and tobacco-growing may no longer happen in Alaçatı, but an old grape and tobacco warehouse has been converted into this lovely high-ceilinged restaurant with bags of character. The breakfast is very good. Don't miss the tango nights.

Sardunaki
Phone: (0232) 716 02 16
www.sardunaki.com
How would you feel about dancing the sirtaki (a dance created for the movie Zorba the Greek)? This place offers music from both sides of the Aegean, with live performances at the weekend.

Tuval Restaurant
Phone: (0232) 716 98 08
Sprawling along the main street, this chic restaurant even has its own small boutique.

Kalamata
Phone: (0232) 716 63 57
Breakfast, mezes and delicious seafood specialties served with a big smile on the side.

Lavanta
Phone: (0232) 716 68 91
The colors and tastes of the Mediterranean.

Evce
Phone: (0232) 716 02 66
www.evcecafe.com
Delicious, home-cooked meals, everything from mantı (Turkish ravioli) to stuffed chard.

İmren Helva ve Lokma Evi
Phone: (0232) 716 83 56
A sweetshop that has been going strong on the same site since 1941. Try the home-made ice cream, especially the mastic and lemon flavors.

Köşe Kahve
Phone: (0232)716 04 13
A lovely place where cakes and cookies are baked by owner Mrs. Tomris.

Kırmızı Ardıç Kuşu
Phone: (0232) 716 65 51
www.kirmiziardic.com
Has its own art gallery.

Shaka
Phone: (0232) 716 05 06
www.shaka-alacati.com
Popular spot for "happy hour" in Alaçatı Harbor.

Sea Side
Phone: (0232) 716 98 99
www.seasidecesme.com
Opened in 1997, this entertainment complex has a Blue Flag beach. With a restaurant and a bar, it also serves as a nightclub.

If you are interested in local flavors, be sure to look out for the Alaçatı pickle house.

E "UGLY" TOWN THAT BECAME "CUTE"

irince

Fatih TÜRKMENOĞLU

Şirince must be one of the loveliest villages in Turkey. Set on a hillside above Selçuk and within easy reach of the ruins at Ephesus, the town retains most of its lovely old wooden houses with their red-tiled roofs, still mercifully undefiled by solar panels. Up here the air feels fresh and the restaurants serve fruit-flavored wines.

Şirince provided the setting for the Greek writer Dido Sotiriou's celebrated book "*Farewell Anatolia*". There she wrote: "If there is a place called heaven on earth, our village of Kırkınca must be a part of it", a sentiment with which many visitors to modern Şirince would surely concur.

Of course much has changed since Dido grew up here. The old village school now houses the Artemis Restaurant and many of the fine old houses, which line up in tiers along the hillside, have been turned into hotels and pensions, or accommodate villagers who make a living out of selling lace to tourists. But modern Şirince is a mesmerizing village and very different from others in the vicinity.

> After a quick supper, you can retreat to a hotel room that will make you feel as if you have stepped straight back into the 19th century.

Originally Şirince was built by the Greeks, but after the population exchange between Turkey and Greece in 1923, the Greeks who had to leave Anatolia were replaced by Turks from Thessalonica. The Greeks had named their village "Çirkince" (which literally means "uglyish"), hoping that the name would deter anyone from bothering them. Eventually, Kazim Dirik, the governor of İzmir, declared "this place is beautiful - it cannot be named Çirkince", and the name was changed to "Şirince" (cute, adorable).

There are still two churches in the village. The Church of St John the Baptist, in the upper village, is being restored by an American foundation. Unfortunately, most of the contents of the second church, Hagia Dimitri, have been stolen; it stands dilapidated and in need of rescue.

In some ways Şirince is timeless. Up ahead Shepherd Mehmet is grazing his three goats. On the hillside the women are selling knitted socks and embroidered tablecloths. Village kids are volunteering as guides, leading visitors up and down the hills. The tourist buses come and go, the digital cameras keep on clicking.

A shopper's paradise

This little village is great for shopping. The local women sell home-made lace, tablecloths, beads, muslin cloth, and dresses, and there is a single remaining woodcarver who still makes beautiful wooden spoons. "Demetrius", the jeweler's shop which manufactured the pieces used in the Brad Pitt-Orlando Bloom movie *Troy*, stocks beautiful individual rings and necklaces.

Şirince's name is associated with the grapes that are produced around here and used to make delicious fruit wines (including strawberry, cherry and peach). There are only two wine producers in the village; much of what is on sale is actually produced and bottled elsewhere but labeled as "from Şirince" regardless. The olive oil produced locally is also incredibly tasty.

HOW TO **TRAVEL?**

Take the Selçuk exit off the İzmir-Kuşadası highway. Traveling by public transport, look for a bus to Selçuk; local minibuses run the last 9km up to Şirince.

WHERE TO **STAY?**

Nişanyan Hotel and Houses
Phone: (0232) 898 32 08
You can immediately tell that this is a hotel born out of love. Co-authors of the celebrated book, "The Little Hotel Book: The Best Small Hotels of Turkey", Müjde and Sevan Nişanyan have been the prime movers in putting Şirince on the map. They take care of every detail in their hotel and "houses". The views are fantastic and their secret sherbet recipe superb. Here you get to rub shoulders with wealthy Americans, European artists and Turkish intellectuals who have traveled all this way just to stay at the Nişanyan Hotel, unquestionably one of "the best small hotels in Turkey".

Kilisealtı Pansiyon
Phone: (0232) 898 31 28
Lovely small pension in the shadow of a church (hence "beneath the church") and with panoramic views over the village.

Şirince Evleri (Houses)
Phone: (0232) 898 30 99
Two houses with inviting Ottoman-style décor and big brass beds.

Kırkınca Evleri
Phone: (0232) 898 31 33
Five delightfully decorated Ottoman-style houses.

Huzur Pansiyon
Phone: (0232) 898 30 60

WHERE TO **EAT?**

Artemis
Phone: (0232) 898 32 40
Şirince's most popular restaurant is housed in an old school-house with a sweeping view. The decoration, service and food are all great. For breakfast, try the otlu ve peynirli börek (pastry filled with herbs and cheese) with a large cup of tea. For dinner, go for the "sac kavurma" (meat and vegetables fried in a wok with herbs). Fruit wines are on sale in the garden.

Ocakbaşı
Phone: (0232) 898 30 94
Mrs. Zeynep's home-cooked dishes are delicious. Try the güveçte kuru fasulye (white kidney bean casserole), the pickles, the kabak çiçeği dolması (stuffed squash flowers) and the peppers with çökelek (dried cottage cheese). The view from the garden is fantastic.

Tepebaşı Gözleme Bahçesi
Phone: (0232) 898 30 83
As the name implies, this is a place to eat "gözleme" (Turkish-style pancakes); try the unusual otlu (with herbs) version. The stuffed vine leaves and home-made baklava are also very good.

Arşipel
Phone: (0232) 898 32 16
Try the house specials made with Aegean herbs, and the patlıcan çorbası (eggplant soup).

Otherwise, Özlem Gözleme Bahçesi is famous for its stuffed vine leaves cooked in olive oil and for its bulgur (cracked wheat) risotto.

The Şirince Sultanhan and Grup Restaurant are best known for their çöp kebab, small pieces of lamb served on thin skewers.

WHAT **TO DO?**

Şirince makes the perfect base for excursions to Selçuk (9km), Ephesus (11km) and Kuşadası (28km). You can just about squeeze visits to Ephesus, the Yedi Uyurlar (the Cave of the Seven Sleepers), the House of the Virgin Mary, Selçuk Castle, İsabey Mosque, the Temple of Artemis, and Selçuk Museum into two busy days.

The Kuantum Yaşam Merkezi (Quantum Living Center) holds seminars on "the reconstruction of the spirit" in Şirince. The program includes meditation, excursions and walking tours, and concentrates on "capturing the spirit". During the four-day workshop, participants stay at the Kırkınca Evleri. Groups never exceed 10 people. For further information, go to www.kuantumdusunce.com or call (0533) 480 16 27.

LAND OF SUN AND CIVILIZATION
037 Ionia

Saffet Emre TONGUÇ

Ionia was the ancient name for an area around İzmir that extended as far north as Foça and as far south as Miletus. Today, it's a region that is littered with reminders of the ancient Greco-Roman civilization, especially in the stunning sites of Ephesus, Priene and Miletus.

The Theater of Ephesus
Saffet Emre Tonguç

Celcus Library of Ephesus

Between the 11th and 6th centuries BC, 12 Ionian "cities" played a pivotal role in history. They were: Miletus, Myus, Priene, Ephesus, Colophon, Lebedus, Teos, Erythrae, Clazomenae and Phocaea, with the two Aegean islands of Samos and Chios thrown in. Later, Smyrna (now İzmir) joined the Ionian confederation to make it a baker's dozen. Theirs was a cultural and religious union, rather than a political one, and all the "cities" retained complete autonomy. Once a year, their representatives would come together to celebrate the Panionic Festival on Mt Mycale, near Priene.

Of all the cities, it was Miletus that made one of the greatest contributions to history, when it bequeathed the alphabet to Athens in 402 BC; albeit with many revisions (particularly the addition of vowels), this alphabet has survived until the present day. The Miletians had picked up the alphabet from trading with the Phoenicians which is why the letters of the Greek alphabet are sometimes referred to as "Phoenician Things".

The Ionians were very advanced in science, art, culture and philosophy.

According to Herodotus, the famous "father" of history, Ionia boasted the best climate in the world, a verdict with which many modern visitors would agree.

HOW TO **TRAVEL?**

The ancient Ionian cities formed a loop around İzmir, with Foça (ancient Phocaea) as the furthest northerly point. Not too far away from Foça, Bergama is nearly 100 kilometers from İzmir and 240 kilometers from Çanakkale. If you travel out to the Çeşme peninsula from İzmir and head south to Kuşadası via Seferhisar, you can visit a couple of the other cities: for example, Ephesus is three kilometers from Selçuk and 20 kilometers from Kuşadası. As you pass Söke on the road from Selçuk to Bodrum, a turning on the right leads to Güllübahçe; from here you will come first to Priene, then to Miletus and finally to Didyma, 20 kilometers after that.

IONIAN CELEBRITIES

HOMER

Homer, the blind poet of Smyrna (now İzmir) who probably lived in the 8th or 7th century BC, is known as the father of western literature. The *Iliad*, in which he tells the story of the Trojan War, and the *Odyssey*, which describes the Greek hero Odysseus's long journey home, are his two masterpieces. For centuries, the *Iliad* was the second most frequently read book after the Bible in the West (allegedly!).

THALES

The astronomer and mathematician, Thales (624-546 BC) was one of the Seven Sages of Greece. His famous aphorism, "Know yourself", was inscribed in the forecourt of the Temple of Apollo in Delphi, site of one of the most important oracles in Ancient Greece. According to Thales, who predicted the eclipse of the sun in 585 BC one year ahead of time, everything was made of water. By focusing on verifiable facts, rather than relying on myths and legends, Thales helped to engineer the birth of scientific thought. Although few of his writings survive, his ideas live on in Aristotle's Metaphysics.

ANAXIMANDER

Anaximander (610-546 BC) succeeded Thales as head of the world-famous Milesian School in Ionia. He was one of the earliest thinkers to develop a theory of evolution and one of the first to realize how far the sun might be from the earth. Recognized as the inventor of the sundial, he was also the first person to deduce that the earth's axis was tilted. Pythagoras was one of his pupils.

ASPASIA

A Miletian, Aspasia was the mistress of the 5th-century BC Athenian statesman Pericles; she taught him the art of rhetoric. An early believer in women's equality, she was hugely influential in Athenian philosophy and literature circles, where the great Socrates also came to know and admire her.

HERACLITUS

Heraclitus (535-475 BC) was one of the earliest dialectic philosophers and, in his famous aphorism "Panta Rhei," proposed the theory that nothing in nature remains the same and is, instead, subject to continual change. He is also known for another aphorism - "You cannot wash in the same river twice". Famous German philosopher Nietzsche once remarked, "The world forever needs the truth, hence the world forever needs Heraclitus," underlining the importance of this philosopher, who argued that it is the constant conflict of opposite elements that creates evolution. Heraclitus, a contributor to Stoic philosophy, is also known to have said, "Water finds life from the earth and spirit finds life from water".

The Miletian philosophers were also the first people to suggest that matter was made up of atoms. One of the world's first logographi (historiographers), Cadmus wrote a book on the city's foundation, while Hecataeus was one of the world's first geographers and cartographers.

The ancient city of Miletus

Refik Ongan

THE GATEWAY TO EPHESUS
038 Kuşadası

Saffet Emre TONGUÇ

Kuşadası is a big, brash port town which is perfectly positioned for visits to Ephesus as well as for trips to the Greek island of Samos. Although the center retains some of its old buildings, including a huge caravanserai, modern development has not been kind to the town which has sprawled in every direction to accommodate its many guests. It's a place to come if you like your nightlife loud but also like to spend your days exploring, with inviting small beaches just a short hop away on the Dilek peninsula.

Kuşadası from the garden of the Kısmet Hotel
Serhan Güngör

Kuşadası was known to the Byzantines as Ania, and then to the Venetians and Genoese as Scala Nuova, a name now attached to the port. Founded as an extension to the ancient city of Ephesus, after the original port had silted up, it takes its present name Kuşadası (Bird Island) from the off-shore islet of Güvercin Adası (Pigeon Island), which boasts a small Genoese Castle.

Every year the port of Kuşadası welcomes hundreds of cruise liners filled with tourists who are coming to see Ephesus.

Around town and out to the beaches

Across the road from Scala Nuova Port, pedestrianized Barbaros Hayrettin Paşa Boulevard wends its way up from beside the 16th-century Öküz Mehmet Paşa Caravanserai to a small arch and tower across the road, a miraculous survivor from the medieval walls. The entire street is lined with shops, banks and estate agents aimed at tourists. Off to the right lies the noisiest part of town: Barlar Sokağı, where all the bars are located! If, instead, you turn the corner beside the PTT (post office) and wander round the side streets, you will stumble upon a few decent restaurants and shops, as well as an ancient hamam (Turkish bath).

There's a public beach on the road leading from the port to the marina but you might prefer to try alternatives such as Kadınlar Denizi and Cennet beach.

The erstwhile lovely Pamucak beach at the mouth of the Küçük Menderes (Little Meander) river is now chock-a-block with newly-built hotels and water-parks.

For something less developed, head for the Dilek Peninsula, which was declared a national park in 1966; it's dotted with small, sandy beaches - İçmeler, Aydınlık Koyu, Kavaklı Burun, and Karasu - which look up at Mt Samsun, a towering 1237 meters high.

On to Selçuk and Samos

Because of its proximity to several major archeological sites, Kuşadası hosts thousands of package holidaymakers every year. Many of them also visit nearby Selçuk to see the sculptures of a many-breasted Artemis in the museum; the scant remains of the Temple of Artemis (one of the Seven Wonders of the Ancient World); the Basilica of St John the Evangelist (one of the four authors of the gospels); and İsabey Mosque (one of Turkey's most beautiful and ornate mosques).

A daily ferry connects Kuşadası with the Greek island of Samos (Sisam). For further information, contact Anker Travel (Phone: (0256) 612 45 98; www.ankertravel.com). Daily excursions cost around €35.

Kuşadası boasts some spectacular sunsets, although the view is equally alluring when the moon is full.

Mehmet Çabuk

WHERE TO **STAY?**

Kısmet Hotel
Phone: (0256) 618 12 90
www.kismet.com.tr
A Kuşadası classic, the hotel stands out for its spectacular view, excellent food and unique atmosphere.

Villa Konak
Phone: (0256) 614 63 18
www.villakonakhotel.com
Twenty-two-roomed hotel with a beautiful garden in the old part of town. Doesn't take children.

Liman Hotel
Phone: (0232) 614 77 70
Comfortable, straightforward hotel with small roof restaurant opposite the Samos ferry landing.

Bakkhos, Kirazlı Village
Phone: (0256) 622 03 37
Four kilometers outside Kuşadası and handy for Ephesus, the 12-roomed Bakkhos is buried in deepest countryside. The decor reflects the arty taste of owners Manuela and Orhan Özbaş. A splendid pool completes a perfect picture. Don't get too comfy on those sun loungers though you may never want to get up again.

Kalehan Hotel, Selçuk
Phone: (0232) 892 61 54
www.kalehan.com
A pleasing hotel with unique decoration and ambience in close proximity to Ephesus. Overlooked by a Byzantine castle.

Nilya Hotel, Selçuk
Phone: (0232) 892 90 81
www.nilya.com
A pleasant surprise down a Selçuk back street. Breakfast is superb. You feel like you're vacationing in a friend's house.

WHERE TO **EAT?**

Tarihi Çınar 2 Restaurant
Phone: (0256) 618 18 47
One of the best seafood restaurants.

Secret Garden Restaurant
Phone: (0256) 618 26 96
The view, the service, the fish, the mezes and the choice of wines are all excellent. It's right next to the Kısmet Hotel.

Cimino Restaurant
Phone: (0256) 614 64 09
In the heart of Kuşadası, this restaurant specializes in Italian cuisine. The view is the icing on the cake.

Değirmen Restaurant
Phone: (0256) 681 2150
Excellent restaurant in extensive grounds eight kilometers out of Kuşadası on the road to Davutlar. Menu features some quirky local dishes such as keşkek (mutton and wheat pounded into a tasty paste).

SHINING A SPOTLIGHT ON HISTORY

039 Ephesus

Saffet Emre TONGUÇ

The largest excavated Greco-Roman city in the world, Ephesus was, like many other Anatolian ancient cities, a cradle first of Greek and then of Roman civilization. Although only 10 percent of the city has been excavated, enough survives of its magnificent buildings for you to get a real sense of what an old Roman town would have looked like. Above all, in the wonderful Terraced Houses, you will feel yourself a guest dropping in on life as it was lived almost two millennia ago.

The Library of Celsus once housed 12,000 books.

Saffet Emre Tonguç

Once a town with a population of nearly 250,000 inhabitants, Ephesus was the capital of the Roman province known as Asia Minor. It was also a flourishing center of religion, culture, and the arts. As one of the Seven Wonders of the Ancient World, the Temple of Artemis was a source of pride and prosperity for the city. Since it was the chief harbor on the west coast, thousands of people from different nations flocked to Ephesus and were mesmerized by its beauty. Later, the city also became one of the most important centers of Christianity. Not far from Lydia where the first coin was minted, the ancient city of Ephesus also boasted the first known bank in history.

THE HOUSE OF THE VIRGIN MARY

The so-called House of the Virgin Mary (Meryemana; "Mother Mary" in Turkish) is a peaceful place where people come to make a wish or to drink from a spring, which is believed to have healing powers. In the 19th-century a paralyzed nun, Anna Katherina Emmerich, saw a vision of the house where the Virgin Mary is believed to have spent her final days, which enabled two Lazarist missionaries from İzmir to locate it in upper Ephesus. Research carried out in the house revealed that the structure dated back to the first century which tended to support the story that, before his death, Jesus entrusted his mother to St John the Evangelist, who brought Mary to live here. Although St John died in Selçuk and was buried there, there are no clues as to the whereabouts of Mary's grave.

The Temple of Domitian was named after a ruthless Roman emperor.
Saffet Emre Tonguç

With such a rich historical and cultural heritage and such extensive remains, it's hardly surprising that Ephesus is regarded as one of the world's most important archeological sites.

From the Odeon to the Library of Celsus

Today, the Ephesus ruins are accessed via two separate gates. The lower gate is on the left-hand side of the road from Selçuk to Kuşadası, on the foothills of Mt Panayır. The upper gate is on the right-hand side of the road up to the House of Mary. Used by the residents of the ancient city of Magnesia on the Menderes (Meander) river, this entrance leads straight to a small theater called the Odeon. Also serving as a meeting hall for the local council, the Odeon stands next to an altar where some especially famous statues of Artemis were unearthed. Artemis was the virgin goddess of the hunt. However, the multiple breasts (or eggs, according to some archaeologists) on the statues emphasized her role as the goddess of fertility. Today, these statues are on display in the Ephesus Museum in Selçuk along with numerous other finds from the site.

The sculptures, busts, and figurines displayed in the Ephesus Museum in Selçuk offer valuable clues to the period in which they were created.

After the altar, you come to a street named after the Curetes (Roman priests), which passes through one of the main squares of the city. Nike, the goddess of victory, who gave her name to the famous sports brand, is only one of the mythological figures to greet you in statue form in this square. Opposite her statue stand the ancient hospital and pharmacy, as well as a bas-relief of Hermes. Do not get this Hermes confused with the famous French luxury brand Hermès; the former was the messenger of the gods and the god of travelers in his own right. Nearby you'll see the foundations of a temple named after Domitian (51-96), a

Nike, who gave her name to a famous sports brand, was the goddess of victory in Greek mythology.
Saffet Emre Tonguç

Terrace Houses
Saffet Emre Tonguç

famously ruthless Roman emperor.

Further ahead you come to the Gate of Hercules, the heroic strongman of Greek mythology; once you pass through this gate, you find yourself in an ancient pedestrian zone where the 1,900-year-old sidewalks of Ephesus have stood up to the test of time remarkably well. As you walk along, you will see, on your right, a fountain dedicated to the emperor Trajan and a temple built for his nephew Hadrian. The public bath complex is behind the temple. At the entrance to the baths stands a headless female statue; meet Scholastica, the city's "madam", who restored the baths with the money she made from her brothel.

Look at a 20YTL banknote and you will find both the Temple of Hadrian and the magnificent Library of Celsus depicted on it.

A toilet block near the baths is particularly eye-catching. These toilets consisted of a series of holes one beside the other - the Romans certainly weren't shy! Joking aside, the baths and latrines were among the most important places for social interaction in Roman times.

The most outstanding feature of Curetes Street is the cluster of private houses, known as the Terraced Houses, which belonged to the more affluent inhabitants of the city. These houses were incredibly luxurious, with central courtyards and fountains, frescoes on the walls and mosaics on the floors.

In the center of the arch at the entrance to the Temple of Hadrian is a bas-relief of Cybele, the Mother Goddess.
Saffet Emre Tonguç

One of the statues of Celsus Library.
Mehmet Çabuk

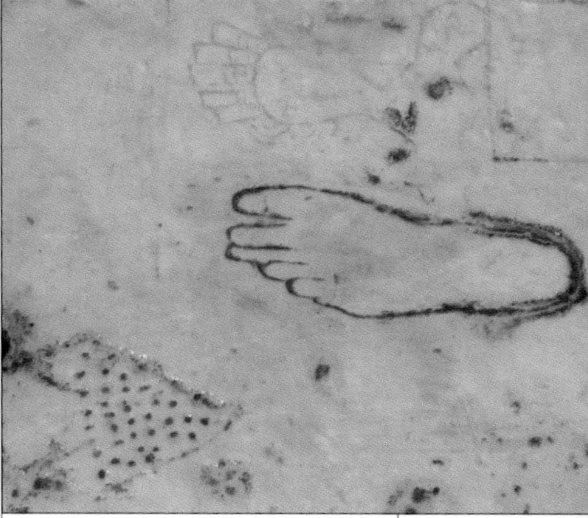
The first advertisement, pointing the way to the brothel.
Saffet Emre Tonguç

A library and a brothel

Beyond the Terraced Houses you arrive in the heart of the city, which boasts some of the most spectacular public buildings. Traditionally, wealthy Ephesians erected such buildings to beautify their town and had their names engraved on the columns of the municipality hall in return.

The Austrians, who had been excavating at Ephesus since 1895, may have been able to create their own Ephesus Museum inside Vienna's Hofburg Palace with what they carried away from the ancient city, but the restoration work they did on the Library of Celsus in the 1970s is still stunning. Often used as an image to promote Turkey abroad, this Library remains in great condition and looks simply astounding. From the frequency with which they visited the library, it may have appeared that the men of Ephesus were very keen on reading. However, later studies revealed that a secret tunnel allowed passage from the library to the building opposite it. It's not that difficult to guess, is it? The building immediately opposite was nothing but the brothel! Lesson? Beware of bookworms!

In order to save money for their dowries, impoverished Ephesian girls practiced the oldest profession in the world, which was socially acceptable at the time...

After leaving the library, you will pass the Agora (Market Place) and head along the Colonnaded Street towards the grand theater. As you go, look out for the clearly visible

Ephesus Theater
Saffet Emre Tonguç

One of the Seven Wonders of the Ancient World

THE TEMPLE OF ARTEMIS

Although, all seven of them once stood inside the boundaries of the Ottoman Empire, only two of the Seven Wonders of the Ancient World were in what is now modern Turkey. One was the Mausoleum of Halicarnassus in Bodrum, the other the Temple of Artemis in Ephesus. Some of the artifacts from these two "Wonders" can be seen in the British Museum in London, so if you are ever there, do make sure to visit them!

Anatolia, which was home to Çatalhöyük, possibly the first Neolithic settlement in the world, was also the birthplace of Cybele, one of the first goddesses known to history. At a time when fertility was still thought of as a miracle, women played the dominant role in society and the Earth Mother goddess Cybele was hugely important. Over time, she became identified with other deities in different cultures, such as Kubaba, Ishtar, Ninoe, Artemis, and Diana.

Boasting 127 columns with Ionic capitals, the Temple of Artemis in Ephesus was originally four times bigger than the Parthenon on the Athens Acropolis. According to some historians, several of the columns were later re-used in the construction of of Hagia Sophia in İstanbul. Legend has it that on the night the Temple of Artemis was destroyed by arsonists, Artemis was preoccupied with the birth of Alexander the Great and so could not protect her Temple! That ´s probably why Alexander the Great wanted to have it rebuilt.

The statue of Artemis was excavated from the State Altar of Ephesus

Saffet Emre Tonguç

sewerage system and admire an infrastructure designed and built some 20 centuries ago. Don't miss the marble figure on your left either - this seems to have been the world's first advertising. Consisting of a left foot, the figure of a woman, and a heart, the message roughly translates as: "If you need a beautiful woman to fill your lonely heart, keep going to the left!" The ad was put here to guide newly-arrived sailors straight to the brothel. One of the most important brothels of this period was in Pompeii, Italy. When you visit this ancient city, you can still see the graphic frescoes on the walls. To overcome possible language difficulties between the prostitutes and their clients, their services and fees were depicted on the walls!

Epistle to the Ephesians

As you walk along Arcadian Street towards the famous port of Ephesus, you will pass the largest ancient theater surviving in Anatolia; this magnificent structure, which had a seating capacity of 25,000, is still in regular use for open-air concerts.

The theater used to be so important that it was even mentioned in one of the books of the Bible, St Paul's Epistle to the Ephesians. St Paul of Tarsus came to Ephesus to try and convert the locals to Christianity, to the fury of some of the residents who much preferred their own goddess; "When they heard [this] and were filled with rage, they [began] crying out, saying, 'Great is Artemis of the Ephesians!'" (Acts 19:28).

The alluvium carried by the river Küçük Menderes (Little Meander) slowly silted up the harbor of Ephesus and mosquitoes spread malaria all over the city, eventually bringing its glory days to an end. During the reign of the famous Byzantine emperor Justinian, who commissioned

The only column left from the Temple of Artemis

Saffet Emre Tonguç

Istanbul's Hagia Sophia, the rocks on the hills were used to build a fortress in Selçuk and the remaining population moved there.

WHAT **TO DO?**

- Apart from the ancient city of Ephesus, you can also visit the Church of Saint John the Evangelist, who is said to have brought the Virgin Mary to Ephesus at the end of her life.
- İsa Bey Mosque was built in 1375. Architecturally, it is one of the most outstanding of all Anatolian mosques.
- The Steam Locomotive Museum in Çamlık houses an interesting collection of old trains in an attractive garden.
- The Selçuk bazaar is fun to walk around.
- If the silted-up harbor of Ephesus still existed today, its beach would have been the present-day Pamucak, which overflows with tourists in summer.

The entrance to the Ephesian Agora

Saffet Emre Tonguç

WHERE TO **EAT?**

Amazon Restaurant

Phone: (0232) 892 38 79

Apart from the dishes majoring on Aegean herbs and vegetables, the menu features ancient Ephesian olive mezes (appetizers). Don't miss them!

A BEAUTY OF THE ANCIENT WORLD
040 Priene

Saffet Emre TONGUÇ

Gloriously situated on the slopes of Mt Mykale, ancient Priene was a marvel of early city planning. Small but breathtaking, the site of its ruins makes a great place to while away a few hours. Nearby Eski Doğanbey is an abandoned Greek settlement slowly finding new life as big-city refugees move in.

Agora (Market Place)

Built on a grid plan of the type first used by the architect Hippodamos in Miletus 2,500 years ago, Priene is one of the rare ancient cities that managed to preserve its original layout, perhaps because the Romans weren't very interested in it. The ancient theater, with a seating capacity of 5,000, is regarded as one of the most beautiful of such structures. The five marble seats near the stage were reserved for prominent people on the city government. The altar inside it was used for sacrificing animals as votive offerings to Dionysus, the god of wine and theater. A clepsydra (water glass) was used to show the actors how much time remained.

Priene frequently played host to Ionian congresses and festivals, and its bouleuterion (council chamber) could house 640 delegates. The Prytaneion near it was used as the administrative headquarters. The town's most magnificent structure, the temple dedicated to the goddess Athena, was commissioned by Alexander the Great who conquered Anatolia during a military expedition of 334 BC; the temple was built by the famous architect Pytheos, who also created the Mausoleum in Bodrum. With 10 Ionic columns on one side and six on the other, the structure is still visible from the road far below.

The city's stadium was used for all kinds of sports, including boxing, wrestling, and the pentathlon.

You can still explore the ruins of a dwelling said to have been the house where Alexander the Great stayed.

Priene overlooks the plain of the Büyük Menderes, the river whose winding path gave the English language the word '"meander".

Demeter and Persephone

Another of Priene's temples was dedicated to Demeter, goddess of the earth and harvest. According to Ancient Greek mythology, Demeter's beautiful daughter Persephone was abducted by Hades, the brother of Zeus and the god of the underworld. Her devastated mother, who was in charge of the changing seasons, stopped work immediately, and life on earth came to a standstill, while her daughter remained in the underworld. In the end, Persephone's father Zeus persuaded Hades to return Persephone to her mother. Before she left, Hades tricked Persephone into eating six pomegranate seeds, which meant that she had to spend half of every year in the underground and the other half on earth, with her mother. At the end of every winter, Demeter turned the earth green to demonstrate her joy at her daughter's return, but at the end of each summer, the green gave way to red and brown, reflecting her sorrow at her daughter's renewed departure…

Towering above the Temple of Athena, Mt Mykale (Samsun) housed a barracks in ancient times.

Saffet Emre Tonguç

WHERE TO **EAT?**

Şelale Restaurant, Güllübahçe
Phone: (0256) 547 10 09
A peaceful place facing the Priene waterfall.

Theater

WHERE TO **STAY?**

Doğanbey Evleri, Eski Doğanbey
Phone: (0532) 590 43 45
www.doganbeyhouses.com
Formerly known as Domaçya, Doğanbey is a semi-abandoned village on the southern slopes of the Dilek National Park, near Priene. After the population exchange between Greece and Turkey in 1923, the Greek residents were forced to leave and by the 1980s, there was hardly anyone left here; reoccupation only started again recently. Visit nearby Karine to enjoy a fish dinner and then spend the night in perfect silence at the restored Doğanbey Evleri (Houses), a handful of delightful self-catering cottages.

A TOWN OF MANY COLONIES AND
A CENTRE OF PROPHECY

041 Miletus and Didyma

Saffet Emre TONGUÇ

One of the oldest and most important Ionian cities was Miletus which went on to found nearly a hundred colonies on the Black Sea. A center of education and art, the town originally stood right on the seashore before alluvium from the River Menderes (Meander) silted up the area and left it stranded inland. To reach Didyma, the seat of an important oracle in ancient times, people would follow the Sacred Way that ran from Miletus.

The town of many colonies

The town of Miletus stood on the banks of the River Menderes, one of the most important rivers of the ancient world which the historian Herodotus dubbed “the laborer”. The English word meander, meaning “to follow a winding course”, was derived from the name of the River Menderes, which followed a convoluted path on its way to the sea.

Miletus was originally established by Neleus, the son of the king of Athens. As soon as the Greeks arrived here, their men slaughtered their Carian counterparts and married their wives. Legend has it that the women vowed never to sit down to eat with their new husbands or to call them by their names!

The town was famed for its many scientists and intellectuals, including Anaximandros, Anaximenes, Thales and Isidoros (one of the two architects of Hagia Sophia in İstanbul). Probably the town’s most beautiful structure was its theater which is still largely intact today; it was expanded to seat 15,000 people during the Roman period. Above it stands a citadel built during the Byzantine era and re-used during Seljuk times.

The Miletians were the first people to establish hegemony over the sea, establishing a string of colonies on the Black Sea coast from Sinop to Trabzon.

One of the world’s oldest known synagogues is located in Sardis, to the east of İzmir, but sources reveal that Miletus also housed a synagogue to cater to the religious needs of its large Jewish population.

The ancient city of Miletus
Saffet Emre Tonguç

Detail from the theater of Miletus

Carved relief of Medusa, Didyma

Saffet Emre Tonguç

The oracle and Medusa

At the entrance to the Temple of Apollo in Didyma there stands a carved relief of the Gorgon Medusa, her hair a mass of serpentine curls; according to legend one glance from this woman was enough to turn the onlooker into stone. In Greek, "didyma" means "twin"; it is possible that the town was given this name to refer to the "twin" temples of Artemis (in Selçuk) and of her twin brother Apollo, who had his own temple in Didyma. According to some archeologists, the town's fame as a center of prophecy preceded the arrival of the Greeks. Certainly, the oracle was second in importance only to the one at Delphi on mainland Greece in Hellenic times.

Originally featuring 108 columns, the Temple of Apollo was one of the great masterpieces of Ancient Greek architecture.

Measuring 109m by 51m, the huge Temple of Apollo was a truly magnificent structure; it could easily have been the eighth wonder of the ancient world had its construction been completed at the time of counting. Over the centuries, it was visited by hundreds of important figures in search of a glimpse into the future; when Alexander the Great arrived to re-consecrate the oracle, the priest in charge of the shrine was able to tell him that he would go on to defeat the Persians.

Traditionally, pilgrims would purify themselves with water from the well, and, after sacrificing an animal (usually a goat) to the gods, would start asking questions like: "Will I ever get married?", "Will I find a new job?" and "What will happen to this country?" Sound familiar? It looks as if the questions that people ask fortune-tellers hardly change over time!

After the coming of Christianity, the oracle was banned as sacrilegious, and a church was built inside the still unfinished temple.

WHERE TO **STAY?**

Medusa House
Phone: (0256) 811 00 63
With less than 10 rooms, this is a small hotel in an old stone house right next to the temple which looks especially beautiful from the garden when floodlit at night.

Club Natura Oliva
Phone: (0256) 519 10 72
www.clubnatura.com
Set amid olive trees on the shores of Lake Bafa on the road to Bodrum. The off-shore island has the remains of a Byzantine a monastery.

WHERE TO **EAT?**

Kamacı Restaurant
Phone: (0256) 811 00 28
It may be a bit touristy but the restaurant offers a great view of the temple.

Temple of Apollo in Didyma

Saffet Emre Tonguç

THE TEXTILE TOWN SURROUNDED BY ANCIENT RUINS

042 Denizli and Laodiceia

Saffet Emre TONGUÇ

According to inscriptions on the tombstones of ancient Hierapolis, Denizli has been turning out textiles for centuries, a tradition which continues even today. This is a great area to come to for a weekend break, both because of the thermal springs in nearby Karahayıt and Pamukkale and because it is full of historic sites. In the Bible the Book of Revelation includes a series of letters addressed to the Seven Churches of Asia Minor. One of those churches was at Laodiceia, in the vicinity of Denizli.

The theater of Laodiceia

Saffet Emre Tonguç

According to the famous 14th-century traveler Ibn Battuta, the brocade-embroidered fabrics of Denizli were unrivalled. Today the city, which was severely damaged in earthquakes in 1710 and 1899, has a population of nearly 300,000 and still makes much of its money out of textile production. Agriculture in general may be very important to it, but Denizli is particularly famous for its roosters, hence the various sculptures around town! Since there is a fair amount of local cotton production, carpet weaving also continues to be a popular craft; there are many sizable carpet manufacturers along the Tavas road.

Towels, bathrobes and other textiles form modern Denizli's main source of income.

Aphrodisias and Hierapolis

Near Denizli are two important archeological sites. One is the ancient city of Aphrodisias, which was dedicated to Aphrodite, the goddess of love and beauty in Greek mythology; the other is Hierapolis, which was founded by the kings of Pergamum on the site of a thermal spring above what is now Pamukkale.

Aphrodisias was home to one of antiquity's most important schools of sculpture.

Excavated by the late great Professor Kenan Erim, who came from New York University in 1961, this beautiful ancient site makes a worthy rival to the more famous Ephesus. The Romans (who called Aphrodite Venus) attached great importance to Aphrodisias, and the emperors granted it numerous privileges. Sculptures created by the most celebrated artists were exported from here to many destinations around the Mediterranean, including Rome.

Hierapolis (Sacred City) was founded by the Pergamene kings in 190 BC. Thousands of people flocked to the city to seek a cure for their ailments in its historic thermal springs. Yet Anatolia's largest ancient necropolis (cemetery) is situated in Hierapolis, right above the natural marvel of Pamukkale! It makes you wonder whether the thermal springs really did have healing qualities or whether people only came here as a last resort. The one consolation is that even if they were not cured in Hierapolis they were at least buried there!

Antalya, İzmir, Kuşadası, Bodrum and Marmaris are all within reasonable day-trip reach of these ancient cities.

One of the Seven Churches

An important center of Christianity and one of the Seven Churches of Asia Minor mentioned in the Biblical Book of Revelation, Laodiceia is just a few kilometers out of Denizli. The other six churches (actually congregations) were all nearby: in Ephesus, Smyrna (İzmir), Sardis, Thyatira (Akhisar), Philadelphia (Alaşehir) and Pergamon (Bergama).

On your way from Denizli to Pamukkale, you will pass a sign pointing to Laodiceia. Ringed by two rivers, the site is also sandwiched between the 2571-meter-high, snow-capped Mt Honaz on one side and the white terraces of Pamukkale (literally, Cotton Castle) on the other.

At the junction of several important trade routes, this ancient city prospered from the wool trade. At first reluctant to embrace Christianity, Laodiceia attracted an interesting reference in the Book of Revelation, the last book of the New Testament, which was written by St John of Patmos.

Anatolia's longest stadium (350m) was in Laodiceia, but since many of the stones were re-used in the construction of other buildings, there is hardly anything left of it today.

His metaphor for the Laodiceians, perhaps derived from the local thermal springs, was intriguing: "I know what you have done. You are neither cold, nor hot, but tepid" (perhaps meaning: "Make up your mind; either be a good Christian or choose another path".) The message must have done its job because the city went on to become an important episcopal see.

Anatolia's longest stadium (350m) was in Laodiceia, but since many of the stones were re-used in the construction of other buildings, there is hardly anything left of it today.

Frequent earthquakes eventually brought Laodiceia to its knees. In recent years, several restoration projects have attempted to restore the site to some of its former glory.

WHERE TO **EAT?**

Mantar Restaurant
Phone: (0258) 266 05 74
www.mantar.com.tr
As the name suggests ("mantar" means mushroom in Turkish), Mantar Restaurant specializes in countless mushroom dishes.

Değirmendere Restaurant
Phone: (0258) 213 30 37
If you can find it, this restaurant in the back streets of Denizli will offer you delicious kebabs and trout specialties.

THE CITY OF THE GODDESS OF LOVE
043 Aphrodisias

Saffet Emre TONGUÇ

As the goddess of love and beauty, Aphrodite was always tempted by the pleasures of life. As well as a husband named Hephaestus, she had a string of lovers, including Hermes, Dionysus, and Adonis, not to mention a string of extraordinary children…

The Tetrapylon, the monumental city entrance
Saffet Emre Tonguç

Located 600 meters above sea level on a branch of the river Büyük Menderes (historically the Maeander), Aphrodisias is one of the oldest settlements in Anatolia. Its museum contains some magnificent sculptures, as well as works from the Neolithic and Bronze Ages. According to a bas-relief discovered here, the city was first named Ninoë, after Ninus, the legendary founder of the Assyrian Empire and the husband of Semiramis. The city first cropped up in history in the 2nd century when its position at the intersection of the important Carian, Lydian and Phyrgian states as well as its support for the increasingly important Roman invaders gave it huge strategic importance. During this period, Mithridates, the King of Pontus, slew nearly 80,000 Romans in Anatolia. His successor, Pharnaces II continued to make life difficult for the Romans. Upset by this continued resistance, the renowned Roman emperor Julius Caesar arrived in Pontus and defeated the Pontic armies. Shortly afterwards at Zile, near Tokat, Caesar used his famous words to describe the short war: "Veni, vidi, vici," - "I came, I saw, I conquered".

Temple of Aphrodite
Saffet Emre Tonguç

Aphrodisias, bas-relief detail

Sarcophagi, Aphrodisias Museum

Saffet Emre Tonguç

From then onwards,

Aphrodisias's luck began to change. Believing that his ancestors could be traced back to the Greek goddess Aphrodite, Caesar offered a golden statue of Eros as a gift to the temple of the goddess. Even when the Roman Emperor Constantine embraced Christianity as the empire's official religion this couldn't dent the goddess's popularity. Hoping to gain more converts to their religion, the Christians transformed the temple (which previously hosted orgies) into a church, which still venerated Aphrodite. The name Aphrodisias was then changed to "Stavropolis", meaning "the city of the Cross."

Among the many sons of Aphrodite were Eros, the lover of Psyche and the personification of the self in psychology; and Bes, who was famed for his outsized male organ.

Hermaphrodite, the son of Aphrodite

Over the coming centuries, earthquakes and invasions buried the city deep in the pages of history. Worse was to come in 1402 when Tamerlane sacked and destroyed much of Anatolia; Aphrodisias never fully recovered from the devastation. Until the excavations of 1961, the villagers of Geyre continued to live among the historic monuments. Then one day, lost on an excursion, the famous Turkish photographer Ara Güler stumbled upon Geyre and was appalled by what he saw. Grabbing his camera, he began to capture images of the columns, bas-reliefs and busts rising up inside the city walls. Thus the first pictures of this ancient city emerged into the Western world. When the time finally came to start restoration, Geyre was moved two kilometers to the west of the ruins.

Aphrodisias is one of Turkey's tidiest and most beautiful archaeological sites. As soon as you enter the ancient city, you come to the town square where the coffee-house of old Geyre used to stand! To the immediate right of the square is the museum, which is no longer big enough to accommodate all the finds from the site. It houses many extraordinarily beautiful sculptures, including one hall

Ionic columns

Saffet Emre Tonguç

Amphitheater

Saffet Emre Tonguç

full of statues of Aphrodite. One statue, which was created in Aphrodisias and rediscovered in Hadrian's Villa in Rome, depicts Antinous of Bithynia (modern day Bursa), who was the lover of Emperor Hadrian.

The most intriguing of Aphrodite's many children was Hermaphrodite. One day, Hermaphrodite, who had inherited his mother's good looks, was bathing in the nude at Bardakçı Bay, near Bodrum (the ancient Halicarnassus). Spotting him, a naiad (sea nymph) fell in love with him, threw her arms around him and held him fast. She prayed to the gods that they should never be parted, and they responded by merging their two bodies into one, thus creating the first hermaphrodite! Despite this, it is hardly surprising that any medicine capable of boosting sexual desire is called an aphrodisiac after Aphrodite, the exquisite goddess of love.

The largest stadium in Anatolia

If you walk to the left of the museum, you can make a full circle around the excavations and return to the same spot. The first monument you will come across is an amphitheater which could seat 8,000 people. The semi-circular section for the orchestra was raised up to accommodate fights between gladiators and wild beasts.

The hill behind the theater offers a panoramic view over the ancient city. Beneath it is the agora, or market place, and right behind this are the Baths of Hadrian which date back to the 2nd century AD. The baths

The Baths of Hadrian

When you look down from the hill behind the theater, you can see the remains of the pool located in the middle of the agora.

Saffet Emre Tonguç

consisted of three sections: the frigidarium (cold bath), the tepidarium (warm bath), and the caldarium (hot plunge bath). An inscription discovered in the baths reads: “Do not leave your valuables in the cabins”!

Next to a building used as the Episcopal Palace in Byzantine times is the Odeon, the city’s most graceful structure. With a seating capacity of 1700, this small theater housed concerts, debates and municipal council meetings. Of the 40 columns in the Temple of Aphrodite immediately behind it, only 14 still remain intact. Although the construction of this temple only began in the 1st century BC, the tradition of worshipping Aphrodite in this area stretches back for 2700 years.

The most famous statue of Aphrodite was created by Praxiteles of Knidos, modern day Datça. This statue was so celebrated in Antiquity that travelers would go out of their way to visit Knidos, thus turning tourism into an important local industry. It gets even better; after admiring the beauty of the statue in the temple, male visitors would make love to the prostitutes working there and so complete the ritual of worship!

Aphrodisias was home to numerous philosophers and intellectuals, and the Philosophy School was located next to the temple. After passing the temple, you encounter the city’s most spectacular structure. The largest and best-preserved of its kind in Anatolia, this 1900-year-old stadium could accommodate 30,000 spectators. With special seating areas for different groups and a total of 30 rows, the stadium measures 262 meters by 59 meters. Behind it stand the city’s 3.5-kilometer-long ramparts, built in the 350s.

The last structure you will see before returning to the square is the magnificent Tetrapylon. Made up of four rows of four columns, this monumental gateway to the city was built across the road leading to the temple. Next to this awe-inspiring structure is the grave of Prof. Kenan Erim, who dedicated 30 years of his life to excavating Aphrodisias. The marble blocks used to build the gateway bear bas-reliefs depicting Eros, the God of Love, and Nike, the Goddess of Victory. Considering their weight one cannot help but appreciate the architectural skill of the Romans.

With a single exception, the names of the planets are derived from those of the Roman gods and goddesses. So Venus is named after the Roman goddess of love who was identical to the Greek goddess Aphrodite. Interestingly, the only exception to this rule is Earth, the planet on which we live and where we once worshipped these gods and goddesses!

One of the best-preserved stadiums in the world, this 1900-year-old structure has a seating capacity of 30,000.

Saffet Emre Tonguç

WHERE TO **EAT?**

Anatolia Restaurant
Phone: (0256) 448 81 38
www.anatoliaturizm.com.tr
After a tour of ancient Aphrodisias, the best idea is to head for the Anatolia Restaurant, 2 km. away. Pide, menemen, and mushrooms au gratin are must-tries on the menu.

Doyurum Restaurant
Phone: (0256) 451 22 90
Located just beyond Karacasu, the Doyurum Restaurant is a good alternative. You will love the yogurt and home-made jams. Beware! Just as in the Anatolia Restaurant, there will be a saz (local guitar) musician, who will play local folk tunes and maybe make you dance the halay.

THE COTTON CASTLE - A GIFT FROM NATURE
044 Pamukkale

Saffet Emre TONGUÇ

The glittering white travertines of Pamukkale make one of the most familiar images of Turkey. Less well known are the extensive ruins of ancient Hierapolis, which line the hillside above the travertines. Together the two sites constitute one of Turkey's World Heritage Sites. Near the entrance to Pamukkale stands the necropolis of Hierapolis. In ancient times, the dead were buried with their personal belongings and bereaved families paid for the maintenance of the huge tombs, which bear interesting inscriptions. One reads: "The thief who tries to dig into my grave shall not find earth to walk on, or sea to look at. When he dies after a childless life of misery, may the wrath of the gods be upon him."

The Colonnaded Street of Hierapolis
Saffet Emre Tonguç

When it came to earthquakes, Hierapolis was particularly unfortunate, and was demolished several times in its history. However, a few emperors, including Nero of fiddling fame, dipped their hands into their pockets and helped rebuild it. They also granted Hierapolis the right to construct temples and organize imperial festivals. As one of the first places to embrace Christianity, the town was also mentioned in the Bible. Philip the Apostle is believed to have lived here and to have been martyred here with his seven sons; the remains of his tomb still survive on the hillside. The Byzantine Emperor Justinian, who commissioned Hagia Sophia in İstanbul, appointed a bishop called John to convert the inhabitants of Hierapolis to Christianity; he converted some 80,000 people and built 98 churches and 12 monasteries. The town was captured by the Turks in the 12th century.

Some of the tombs in Hierapolis are adorned with the symbol of a male organ intended to represent power.

The ruins and the flesh-eating tombs

The Roman theater at the top of the site dates back to the 2nd century AD and is still in very good condition. Septimius Severus (r. 193-211), who commissioned the Hippodrome in İstanbul, also oversaw the restoration of this theater which had a seating capacity of 10,000 in 46 rows, plus a special box close to the stage, which was reserved for the imperial family. Among the bas-reliefs decorating it is a fine one of the god of wine and theater, whom the Greeks called Dionysius and the Romans called Bacchus.

After you finish walking along Hierapolis' recently-excavated Colonnaded Street, which was

Pamukkale is a miracle of nature with few equals in the world.

Saffet Emre Tonguç

The theater of Hierapolis
Saffet Emre Tonguç

dedicated to the Emperor Domitian, you will come to some gigantic Roman baths that are now used as a museum. The museum is relatively small, but the contents, including sculptures, bas-reliefs and ancient coins, are interesting and well displayed. Note in particular the tombs in which wealthy individuals were buried. These were called sarcophagi, which meant literally "eaters of flesh". Once people realized that the corpses placed inside these tombs disappeared within a few years, they chose this interesting name for them!

Septimius Severus, who commissioned the İstanbul Hippodrome, also oversaw the restoration of the theater of Hierapolis.

The shimmering travertines

Beneath the museum lies the famous natural wonder that is Pamukkale (literally, the Cotton Castle). As the dissolved calcium carbonate from the thermal springs of Mt Çal flows down from the hills, it sheds carbon dioxide and forms these chalk-like travertine terraces that have accumulated over the centuries. Taking your shoes in your hand, you can walk on some of them, although swimming is no longer allowed.

The "Sacred Pool" inside the Pamukkale Motel has been in use since Roman times. Don't forget to bring your bathing suit; after paying the entrance fee, you can jump in and enjoy yourself in the warm waters of the pool, which contains fragments of marble and ancient columns.

A church ruin

Mehmet Çabuk

The sacred pool

Saffet Emre Tonguç

HOW TO **TRAVEL?**

Denizli is 250km from İzmir and 215km from Kuşadası. On the way you pass through Aydın and Karacasu, which is 13 kilometers from Aphrodisias. Pamukkale is 20 kilometers from Denizli. If you start out from Antalya, it's 300km to Denizli via Korkuteli. If you start out from Marmaris, you can drive to Denizli via Muğla and Tavas.

WHERE TO **STAY?**

A long time ago, several hotels were built above the Pamukkale travertines, but they have since been torn down. Just south of the travertines Pamukkale village offers many affordable small hotels and pensions. Nearby Karahayıt is not pretty but does have many larger hotels with their own thermal pools. Pamukkale is often included as an overnight stop on Anatolian tours.

The hotels are usually packed in the afternoons, with long queues at the open buffets, but by 9am the next morning everywhere is deserted. There are far fewer groups in winter, if you'd prefer to visit at a less crowded time.

Richmond Pamukkale Hotel
Phone: (0258) 271 42 94
www.richmondhotels.com.tr

Herakles Termal Pamukkale
Phone: (0258) 271 44 25
www.heraklesthermal.com

Colossae Thermal Hotel
Phone: (0258) 271 41 56
www.colossaehotel.com

Lycus River Hotel
Phone: (0258) 271 43 41
www.lycusriver.com

Laruj Polat Thermal Hotel
Phone: (0258) 271 41 10
www.laruj.com

Allgau Hotel
Phone: (0258) 272 27 67
Pleasant pension set around an inviting garden and pool in Pamukkale village.

Koray Hotel
Phone: (0258) 272 23 00
Larger hotel with small pool and courtyard restaurant in Pamukkale village.

THE MOST UNSPOILT BAY IN THE BODRUM AREA

045 Iassos

Fatih TÜRKMENOĞLU

North of the Bodrum peninsula, at the far end of the Gulf of Güllük, you will come across perhaps the most unspoilt bay in the southern Aegean - Kıyıkışlacık, or Iassos as it was known throughout history. There may only be two restaurants, five pensions and a couple of grocery shops here, but the history, the mythology and the sea views are amazing. And that goes without mentioning the delicious olive oil squeezed from the local olives.

Iassos is one of the bays closest to Bodrum airport.

Bünyad Dinç

Although it is now called Kıyıkışlacık ("Little Barracks on the Coast"), many people prefer to stick with the ancient name of Iassos, when referring to this heavenly corner of Turkey. The Güllük peninsula is generally crowded with baking bodies, but Iassos, at the far end of the peninsula, is often almost deserted, which means no blasting music and no razzle-dazzle from the tour boats. Such tranquility may catch you off guard at first. It takes a while, before the soul grows accustomed to the silence, before it begins to distinguish the whisper of the waves, the rocks, and the ruins.

The present-day village was established in 1929. Before that, the area was a large farm run by the Greeks on the site of a 3,000-year-old Carian city, where the locals made their living from the sea and from their olive groves. Their children swam so well that the dolphins would often come to accompany them. One story tells how a dolphin fell in love with a youngster from the village and led him out to sea. Some time later, the animal returned the boy to his family, a story which reached the ears of Alexander the Great, who had the boy appointed a priest of Poseidon, the god of the sea. After that, the image of a youngster swimming with a dolphin began to appear on the coins of Iassos.

The 500-year-old olive trees in the village are living proof that this was an olive-growing center for centuries. The olives are still crushed in old-fashioned presses, and the end result is so delicious that the taste seems to linger on your tongue forever.

A couple of books, an iPod, and a travel companion are all you need. Long walks, lots of history, the stars, the azure sea - they are all yours for the asking.

With the exception of a few pensions, there is nowhere to stay in Iassos, nor any places to hang out at night. What's more, you end up eating in the same places day and night. You can go swimming off the shore near

the ruins, but the nearest decent beach is 20 minutes away by car.

Nonetheless, Iassos makes a perfect spot for a vacation. Since the locals see fewer tourists, they are not as pushy as their counterparts in other resorts around Bodrum.

Ancient Iassos

Italian archaeologists have been carrying out excavations on the site of ancient Iassos since the 1960s; the ruins are scattered over a headland overlooking the sea. The remains of a Greek theater and the 2nd-century temple to Artemis Astias are impressive and well-signed, but you can also see an old agora (market place), a bouleuterion (meeting place) and a gymnasium. The breakwater and the watchtower, both of which are now under water, were a continuation of ancient Iassos. Remains of several Byzantine churches and of a medieval castle are also visible at the site.

The sign for Iassos Museum is broken, so you may have to ask for directions. What was once an old covered fish-market building, now houses a collection of artifacts from the Hellenistic, Roman and Byzantine periods, as well as inscription tablets and old tombstones. In the grounds, you can also inspect a vast old Roman tomb.

The healthy way of life of the Iassos locals comes from a diet rich in fish and olive oil.

Bünyad Dinç

HOW TO **TRAVEL?**

The easiest way to get here is to fly to Bodrum, and take a cab from the airport, which is only 26km away.
If you are driving, you can reach Iassos via the Milas-Bodrum motorway; take the Akbük and Kıyıkışlacık exits.
If you are taking the bus from Bodrum, you get off in Milas and hop on the Kıyıkışlacık minibus.

WHAT TO **EAT?**

Fish, of course! It's both cheap and fresh. The seafood and home-cooked olive oil dishes at the Iassos restaurants are mouth-watering. The çipura (gilthead bream) is especially good in season.

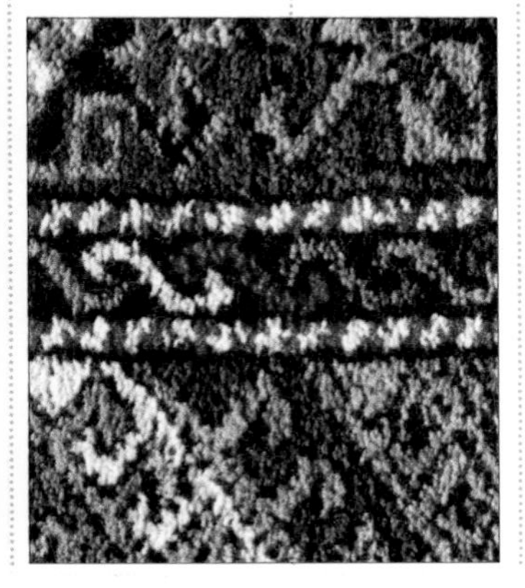

WHERE TO **STAY?**

Rönesans Pansiyon
Phone: (0252) 537 74 12
This 11-room pension with a pool is run by a couple from Istanbul, who have been living in Iassos for the past few years. For breakfast, they offer home-made olive-oil and three different types of olives. The pension is frequented largely by foreign tourists and has a spectacular view.

Zeytin Pansiyon
Phone: (0252) 537 70 08
The owner is artist İbrahim Örs, who spends half the year in Denmark. He hosts a steady flow of artistic groups at the pension.

Kaya Pansiyon
Phone: (0252) 537 74 39

Zürih Pansiyon
Phone: (0252) 537 70 12

WHAT **TO DO?**

There is no beach in town but it's fun to jump into the water from the ancient ruins. A swim in the pristine sea is highly recommended for those who like cold water!

The town has no market, so the locals head for Milas, 18 kilometers away, to go shopping. The popular Milas market takes place on Tuesdays.

You can join a tour to visit Lake Bafa, Bodrum town center or the temple of Apollo in Didyma.

Zeytinlik Koyu (Bay) is 20 minutes away by car and should be on your must-see list. Enjoy daydreaming on the beach at sunset or during the full moon.

For bird-lovers, there is also a local "bird paradise" (a nature reserve for bird-watching).

TRAVELLING BACK IN TIME FOR A DAY

046 Milas

Fatih TÜRKMENOĞLU

As the capital of Caria, the ancient city of Mylasa - or Milas as it is now called - deserves more than the usual brief visit on the way to or from Bodrum airport. The town center retains a surprising number of lovely old Ottoman houses, as well as several interesting old mosques, and an ancient tomb that may have been modeled on the famous Mausoleum of Halicarnassos. The Tuesday market is especially worth visiting.

Gümüşkesen Mausoleum.

Nil Yüzbaşıoğlu

For many years, Mylasa was the capital of ancient Caria, except during the period when King Mausolus ruled the area from Halicarnassus (present-day Bodrum). In the western Luwi (Hittite) language, "Mylasa" means "mill."

The mosques and monuments of Milas

According to the famous geographer Strabo, Mylasa was one of Caria's three largest cities. Its days of glory came in the 4th century BC, but when King Mausolus relocated the capital to Halicarnassus to be closer to the sea, Mylasa lost its old importance. It did, however, revive in Roman times. Later, under the Beylik (Chiefdom) of the Menteşes, Milas became one of the most important towns in all Anatolia.

Don' t leave before visiting the famous Milas market which even has a leech vendor! If you stumble upon a "kız alma" ceremony, do stop and watch the ritual of "taking on a bride".

You can start exploring ancient Mylasa at the Baltalı Kapı (Axe Gate), which would once have been set into the old city walls, but now stands alone with a model of a Roman soldier guarding it. Mylasa's best-known monument is the Gümüşkesen Mausoleum which dates back to the 2nd century AD and is believed to

The ancient city of Euromos, with a huge Temple of Zeus at its heart, is only 12km from Milas.

Mehmet Çabuk

look like a smaller version of the famous Mausoleum of Halicarnassus. Of the 1st-century BC Temple of Zeus, only one column with a stork's nest on the top survives. Other reminders of ancient Mylasa can be seen in the small Milas Museum.

The most interesting survivors from the Menteşe period are Milas' mosques. The Ulu Cami, which was built in 1378, and the Orhan Bey Cami, which was built in 1330, are both extremely beautiful, but the most spectacular of them all is the Firuz Bey Camii, completed in 1394, with pieces of old Roman marblework incorporated into its walls. From Ottoman times, the most interesting relics are the many lovely old wooden houses with their interesting double doors and soaring chimneypots; the restored Hacı Ali Konağı, now used as the tourist office, is typical of what a Milas home would have looked like in its heyday. Nearby, the Çöllühanı is a wonderful, crumbling 18th-century caravanserai crying out for some tender loving care.

A Nomadic woman from Çomakdağı

Mehmet Çabuk

HOW TO **TRAVEL?**

Milas is 165km from İzmir and 45km from Bodrum town centre. You can always drive, but remember that the airport is nearby.

WHERE TO **STAY?**

Milashan Otel
Phone: (0252) 513 79 01

WHERE TO **EAT?**

Milas is hardly gourmet central although it has its fair share of routine pide and kebab restaurants.

WHAT **TO DO?**

The Temple of Zeus at Euromos should be on your must-see list. It probably dates back to the 2nd century AD, and is in very good condition, although the unfluted columns suggest that it was never completed.

Also well worth visiting is ancient Labranda which boasts two grand dining halls and the remains of another Temple of Zeus in a beautiful hillside location.

If possible, try and get yourself invited to a wedding in one of the villages around Milas. It is an absolutely fabulous experience.

The Tuesday market in Milas is the largest in the area. Tourists pour in from the local resorts, all the signs are in English, and the vendors are multilingual.

HOME TOWN OF THE MAUSOLEUM

047 Bodrum Bodrum...

Fatih TÜRKMENOĞLU

Bodrum is an exquisitely beautiful resort in the south-west corner of Turkey, which has become the haunt of the rich and famous. Its waterfront is dominated by the magnificent Castle of St Peter, which houses a unique Museum of Underwater Archeology. There are regular ferries from Bodrum to the island of Kos in Greece.

Bodrum Castle
Mehmet Çabuk

Years ago, one of Turkey's most famous pop-rock groups, MFÖ, released a song entitled, "Bodrum, Bodrum"; "How do I describe it, where do I begin, Bodrum, Bodruuuum," was how it started. Since then, it has become the unofficial anthem of this popular summer resort.

Most Turks have a Bodrum memory; the town is like an autonomous region inside Turkey, with its own private set of rules, one of which is that the evening doesn't start until midnight!

In ancient times, a small town called Zephyria stood on the site of the Castle. Today, Bodrum is nearly a metropolis!

A wonder of the ancient world

Bodrum's original name was Halicarnassus. According to the celebrated historian Herodotus, who was a native of this town, the city was first founded by the Dorians. In 650 BC, the Megarans took it over, expanded it, and renamed it Halicarnassus. In the 4th century BC, the city became the capital of Caria, and went on to become prosperous and successful. One of the Seven Wonders of the Ancient World, the Mausoleum of Halicarnassus was built by Queen Artemisia in honor of her husband Mausolus, who died in 353 BC. Today, only scant ruins of the great tomb remain.

An ancient theater beside the road to Turgutreis has been beautifully restored and is worth a quick look. Work on it started during the reign of Mausolos, although it was extended by the Romans.

Later, Bodrum was conquered by the Romans and Byzantines. In 1415, it was captured by the Knights Hospitaller of Rhodes, and in 1522, during the reign of Sultan Süleyman the Magnificent, it became a part of the Ottoman Empire.

Bodrum and the "Blue Voyage"

The development of tourism in Turkey is still relatively recent. Nonetheless, Bodrum was one of the first seaside towns to gain both local and international fame. Back in the days, when there were no hotels to speak of and, when this whole area was still "the country", a handful of Turkish intellectuals and socialites began to explore the coves around Bodrum by boat. Stories about the first blue voyages taken by the likes of Azra Erhat, Cevat Şakir Kabaağaçlı and Mina Urgan, and about the beauty of the surrounding area spread rapidly by word of mouth. Today, no visit to the Aegean is really complete without going on a "Blue Voyage", which offers a perfect opportunity for self-discovery. As the famous Turkish writer Cevat Şakir Kabaağaçlı, otherwise known as the Fisherman of Halicarnassus said, you return as a different person...

Bünyad Dinç

The Castle of St Peter

The castle was built by the Knights Hospitaller of Rhodes in the 15th century; its former name, the "Petronium," eventually evolved into Bodrum. Not only is the building itself absolutely magnificent, but the museum inside is spectacular, with its contents displayed in an inviting, modern way. One of the most interesting sections displays the remains of the Carian princess Ada, who was buried with all her golden finery in the 4th century BC. The award-winning Museum of Underwater Archeology has a beautifully displayed collection of some of the oldest shipwrecks ever dredged from the seabed.

The celebrated Turkish author known as the Fisherman of Halicarnassus was imprisoned in the castle for three years from 1924 to 1927. Even after being pardoned, he continued to live beside the Aegean, until his death in 1973, when he was buried in Bodrum. As you walk through the castle, you cannot help but ponder his punishment - it might even have been a blessing to live here…

Bodrum Marina

Saffet Emre Tonguç

The Marmara Hotel

WHERE TO **EAT?**

Try the dönerli dürüm (döner in pitta wrap) in the Bodrum bazaar. The best time to have it is after a long night of partying.

Marina Yacht Club
Phone: (0252) 316 12 28
www.marinayachtclub.com

Gemibaşı
Phone: (0252) 316 12 20
A laidback place where you can tuck into great seafood.

Yağhane
Phone: (0252) 313 47 47
Very trendy restaurant in an old olive-oil factory.

Kocadon
Phone: (0252) 316 37 05
One of Bodrum's best restaurants with a romantic garden.

Liman Köftecisi
Phone: (0252) 316 50 60
Extremely popular meatball emporium.

Berk Café & Bar
Phone: (0252) 313 02 39
Pleasant taverna-style seafood restaurant near the Halikarnas Disco.

WHERE TO **STAY?**

The Marmara
Phone: (0252) 313 81 30
www.themarmarahotels.com.tr
Offers a spectacular view and superb design. To top it all, there is a watchtower from the 4th century BC in the garden.

Su Hotel
Phone: (0252) 316 69 06
www.suhotel.net
Modeled on an old Kos house, the Su Hotel offers a wonderful surprise down a Bodrum back street near the Mausoleum. Think of a garden covered in bougainvillea, a big swimming pool and walls painted in Bodrum white. Stir in reds, yellows, and blues as part of the décor. The Su provides a cozy, relaxed atmosphere, far from the madding crowds of Bodrum.

The Butterfly
Phone: (0252) 313 83 58
www.thebutterflybodrum.com
A perfect getaway stashed in the residential streets above Bodrum Marina with very friendly owners. The swimming pool on the terrace offers a glorious view. There is a large sitting room, and the bedrooms are tastefully decorated. Here, you can blend into Bodrum's crazy nightlife or seek refuge in your "castle" retreat any time you like.

Pink Life Apart Hotel, Yalıkavak
Phone: (0252) 385 20 22
www.hotelpinklife.com
Right beside the sea in a quiet location on the Bodrum Peninsula.

WHAT **TO DO?**

Bodrum is nightlife heaven - the Turkish answer to the Greek island of Mykonos. The hundreds of bars and discos between the Castle and the Halikarnas Disco stay open until the wee small hours of morning. The all-time favorites are Mavi, Hadigari, Küba, Halikarnas in the town center, and Ship a Hoy out in upmarket Türkbükü.

Take a boat trip to see and swim in the surrounding bays, especially Akvaryum (Aquarium) Bay.

If you want to be a true "Bodrumlu" (Bodrumite), purchase a pair of leather sandals from the internationally famous sandal-maker Ali Usta who has a shop in Bodrum Çarşısı (Market). Remember to visit on the first day of your stay as he needs time to custom-make your footwear.

Extending beyond Bodrum town is the Bodrum Peninsula where each bay seems more beautiful than the last one - be sure to visit Göltürkbükü, Yalıkavak and Gümüşlük. Geriş village, near Gümüşlük, is known as the "Tibet of Bodrum", a place to come if you're into classical music, incense and meditation.

Take a trip to Milas on Tuesday to explore the famous Salı Pazarı (Tuesday Market).

Some of the smaller villages around Bodrum, such as Çökertme, Sazköy, Mazı, Etlim, Çiftlik, are fun to visit. Mumcular is a good place to buy olive oil.

A goddess figurine

Saffet Emre Tonguç

BODRUM'S QUIETER CORNER
048 Bitez

Fatih TÜRKMENOĞLU

Bitez is one of the least pretentious bays on the frequently pretentious Bodrum Peninsula. The beach and the sea are beautiful, and prices in the hotels and restaurants are very reasonable compared to those in other nearby resorts. It's a place for doing very little and is especially good for families with children.

It's possible to surf or water-ski in Bitez.
Saffet Emre Tonguç

Also known as "Ağaçlı" (the Place of Trees), Bitez is a favorite with people who enjoy swimming in pristine waters, and are in search of a peaceful holiday. Despite the newly-built hotels and apartment complexes, this little bay somehow manages to hang onto much of its beauty. The beach is lovely, and although the local authorities have permitted the hotels and restaurants to put out cushions, chairs and tables, they have also insisted that they allow free access to the sands, which means that you can take your towel and suntan lotion and set up camp wherever you like.

If you say, "I want to be in Bodrum and still have a peaceful holiday", then Bitez is the right place to come.

If you wine and dine at the restaurants that provide "beach accommodation" during the day, all is well and good. If not, no one asks you to buy anything. In short, you are at a public beach that has a "beach club" feel to it. The sea is great and very shallow, which is what makes Bitez so popular with families, who have small children.

A popular folk song refers to a "Bitez yalısı". The word "yalı" generally means a seaside mansion in Turkish, but in this particular song it refers to a beach in Bitez. A story tells how the lovers Gülsüm and Halil decided to run away together to the island facing the town. Halil had killed his sister and Gülsüm was married to another man, who was Halil's close friend. Halil had served seven years in prison and was still on probation when the couple decided to meet at Bitez yalısı. A boatman got word of their escape, and informed the authorities, and Halil was caught and killed in the dungeon below the Belediye (Municipality) building. It was Gülsüm and Halil's great love that inspired this folk song. Years later, the Belediye held a sculpture competition and erected the winning statue at the point where Gülsüm and Halil tried to embark.

Walking the hills

It is possible to hike to Upper Bitez, where there are some lovely stone houses and paths through the tangerine groves.

The village has separate tea-houses for men and women; if you drop in on them, you will feel yourself a world away from the coastal goings-on.

On the way, you can visit the ruins of a small, forgotten church with its floor decorations still intact.

The music is not too loud!

Bitez makes the perfect choice for a peaceful holiday, with many hotels and restaurants located immediately behind the beach. The fact that no cars are allowed along the waterfront is a life-saver for families with small children.

If you must see some "action", you are only two bays away from Bodrum. Minibuses run into town every five minutes, so you can manage without a car.

The Bitez café owners keep the public beach clean. If you take an early morning walk, don't be too upset about the clutter on the sand - it will be gone by the time you want to go swimming.

Refik Ongan

HOW TO **TRAVEL?**

If you arrive by bus or plane, you can easily reach Bitez by minibus from Bodrum Otogar (Bus Terminal). Bitez is only 42km from the Bodrum-Milas airport.

WHERE TO **STAY?**

There are some beautiful little hotels in the area. You can explore the options at www.bodrum-bodrum.com.

Bora Bora Apart Hotel
Phone: (0252) 363 79 42
www.boraapart.com
A cozy atmosphere, good food, and close proximity to sea.

WHERE TO **EAT?**

The water-front restaurants are quite decent although there is a bit of a culture clash - Chinese versus kebab, etc. You should be able to find something good enough to eat.

WHAT **TO DO?**

There are diving schools for those interested in exploring the underwater wonders of the area.

The Ortakent and Milas markets are lovely; don't miss them if you want to soak up some local color.

THE "SILVER" RESORT ON THE BODRUM PENINSULA

049 Gümüşlük

Fatih TÜRKMENOĞLU

Of all the resorts on the Bodrum Peninsula, probably the most appealing is little Gümüşlük on the far western side. A small sandy beach, some inviting restaurants and a string of ruins on and off-shore all add up to a place, where you will be happy to spend a few days relaxing. For the more thoughtful, there is a meditation center up in the surrounding hills.

Sunset in Gümüşlük.

Nil Yüzbaşıoğlu

Gümüşlük was founded on the site of the ancient city of Myndos. The first settlers in the area were the mysterious Leleges. Legend has it that during the siege of Halicarnassus, Alexander the Great stayed here. In the course of history, the town fell under the domination of the Dorians, the Persians, and the Carians. In 1523, during the reign of Sultan Süleyman the Magnificent, it was finally conquered by the Ottomans.

The ruins of Myndos are not very extensive – just a few pieces of masonry on the shore and on the island. Still, this historic site is a favorite with those, who enjoy exploring the quieter bays of the Bodrum Peninsula.

One of the most beautiful spots in Gümüşlük is the Limon Café, which offers a view out over Tavşan Adası (Rabbit Island). It's the perfect place to come to watch the sun set and the sky change color at the end of the day. Some would argue that the sunsets here are at their most beautiful during the fall.

Gümüşlük is set on one of the most beautiful bays of the Bodrum Peninsula. Words can barely describe the magnificence of the sunsets…

Art and meditation

An old church overlooking the village is used as an art house called Eclisia; internationally-renowned artists come to hold special workshops here. There is also an Art Academy (Phone: (0252) 394 43 01) at the entrance to the village - it is so big that it almost resembles a college campus. Painting, sculpture, photography, and video-art workshops are held here. Artists from all over the world come to live at the Academy and participate in workshops with fellow Turkish artists.

Further uphill, the village of Karakaya hosts a meditation and yoga camp (www.oshokun.com). Accommodation is provided in rooms or in tents set up on the grounds. Come here to meditate, do yoga, have regular massages, and feast on vegetarian meals, while also enjoying the company of a dedicated band of international guests.

No matter how long you stay in Gümüşlük, it won't be long enough...

Bünyad Dinç

WHERE TO **STAY?**

For further information on all Gümüşlük's hotels and pensions, click on www.bodrumlu.com.

Mandalinci Myndos Hotel
Phone: (0252) 394 31 51
Large, modern hotel, at one end of the beach.

Club Gümüşlük
Phone: (0252) 394 3401
maporg@superonline.com
Collection of beach chalets in a central location on the beach.

Mandalinci Studios & Cottage
Phone: (0252) 394 3151
www.mandalincimyndos.com
Self-catering apartments right beside the water.

WHERE TO **EAT?**

You really must try tuzda balık (fish baked in salt). All the restaurants on the waterfront are good, but Laz Selo is especialy popular. The "Laz" are an ethic group from the Black Sea region, and, as the epithet suggests, Selo is a typical Black Sea fellow. He mixes vinegar with salt, wraps any kind of fatty fish in it and throws it in the oven. The fish are delicious, as are the mezes (appetizers). His restaurant sits right over the water at the far end of the bay, but, most importantly, it's his jovial presence that adds character to the place.

Mimoza Restaurant
Phone: (0252) 394 31 39

Siesta
Phone:(0252) 394 38 16

Aquarium Restaurant
Phone: (0252) 394 36 82

WHAT **TO DO?**

Walk over to Tavşan Adası and try to spot the rabbits – you stand a better chance after dark!

The windmills on the hills on the way to Gümüşlük from Bodrum provide a great photo opportunity.

AWARD-WINNING ARCHITECTURE BESIDE THE SEA

050 Akyaka

Fatih TÜRKMENOĞLU

Backed by Mt Sakartepe, Akyaka grew up beside one of the most tranquil and beautiful bays of the Gulf of Gökova. Here, architect Nail Çakırhan's award-winning house blended modern development with natural beauty, inspiring other developers to build in sympathy with an idyllic location where the Kadın Azmak and Akçapınar Azmağı streams run down to the sea.

The first thing that comes to mind when thinking about Akyaka is Nail Çakırhan and the style of architecture he created here.
Fatih Türkmenoğlu

Akyaka (aka Gökova) is the perfect place for those in search of complete peace. Here, there is no noise, no blasting music, and no irritatingly persistent vendors. It's a "town", which only really took to tourism over the last 10 years. The one downside is a strong wind, called, appropriately, "Deli Mehmet" (Crazy Mehmet), that whips through the streets every 10 to 15 days.

A beautiful pine forest flows right down to a sandy beach, where the sea stays shallow for hundreds of meters. Nearby are the Gökova Plain and wetlands, where some of the last European fish otters (lutra lutra) live and where you can sometimes spot herons, flamingoes and pelicans.

There's not much that's old to see in Akyaka, but the landing stage on the way to Çınar Beach was used for exporting chromium until recently; it stands on the same site as a pier supposedly used by the ancient Egyptians to import tropical fruit, dates, spices, and fabric.

The Aga Khan Award for Architecture

The houses of Ula, an old town near the provincial capital of Muğla, provided the inspiration for the architecture of Akyaka. Here, each building is detached, and most were designed with lovely wooden balconies and overhanging roofs in a way that makes them look both modern and historic at the same time. The "father" of this style of fusion building is Nail Çakırhan, who was given the Aga Khan Award for Architecture for his own home in 1983. Unlike most winners, Mr. Çakırhan had no formal training in architecture. But for someone, who not only created such beautiful buildings, but also pioneered the preservation of such a beautiful place, no awards will ever be enough.

Every day boats leave Akyaka to visit the bays around Sedir Island. Don't miss your chance!

The story of Pan and Syrinx

According to Greek mythology, Pan, the impish nature god, who was half man and half goat, was wandering through the reedbeds near the mouth of the Kadın Azmağı river, when he spotted and fell in love with the nymph Syrinx. Syrinx resisted Pan's charms and prayed for rescue, whereupon her fellow nymphs changed her into a reed. Hearing the whisper of the wind rustling through the reeds, the mournful Pan went ahead and fashioned the first "Pan pipe" out of his erstwhile beloved.

Scenes from the celebrated Turkish movie Dondurmam Gaymak ("Ice-Cream, I Scream")" were shot in Akyaka. Some of the extras were chosen from among the locals.

Fatih Türkmenoğlu

HOW TO **TRAVEL?**

The nearest airport is at Dalaman, 65km away; most of the hotels have shuttle services from the airport. If you are coming by bus, there is a minibus from Muğla every half hour. Marmaris is 32km away, Köyceğiz 30km away and Dalyan 45km away.

WHERE TO **EAT?**

Fish, pine-scented honey, sourdough bread, fried eggplants, and green peppers with yogurt, followed by ada cayı (sage tea) from the mountains.

Pick fresh herbs to eat straight from the water at Nadir Usta's place in Azmakbaşı.

WHERE TO **STAY?**

There are pensions, and a large camp and caravan site in the surrounding forest.

Club Asuhan Çobantur
Phone: (0252) 243 45 50
Pleasing hotel with a stream running through the grounds in a particularly quiet corner of Akyaka.

Yücelen Hotel
Phone: (0252) 243 51 08
Yücelen is a Nail Çakırhan building with a lovely view. There are also wooden houses on the beach.

Ottoman Residence
Phone: (0252) 243 59 01
www.ottomanresidence.com

Sitar Apart Otel
Phone: (0252) 243 43 39
Two or three people can stay in each room. No breakfast provided.

WHAT **TO DO?**

As you drive down to Akyaka, take several breaks to soak up the scenery.

Go paragliding off Sakartepe.

Dive off Boncuk Bay.

The archaeological sites at Priene, Miletus, Didyma and Caunos can all be visited on day trips.

Make sure to visit Ula, the inland town, which inspired Nail Çakırhan.

Take a boat trip to Sedir Island ("Cleopatra's Island") and the surrounding bays. Hidden in the middle of the island are the remains of ancient Cedreae, including a lovely overgrown theater amid olive trees. On the east coast is a bay, where sand is so soft and white that it has a preservation order on it. The island takes its name from a belief that Mark Anthony had the sand brought here from Egypt especially for his lover, Cleopatra. Sad to say, it's almost certainly not true.

THE TOWN AT THE END OF THE PENINSULA

051 Datça

Fatih TÜRKMENOĞLU

"Bury me, dear, in Datça. /Forget about Ankara, İstanbul / They are full to the limit/ And equally expensive," wrote renowned Turkish poet Can Yücel, and when you glimpse Datça, with the Aegean on one side and the Mediterranean on the other, you will immediately understand, what it was that so inspired him. At the far end of the Reşadiye Peninsula, Datça is a reminder of what Marmaris must have been like before the arrival of mass tourism. Just inland, Eski Datça is a dream of a place with the aura of an Aegean island. Yücel was so right...

Historians believe that Datça's original name was Stadia.

Nil Yüzbaşıoğlu

Datça lies at the far end of the Reşadiye peninsula, a long finger of land, which extends into the Aegean southwest of Muğla, with the gulfs of Gökova and Hisarönü on either side. Don't believe anyone, who tells you that the road there is too crooked or too dangerous to be taken. In fact, it is absolutely beautiful, long and winding and with the prize of a leisurely supper waiting at the end. Luckily, tourism is not overly developed here, and the area remains mercifully free of the madding crowds except at the height of summer. If anything, it's a settlement that is shrinking - the population, which may have exceeded 100,000 during the period, when it was a Dorian stronghold, is now just 40,000.

Stroll through the streets of Old Datça, sit at a café and recite a few lines of Can Yücel just a few feet away from his house.

In Greek mythology, this area was called "the place with surreal qualities", and the famous geographer, Strabo of Amasya, wrote: "If God wants one of his creations to lead a long life, he leaves him on the peninsula of Datça". Some of the oldest medical schools in history were founded here. Locally-grown chamomile, oregano and sage must have healed many, many ailments in the past, just as they supposedly do today.

Electricity only reached Datça in 1978; the poorly-constructed road made access to the rest of Turkey too difficult. In spite of this, the Datça locals tend to be a well-read and intellectual bunch. They have always had close ties to the island of Simi, which lies just a short distance away across the sea. Today Simians are the best customers at Datça's Saturday bazaar.

Datça summers tend to be long, often running into November or December (the locals call this the "Sarıca summer," the local equivalent, presumably, of an Indian summer). This is a blissful time of year when tourists are scarce, the breeze drops, and dinners run on deep into the night.

Eski Datça

If Datça is pleasant, Eski Datça, just five kilometers inland, is a dream, its narrow cobbled streets lined with perfect stone houses, their walls draped with bougainvillea and hiding lovely small gardens. Here, the home of the renowned Turkish poet Can Yücel (1926-99) has been turned into a museum.

Datça's three "B"s - bal, badem and balık

People say that Datça lives off "three Bs" - bal (honey), badem (almond) and balık (fish). The honey is for sale all around town, and the fish graces the menus of the harbor-facing restaurants. The blossoming almond trees certainly provided inspiration for some of Yücel's poetry.

Yet another "B" is nearby Balıkaşıran where, after a strenuous walk, you can watch the Aegean and Mediterranean seas merge into one another.

HOW TO **TRAVEL?**

The easiest way to get there is to fly to Bodrum. A ferry runs from Bodrum to Datça three times a day from May through October. The crossing takes about an hour and a half. Phone: (0252) 316 08 82

If you are driving, Datça is ..0km from İzmir and ..0km from Istanbul. There are buses from Istanbul, Ankara and İzmir but normally you must change in Marmaris. Daily minibuses also run between Marmaris and Datça.

WHERE TO **EAT?**

Interesting local dishes include dallampa, karaville, gışıyak, ilabada and bademli incir tatlısı (fig dessert with almonds). The oregano honey is very good.

..da Lokantası
Phone: (0252) 712 05 18
Restaurateurs Aliman and Kamil Erdem used to run Café Kafka in Istanbul and their small Datça town-center venture makes extensive use of local herbs in its cooking. "Dalleme", as the locals call it, is a kind of salad made from chamomile which can only be picked in April and May. By summer, the only herbs left to gather are "sirken otu" (fat hen) and "kaya koruğu/genevir" (stone orpine) which are fried or used in salads and pickles.

Liman Kahve, by the sea, is Datça's most beautiful cafe.

WHERE TO **STAY?**

Hotel Olimpos
Phone: (0252) 712 28 00
Rooms have TV and air-conditioning. Just 10 meters from the sea.

Hotel Mare
Phone: (0252) 712 32 11

Villa Carla
Phone: (0252) 712 20 29
Double room, breakfast and five o'clock tea included in price.

Dede Pansiyon, Eski Datça
Phone: (0252) 712 39 51
Delightful artistic bolt-hole set round an inviting pool.

Yağhane Pansiyon, Eski Datça
Phone: (0252) 712 22 87
Small, secluded yoga centre with large library for its guests.

Mehmet Ali Ağa Konağı, Reşadiye
Phone: (0252) 712 92 57
www.kocaev.com
How would you like to become an Ottoman Pasha, if only for a few days? This treasure of a place in a tiny inland settlement revels in the understated magnificence of the Ottoman era. The garden is fantastic; why not throw a wedding party here and spend your honeymoon in one of the fresco-decorated bedrooms? The mansion was admitted into the prestigious Relais & Chateaux chain in 2007.

WHAT **TO DO?**

Datça is perfect for windsurfing. There are also several diving schools around here.

Walk to Hastane Altı, Kumluk, Taşlık and Şifalı Göl to enjoy the sea at its most beautiful. The bays around here are pristine and gorgeous: Palamutbükü, Kargı Koyu and Ovabükü are perfect for complete escapism.

The sleepy inland villages of Hızırşah, Mesudiye and Reşadiye are lovely places, where you can sit in the tea-houses and strike up a conversation with a local.

Ancient Knidos, a 5th-century BC Dorian settlement, is 35km away on remote Cape Tekir; getting there by boat round the windy cape is half the fun. This is where Praxiteles created his famous sculpture of the naked Aphrodite, sadly known to us only from later copies. The sundial of the celebrated 4th-century mathematician and astronomer Eudoxus is worth tracking down on the site.

In high summer there are boats to the Greek islands of Rhodes (Rodos in Turkish) and Symi (Sömbeki) several times a week.

Mehmet Ali Ağa Konağı (Mansion)
Saffet Emre Tonguç

WALKING ON WATER
052 Orhaniye and Kızkumu

Fatih TÜRKMENOĞLU

Orhaniye is a wonderful small resort on the northern side of the lovely Hisarönü Peninsula, which juts out west of Marmaris. Here, a spit of sand called Kızkumu (Maiden's Beach) extends 600 meters into the sea in such a way that people who walk along it seem to be walking on water. It's a great place to come for a completely relaxing holiday.

Locals believe that if you make a wish in Kızkumu, it will come true.

Kamil Yılmaz

Backed by rugged mountains and with the azure sea stretching out in front of it, Orhaniye is a little piece of heaven on earth. Jutting out from it is a 600-meter-long reddish sand strip that appears and disappears with the tides. It's known as Kızkumu, the Maiden's Beach.

Can humans walk on water? The answer, perhaps, is that, yes, they certainly can, at least at Kızkumu. The story goes that a young local beauty was being harassed by pirates. To escape their attentions, she filled her pockets with sand, and scattered it beneath her feet to make a causeway on which she could walk through the sea. Eventually, her sand supply ran out, whereupon she supposedly drowned herself rather than surrender. Even today, the sand spit off Orhaniye makes the water so shallow that people can wade far out to sea before they need to start swimming – thereby creating the illusion that they are walking on water!

Kızkumu is ideal for a peaceful holiday. The sea remains only ankle-deep for some way off shore. And there is always a cool breeze at night.

Just 28 kilometers from Marmaris, Orhaniye has a few hotels and pensions, three restaurants and then just the sea,

Kamil Yılmaz

the mountains, and the sand. It's the perfect place for a complete getaway, with only a few hundred villagers and their boats to disturb you. The bay is popular with yacht lovers, because it is sheltered from the winds. There is a fee to use the small marina. Early in the morning, the fishermen scoop sea bass, sea bream, and gray mullet from the sea. The water is so shallow that you might well be able to catch your own fish supper too.

The off-shore Keçi Adası (Goat Island) is supposedly inhabited only by goats.

HOW TO **TRAVEL?**

The best way to get here from İstanbul is to fly to Dalaman; then you can take one of the half-hourly minibuses for Marmaris.

Transport out to the peninsula is much thinner on the ground, but there are several daily dolmuşes to Orhaniye in summer. Driving, you take the "Hisarönü-Orhaniye-Selimiye" turning 29km out of Marmaris. It's another three kilometers to Hisarönü, and then, another kilometer or so to Orhaniye.
Boat tours from nearby resorts also moor in Orhaniye.

WHERE TO **EAT?**

Right next to Kızkumu is Kızkumu Beach Club which serves grills, salads, and sigara böreği (stuffed savory pastry), as well as all kinds of drinks, for very reasonable prices.

The waterside Kadir Restaurant is a cozy, family-run place. Much has also been written about the Emine Teyze (Aunt) Restaurant in the Palmiye Hotel whose owner goes all out to please. Fish, casseroles, olive oil dishes - each is more delicious than the next.

WHERE TO **STAY?**

Palmiye Hotel
Phone: (0252) 487 11 34
Pleasant boutique-style hotel with its own hamam and pool.

Doğan Motel
Phone: (0252) 487 10 74
A clean, modern motel next to the Marina which produces much of its own food.

House Apart Hotel
Phone: (0252) 487 12 16

İskele Motel
Phone: (0252) 487 10 13

Evcan Pansiyon
Phone: (0252) 487 11 95

Kaptanköy Pansiyon
Phone: (0252) 487 11 64

WHAT **TO DO?**

This is a great area for waterskiing.
The bays of İnbükü, Kamelya, Dişlice Adası (Island), Artur and Selimiye are all equally splendid.

A great trekking trail leads to the ruins of Loryma, an ancient hillside city with the remains of an impressive fort.
Wild oregano and sage grow on the hillsides. Why not drop into one of the villages to try some oregano tea in the tea-house?

Pick some oregano from the mountains, then brew and drink it. Eat some fresh red mullet or sea bream and listen to the waves...

A SMALL TOWN GROWN UP

053 Marmaris

Fatih TÜRKMENOĞLU

Once a picturesque fishing village, Marmaris is now a grown-up town which exceeds Muğla, the provincial capital, in size. This is a place to come if you like your holidays loud and lively. At one time, Marmaris was said to have more than 3,000 restaurants. This is not somewhere you can expect to get bored.

Today, Marmaris exceeds many towns and the provincial capital of Muğla in size.
Saffet Emre Tonguç

Marmaris has an unbeatable natural setting, its harbor backed by mountains and surrounded by forests. Unfortunately, history has been less kind to it; apart from the tiny castle, built for Sultan Süleyman the Magnificent's conquest of Rhodes, and the quaint streets leading up to it, together with an inland rock studded with tombs, almost nothing remains of old Marmaris, making this somewhere for vacationers, who play for today, rather than hankering after times gone by.

Söğüt, Çiftlik Köyü, Bozburun, Orhaniye, İçmeler, Armutalan, Selimiye, Bayırköy, Turgut, Turunç, Kumlubük, Çubucak, İnbükü... Marmaris is vast. Much like a metropolis, it can't be squeezed into two short pages. Think of this as a "sneak-preview". Each bay or village should be the subject of another article.

Every year, sees the bazaar in the town center grow that bit larger. Where once it was mostly undercover, now it flows out into the surrounding streets, selling an astonishing array of goods, almost entirely aimed at tourists.

An outsize harbor

In the annals of Byzantine historian Doukas, Marmaris was mentioned as a Carian port. The modern town still boasts a flash marina, although nowadays the traders have given away to yachties and day trippers. How many of them know, though, that the harbor is big enough to have accommodated a fleet of more than 700 ships in 1522, when Sultan Süleyman the Magnificent arrived at the head of 140,000 troops for the siege of Rhodes? Or that the British Admiral Nelson holed up here, when he was preparing to try and drive the French out of Egypt in 1798?

Bars and restaurants

As befits such a busy place, Marmaris is overflowing with restaurants, more than 3,000 of them according to one recent count. Most of them sell Turkish staples although there are also "Indian" and "Chinese" restaurants to suit the palates of the largely British clientele. The most picturesque settings are round the harbor, where you can eat your meals while watching the sunset. Don't expect the prices to be anything other than tourist-oriented, though.

Nor is there any shortage of bars, with most of them tucked into what is generally known as Barlar Sokağı (Bar St), one street back from the harbor. The "day" doesn't kick off until around midnight here!

HOW TO **TRAVEL?**

Marmaris is 780km from Ankara and 900km from Istanbul. The best way to get here is to fly to Dalaman; it's 120km from Dalaman to Marmaris, which should take about an hour and a half to drive. The major bus companies offer services to Marmaris from all the big western cities.

WHERE TO **EAT?**

Marmaris is hardly gourmet heaven, although the strangely named **Mona Titti** (Phone: (0252) 455 40 46) in neighboring İçmeler serves decent food. **The Drunken Crab** (Phone: (0252) 412 39 70) in Barlar Sokağı has also been dishing up interesting fish suppers since whenever.

WHAT **TO DO?**

Take a boat tour out to Sedir Island (aka Cleopatra's Island) or along the coast to Dalyan.

Akyaka (Gökova) is near enough for a day trip. On the way, you could get out and walk along the famous "Eucalyptus Path", a rather unlikely stand of eucalyptus trees which line the old road right beside the new one. The trees are thought to have been planted by the famous Turkish author Halikarnas Balıkçısı ("the Fisherman of Halicarnassus") decades ago.

There are daily boats to the Greek island of Rhodes (Rodos); it takes just 45 minutes to get there.

Out on the Hisarönü Peninsula there are some minor archeological sites for die-hard ruins' fans. In particular, near the uninspiring resort of Turunç, on the south side of the peninsula, there are traces of the old settlement of Amos: a stretch of Byzantine wall, and remains of a temple and theater.

If you have a car, explore the remote Reşadiye and Hisarönü peninsulas, stopping off, perhaps, in Selimiye, Orhaniye, Hisarönü, Bozburun and Söğüt, all of them with pleasant restaurants and lovely views.

© Bunyad Dinç

WHERE TO **STAY?**

Marmaris and adjoining İçmeler are full of package-holiday hotels, some of them likely to be quite noisy.

Pupa Yat Hotel
Phone: (0252) 413 3566
Pleasing yachties' hideaway on the outskirts of town with a lovely view from its dining room. Far enough away to avoid the Bar Street decibels.

16 MUST-SEE PLACES
IN THE MEDITERRANEAN REGION

THE MEDITERRANEAN REGION

TURQUOISE WATERS
054 Blue Voyage

Saffet Emre TONGUÇ

Surrounded by sea on three sides, Turkey is the perfect place to enjoy the never-ending turquoise-blue of the Aegean and Mediterranean seas during the day and then to sleep under the stars at night. In the morning, lucky Blue Voyagers will be ready to set sail again in search of new adventures.

Kaleköy, a modern-day sleeping beauty.

Saffet Emre Tonguç

Blue nostalgia

In 1925, the government of the day sent famed author Cevat Şakir Kabaağaçlı into exile in Bodrum, because of an article he wrote. Of course, when the authorities realized that the author had turned his punishment into a pleasurable holiday, they decided that he should serve out the remaining part of his sentence in İstanbul. Yet the author sprinted back to Bodrum as soon as it was complete. Along with his friends Azra Erhat, Sabahattin and Bedri Rahmi Eyüboğlu, Cevat Şakir - who used the alias "Halikarnas Balıkçısı" (The Fisherman of Halicarnassus) - initiated the first Blue Voyage in 1957. Back then, the starting point was Kuşadası, the boats were old and dingy, and their passengers were completely carefree, sleeping in sleeping bags and waking up with the first rays of the sun. The point was not just to sail around, but also to explore history in the heart of nature, to discover Anatolia's rich cultural heritage and create a philosophical platform for intellectuals.

The passing years have added color and technology to the whole experience and today the Blue Voyage has become a particularly popular holiday choice. The turquoise waters of Turkey are perfect for helping you forget time as you sail away to freedom in a gulet (a graceful wooden yacht).

Kuşadası, the original starting point for the Blue Voyage, is no longer so popular. The rough sea, the pollution created by fish farms, and the sparse amenities there have diverted most Blue Voyagers to the area between Bodrum and Antalya, where it is still possible to spend whole days soaking up glorious blue and green scenery, and completely escaping from the stress of everyday life.

One of the most attractive aspects of a Blue Voyage is that it offers natural beauty on one side and a rich mix of history on the other…

In his verses the poet Bedri Rahmi Eyüboğlu describes the Blue Voyage this way: "The Blue Voyage is a fairy tale, never told, never written, never depicted…" The information is there - it is up to you to tell, write and depict it…

Bünyad Dinç

THINGS TO CONSIDER...

If you are a group of 8 or more, you can rent a boat through a company that specializes in Blue Voyages and determine your own route. If you are traveling alone, you can rent a cabin in a boat with a set itinerary.

The age, durability, comfort and construction of the boat are all important factors in determining the cost. The cheaper boats built in Bozburun are not usually very popular with serious sailors. Today, most boats have air-conditioning, another factor that affects prices. The June, July, and August heat make it very hard to sleep in the cabins. You can keep the stars company at night by sleeping on the deck, but the early morning dew can be uncomfortable. The covered stern is often a better bet.

If you have a Turkish cell phone, be careful about roaming costs. Make sure that you switch the "select network" command from automatic to manual. In many places, the Greek network emits a stronger signal and before you know it, you might find yourself keyed into that network and paying roaming charges! On some Greek islands such as Chios, Kos, Rhodes, and Simi, the Turkish networks are also available.

Try to travel light and bring only small suitcases; it might be difficult to find space for lots of luggage on the boat. Don't forget to pack anti-mosquito spray and ear-plugs - there may be thoughtless neighbors in the bays where you anchor overnight, who blast out music until the wee hours.

Be careful about whom you choose to travel with. The heat of the cabin and the relatively limited space on deck can narrow down your personal space, and you might not want to vacation so closely with people you've only just met. Traveling with the "wrong" people can rapidly turn a heavenly vacation into hell.

The ideal length for a Blue Voyage is probably between five days and a week. The longer your journey, the more you may find the days becoming monotonous.

You can walk up to the citadel in Bozukkale.

Saffet Emre Tonguç

ROUTES

The most popular routes for a Blue Voyage are usually the ones between Bodrum and Antalya. If you intend to relax and be at one with nature, put Gökova and Hisarönü onto your itinerary. If you prefer nature walks and history, and want to move about instead of basking in the sun all day long, go for the stretch from Marmaris to Antalya instead.

BETWEEN BODRUM AND MARMARIS

Day 1: Leave Bodrum early and head over to Çökertme. After lunch, anchor at Çamaltı and see the ruins of Keramos, half an hour away on foot.

Day 2: You can visit Sedir (Cedar) Island in the morning and swim off a beach renowned for its fine sand, allegedly imported for Cleopatra's pleasure. You can eat lunch at "İngiliz Limanı" (the British Harbor),

GET READY FOR BOAT RULES!

Food is served as soon as it is cooked on the boat, so it is always incredibly fresh and delicious, and unfortunately an invitation to those unwanted extra pounds! Lunch and dinner times are usually determined at the start of the tour. The boat usually has a captain, a chef and a sailor, who doubles up as a waiter.

Removing your shoes as soon as you board the boat is always the first rule. Most boats have 12 or 24 volts of electricity, supplied by batteries, so try to be economical; when the 220-volt generator is working, you can charge up your electrical appliances. Since water is provided from a reservoir, try and use it sparingly. In order to avoid blocking the toilets, you must throw toilet paper into the wastebasket.

When you anchor in the bays, locals may row up to your vessel selling ice cream, bread, newspapers, pancakes, bandanas, pareos and fish, or offering their services for water skiing, banana and parasailing. Don't assume that your gulet will ever actually use its sails. These days most of the cheaper boats cruise along quite adequately (if noisily) with a diesel engine and only raise the sails briefly to show you how it's done.

so named because it was the hideaway of the British fleet during World War II. At the entrance to the bay is a statue of a mermaid - similar to the famous sculpture of the Little Mermaid at Langelinie Quay in Copenhagen. Beneath it is a text by Sadun Boro, who toured the world in his boat Kısmet. You can spend the night in nearby Mersincik.

Day 3: Your stopover for today will be Datça. The Knidos ruins used to house a famous statue of the naked Aphrodite, created by the Greek sculptor Praxiteles in c. 360 BC. You can stay overnight in Bencik bay or Hisarönü.

Day 4: Do not miss Orhaniye and Selimiye. Located at the end of Orhaniye bay, Kızkumu is a beautiful place that gives people the impression that they are walking on water. You can spend the night in Bozburun and dine at Sabrina's House (Phone: (0252) 456 20 45) or Orfoz Restaurant (Phone: (0252) 456 22 09). Villa Julia in Söğüt (Phone: (0252) 496 50 01) and the nearby Denizkızı (Mermaid) Restaurant are other good choices.

Day 5: Visit the remains of Loryma Castle in Bozukkale bay in the morning, then sail into Serçe Limanı (Harbor) two miles off Bozukkale - some of the glass amphorae displayed at Bodrum Museum were excavated here. Then you can spend the night at Kadırga Limanı (Harbor) surrounded by olive trees and move on to Marmaris the next morning.

CRUISING ON BOUTIQUE BOATS...

Technology is always introducing new concepts into our lives; as we grow more and more accustomed to cell phones, the internet, text messaging, WAP, zapping, rating, etc., things like "boutique hotels" that we had never even heard of just a short time ago suddenly become a crucial part of our lives.

Most of the boat captains are self-taught and service is often no more than average. There are a few exceptions, however. Named after an old sponge-fisherman from Bodrum, Cavur Ali is an unconventional and very "boutique" boat. The owner and captain, Tosun Sezen is a graduate of Robert College (a renowned American high school in İstanbul) who moved to Bodrum at the end of the 1950s with his Swiss wife Josette. His name crops up in several foreign publications as a famous diver of the past.

Built entirely of teak like the old sponging boats, Cavur Ali has only four cabins and includes a compressor for scuba-diving. The food, the table setting and the refined decoration offer five-star hotel service at sea. The most enjoyable part of the journey is often just talking to the captain in the evening. The stories he can tell, filtered down through the years, soon carry you off into a world of reverie. The setting is a boat, with the stars, the vast sea, and the dark night as the backdrop. After a few glasses of wine, everyone becomes an actor in a surreal play.

Phone: (0542) 595 73 77 or (0242) 419 24 41

www.cavurali.com

If your group is large, you might want to opt for the eight-cabin Grand Acar. Captain Ahmet stops at nothing to provide his guests with a good time. The cabins and common areas are all very spacious, and the delicious food is a topic of conversation in all four corners of the globe.

Phone: (0532) 436 34 73

www.kaptanacar.com

Cavur Ali
Saffet Emre Tonguç

BLUE VOYAGE PRICES

Blue Voyage prices are always subject to change. Everything from the month of your voyage and the size of the boat, to the itinerary and the number of people in your group will affect the cost. The more luxurious the boat, the higher the price. If you can find a boat that can accommodate 10 to 12 people for less than 700-1000 € per day, you are either very lucky or your expectations are pretty low. In Turkey, many boats are available for more than 4000 € per day. Some of them work on an all-inclusive basis, with prices including the cost of locally-produced drinks. Some leave the provisioning up to you, while others only charge for alcohol to generate some extra income for the crew. The most expensive months are usually July and August, followed by June and September.

BETWEEN MARMARİS AND ANTALYA

Day 1: When Sultan Süleyman the Magnificent set out to defeat the Knights Hospitaller of Rhodes, he ordered that a new castle should be built. When he saw its unsatisfactory small size, the Sultan flew into a temper and ordered that the architect be hanged. The name of one of Turkey's most popular resorts is derived from the Sultan's command: "Mimarı as!" (Hang the architect). Leaving Marmaris and its unfortunate castle behind you, a three-hour cruise will bring you to Ekincik. As soon as you get there, jump on a small boat to Dalyan where you can visit the ruins of Caunos and İztuzu Beach (Turtle Beach) where Caretta caretta (loggerhead turtles) still lay their eggs. Life will seem particularly beautiful.

Day 2: Leave early in the morning for Ağa Limanı (Harbor) and take a leisurely after-breakfast walk. Climb up to Lydae and sip some of the sage tea that the yörüks (nomads) will offer you - now, you are officially in Lycia, the ancient Land of Light. Here, you can snap a few temple ruins and then walk down through the woods again, following part of the famous Lycian Way. At the end of the road, you will find yourself at the Batık Hamam (Submerged Bath) in Göcek. The boat will follow you there and, having burned off the calories in advance, you will be able to enjoy your meal with a clear conscience. Continue to Bedri Rahmi bay in the afternoon, looking out for the spirits of the first Blue Voyagers along the way.

Day 3: It takes about an hour and a half to get to Fethiye from Göcek, so continue on to Ölüdeniz immediately. After soaking up the sun on one of Turkey's most beautiful beaches, continue on to Soğuksu and walk to Kayaköy. At the end of the 45-minute walk through beautiful scenery, you will arrive in a derelict and truly sad place: an old Greek village with hundreds of houses abandoned during the 1923 population exchange between Turkey and Greece. As you walk among the churches and the houses you will be traveling back to past centuries. Then, you can spend the night at Gemiler Adası (St Nicholas island), which boasts the remains of a monastery.

The Lycian Way walking trail is marked with red and white flashes, so you don't need to worry about getting lost while out trekking.

Day 4: The reward for a three-and-a-half hour cruise is Kalkan, one of the most beautiful coastal towns, now chock-a-block with British settlers. If you call Mehmet Tanç (Phone: (0532) 783 24 15), he will take you to the ancient city of Patara, which has the best sandy beach in the area, and then to the village of Bezirgan perched above Kalkan. Don't forget to try the tasty "gözleme" (pancakes) his wife makes.

© Bünyad Dinç

Day 5: A two-hour cruise, bypassing Kaputaş Beach and Castellerizo (Meis) Island, brings you to Kaş which has several diving schools. Enjoy a cup of coffee at inviting Café Merhaba, then walk through Uzun Çarşı (the Long Bazaar), one of Turkey's loveliest shopping streets. If you're interested in antiques, take a look at Turqueria which offers a great selection. Then stop for lunch at Bahçe Restaurant in a

The sheltered bays of the Aegean and Mediterranean provide natural harbors for boats.

Saffet Emre Tonguç

shady garden. If you are staying overnight, try the French delicacies at Chez Evy (0242 836 12 53). Alternatively, you can stop the night in Bayındır Bay.

Day 6: After leaving Kaş, you will pass Uluburun, where the oldest shipwreck in the world was excavated. Right now, it is exhibited in Bodrum. Be sure to stop at Aperlae. Diving is prohibited in Kekova, but allowed here. You will be amazed at the ruins visible under water. After lunch, you will reach Simena (Kaleköy) in an hour. Climb up to a citadel dating back to Crusader times at the top of the village and enjoy the view from what must be one of the most beautiful villages in Turkey. Then sail out over the extraordinary remains of a submerged city called Kekova. As the boat slowly cuts through the water, watch out for the wonders - both underwater and on land - of this magnificent city that was destroyed by an earthquake. Then spend the night in Karalos bay. Should there be a full moon, you really are in luck; it doesn't get any better than this.

Day 7: From Myra's harbor Andriake (Çayağzı), take a trip to the Church of Saint Nicholas (Santa Claus) in the town centre. Myra is the last place Saint Paul visited, before he was taken to Rome as a prisoner. The ruins of the theater and the tombs carved into the rocks will give you some clues to the ancient architecture of this area. You can also arrange for a minibus to take you to beautiful, little-visited Arycanda (Arif), just beyond Finike. Before visiting one of the best-preserved Greco-Roman theaters in Anatolia, you can also treat yourself to some trout at one of the local fish farms. Your overnight stay will probably be in the marina at Finike.

Day 8: A three-hour morning cruise will first take you to Adrasan Bay and then to Olympos. Olympos, where the ruins peek out from amid the undergrowth, is one of Turkey's most intriguing ancient cities; it makes you feel as if you are in an Indiana Jones movie. Up above, the Chimaera (Yanartaş) is a breath-taking sight, both because of the myths attached to it and because of its mysterious, ever-burning light. Afterwards you can spend the night at Port Ceneviz (Genoese).

You can travel by boat from Kaş to Meis island, which has very few residents. The Blue Cave at the back of Meis might be worth a quick look.

Day 9: Today, you should reach the romantic ancient city of Phaselis which is best visited in the morning - by noon, the site is overrun with day trippers. As you sit in the ancient theater, lift your head and look up at Mount Tahtalı. Perhaps, it will share one of its thousand-year-old secrets or recount the story of Bellerophon, who rode his winged horse Pegasus over the Chimaera to slay it.

BLUE VOYAGE YACHT AGENCIES

Some of the yacht agencies organizing Blue Voyages offer both cabins in boats and private group rentals. Some only rent out the boats and leave you to organize the group. There are also individual boat owners, who market their own boats. The list below gives just some of the innumerable possibilities:

YACHT AGENCIES RENTING CABINS AND BOATS

İSTANBUL
Credo Tours
Phone: (0212) 254 81 75
www.credotours.com
Credo dedicates itself to create experiences that combine the best Turkey has to offer with style, understanding and sophistication. Credo offers some of the most luxurious boats with an excellent service.
Setur
Phone: (0216) 474 06 00
www.setur.com.tr
As the operator of numerous marinas across Turkey, Setur is one of the best companies offering Blue Voyages.

BODRUM
Arya Tur
Phone: (0252) 316 15 80
www.aryatours.com
Neyzen Tur
Phone: (0252) 316 72 04
www.neyzen.com.tr
Mizana Tur
Phone: (0252) 313 24 65
www.mizanayachting.com
Egeyat
Phone: (0252) 316 57 49
www.aegeanyacht.com
Egeyat owns almost 30 boats and organizes tours which offer everything from a classic Blue Voyage to a luxury cruise.

BOAT RENTAL COMPANIES

BODRUM
Seagull
Phone: (0252) 313 48 83
www.seagullyachting.com
Founded by partners who have been sailing for 20 years, Seagull offers six high-standard boats. Most of its owners also captain their own boats. The crews are excellent.
Pruva Yachting
Phone: (0252) 313 76 63
www.pruva.com.tr
Some of the best and newest boats in Turkey.
Salmakis
Phone: (0252) 316 28 77
www.salmakis.com.tr
They have four boats, some with six and some with eight cabins. In June, daily prices range between 750 € and 2250 €; for full board, calculate an extra 22 € per person per day.
Admiral Tours
Phone: (0252) 316 17 81
www.admiralyachting.com
S&J Yachting
Phone: (0252) 316 05 61
www.yacht-turkey.com
Apak Tours
Phone: (0252) 316 52 44
www.apaktours.com
Barbaros Yachting
Phone: (0252) 316 39 19
www.barbarosyachting.com

FETHİYE
Alesta Yachting
Phone: (0252) 614 18 61
www.alestayachting.com

MARMARİS
Yeşil Marmaris
Phone: (0252) 412 64 86
www.yesil-marmaris.com
Gino Yachting
Phone: (0252) 412 52 20
www.ginogroup.com
Megamar
Phone: (0252) 412 08 97
www.megamar.com
Contact
Phone: (0252) 413 63 13
www.contactturkey.com

GÖCEK
Arinna
Phone: (0252) 64 52 682
www.veladare.com
Hatsail
Phone: (0252) 645 17 65
www.hatsail.com
Galeo
Phone: (0252) 645 20 32
www.galeoyachting.com

LUXURY YACHTS

Boats are available to suit all budgets. The most expensive yachts are often rented by foreigners. Rich Turks, on the other hand, prefer to head for the Caribbean or France, in order to stay out of sight! The most luxurious gulets used for Blue Voyages are often built in Bodrum; some even boast Jacuzzis and plasma TVs. While the boats built in Bozburun cost a few hundred thousand US dollars, these luxury gulets cost upwards of a million US dollars. Below are a few addresses for further information.

Cobra Queen
Phone: (0252) 316 31 89
www.cobrayachting.com

Kaya Güneri IV
Phone: (0252) 319 04 85
www.kayaguneriyachting.com

Lady Christa
Phone: (0532) 324 80 58

Palmyra
Phone: (0532) 748 54 60

Carpe Diem II
Phone: (0252) 316 21 48
www.viyayachting.net

Eylül Deniz II
Phone: (0252) 313 67 78
www.eastyachting.com.tr

Enderim A
Phone: (0252) 244 06 10
www.enderim.net

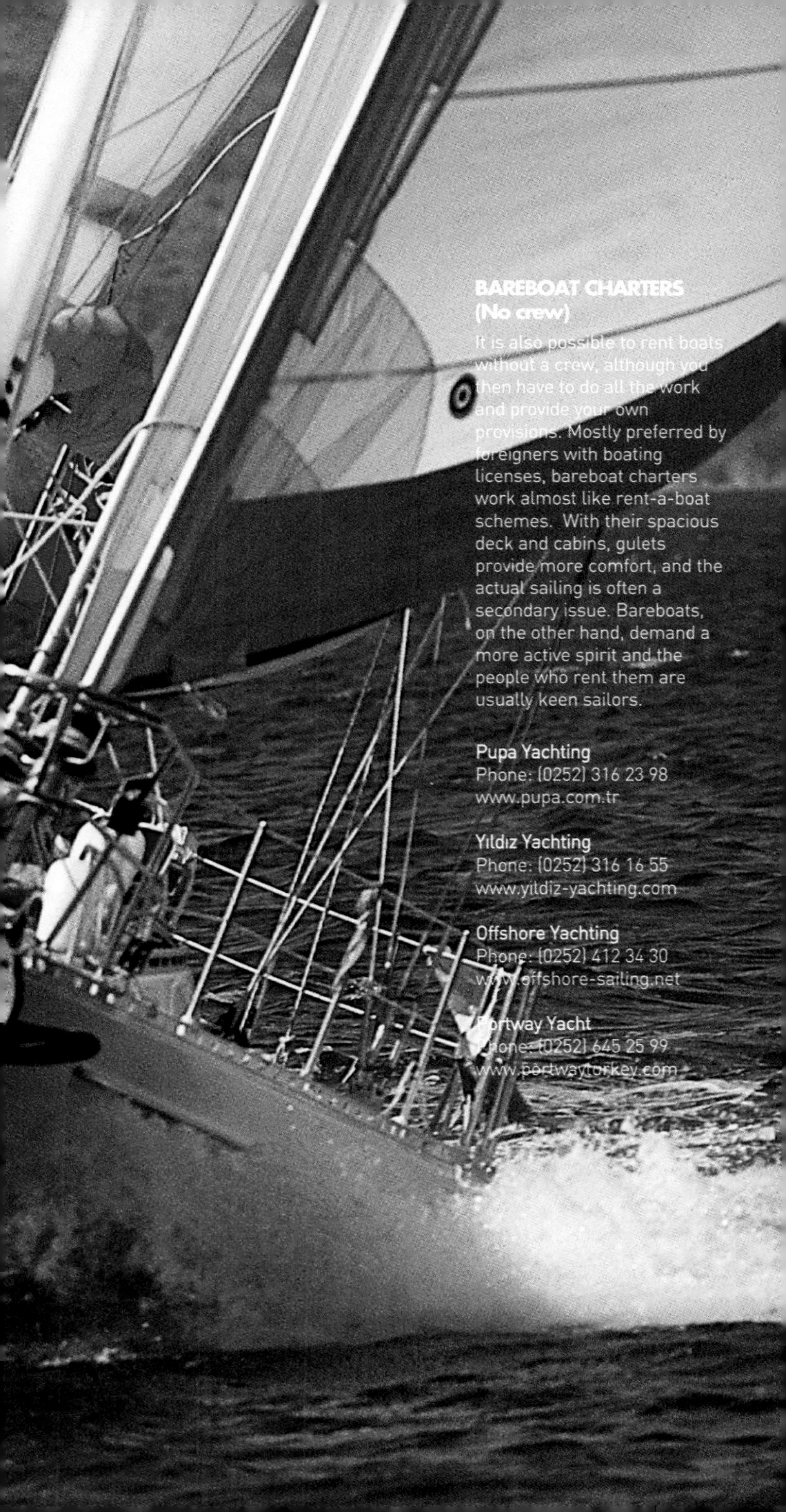

BAREBOAT CHARTERS (No crew)

It is also possible to rent boats without a crew, although you then have to do all the work and provide your own provisions. Mostly preferred by foreigners with boating licenses, bareboat charters work almost like rent-a-boat schemes. With their spacious deck and cabins, gulets provide more comfort, and the actual sailing is often a secondary issue. Bareboats, on the other hand, demand a more active spirit and the people who rent them are usually keen sailors.

Pupa Yachting
Phone: (0252) 316 23 98
www.pupa.com.tr

Yıldız Yachting
Phone: (0252) 316 16 55
www.yildiz-yachting.com

Offshore Yachting
Phone: (0252) 412 34 30
www.offshore-sailing.net

Portway Yacht
Phone: (0252) 645 25 99
www.portwayturkey.com

055

AN ANCIENT CITY ON THE BANKS OF A RIVER
Caunos and Dalyan

Saffet Emre TONGUÇ

When Caunos, the son of Miletus and grandson of Apollo, fell in love with his twin sister Byblis, he fled the country to mend his broken heart and founded a new city near present-day Dalyan. Built beside the aqueduct that connects Lake Köyceğiz to the Mediterranean, the old city on one bank of the Dalyan river was named Caunos after its founder. The fast-expanding modern resort of Dalyan sits on the opposite bank of the river and offers magnificent views of ancient Lycian tombs cut into the rock-face above it.

Dalyan River
Bünyad Dinç

Dalyan was once right on the border between Caria and Lycia, which lay to the east. Today, Caunos/Kaunos, with its theater, temples, city walls, and tombs of the kings, is an important archaeological site which also houses an intriguing structure used to measure the speed and direction of the wind, as well as several baths. If you're up for a bit of adventure, you can climb up to the Acropolis (the city's highest point) and enjoy the spectacular view.

Across the river from Caunos, Dalyan is a busy holiday resort in the summer and a tranquil Mediterranean town in the winter. Although the Caretta carettas (loggerhead turtles) are not visible throughout the year (and, in any case, should not be disturbed), Turtle Beach always offers a lovely six kilometer walk from one end to the other. The hotels stay open in the winter and offer fireplaces where you can relax in front of a blaze after a busy day.

To the west of Dalyan are the Sultaniye Kaplıcaları (thermal springs), Ekincik, Marmaris and Gökova. To its east lies Göcek, hidden amid pine trees. A major yachting center, Göcek is warm even in the winter and with the few restaurants on its shore, offers a perfect getaway for those who enjoy the delights of the off-season.

İztuzu Plajı (Turtle Beach)
Rıfat Yüzbaşıoğlu

If you are staying in Dalyan, you can easily get to İztuzu Plajı (Turtle Beach) by boat. It's a wonderful ride along a rush-lined river with the 2500-year-old, mini-temple-like Royal Tombs staring down at you from a looming cliff-face. Unlikely as it may seem, as you float along the river, you may well be reminded of Humphrey Bogart's famous movie The African Queen.

Saffet Emre Tonguç

WHERE TO **STAY?**

Sedir Resort
Phone: (0252) 284 33 64
www.sedir.co.uk
Far from the Dalyan crowds, this is a family-run establishment in the woods. After picking them from her back garden, Filiz Hanım transforms fresh vegetables into truly splendid dishes. Meanwhile, husband Baki Bey will be busy grilling fish, while the boys of the household hover ready to serve. The large pool is all yours; enjoy it as much as you want. You will feel completely at home here.

Swissotel Göcek, Marina & Resort
Phone: (0252) 645 27 60
www.gocek.swissotel.com
Göcek is one of the most beautiful places in Turkey. This establishment is small and elegant, and accessible by boat or car.

Montenegro
Phone: (0252) 644 01 81
A heavenly place to stay on top of a hill in Göcek. Ideal if you want to forget everything and relax in the arms of nature.

Kamarca House
Phone: (0252) 284 45 17
This six-room hotel is perfect for an unconventional vacation. Hostess Kamer Hanım's meals will leave you begging for more.

WHERE TO **EAT?**

Ley Ley (Phone: (0252) 284 46 69) and **Gölbaşı** (Phone: (0252) 284 44 10).
Both these restaurants are outside the town center and surrounded by nature. At Ley Ley you are guaranteed to see nesting storks in summer. Alternatively, try **Ramazan Han Restaurant** (Phone: (0252) 284 41 83) **Zeugma** (Phone: (0252) 284 21 41) or **Metin Pizza** (Phone: (0252) 284 28 77) in town.
Riverside (Phone: (0252) 284 31 66) is on the outskirts of Dalyan and can be accessed by boat. Here you can sample the seafood while saluting the kings lying in their tombs just across the river.

Caunos, theater

WHAT **TO DO?**

After slathering your entire body with mud at the local mud baths, take a boat to Lake Köyceğiz and jump into the water.
You will look like a zombie on the way over, but afterwards your skin will be as soft as a baby's bottom.
Sadık's boat "**Fok**" is perfect for this trip (Phone:0543 630 02 32).

The small beach resort of Ekincik, 30 kilometers south of Köyceğiz, is a secret treasure in the summer months when Dalyan itself can be too busy for comfort.

AT THE HEART OF LYCIA

056 Fethiye

Saffet Emre TONGUÇ

Foreigners often refer to the southern coast of Turkey as the "Turquoise Coast", and in fact the name of the lovely gemstone called "turquoise" comes from French, and means "Turkish". Apart from some chrome mining and orange and tomato farming, Fethiye, the attractive capital of the Turquoise Coast, has mainly grown fat on the proceeds of tourism. Located in a beautiful bay, dotted with twelve idyllic small islands, it makes an ideal kicking-off point for a Blue Voyage.

Xanthos, Byzantine Basilica

Şemsi Güner

Fethiye stands on the ruins of Telmessus, an ancient Lycian city. It is, therefore, small wonder that there are plenty of rock-cut tombs and a recently-restored ancient theater right in the town center. The historic citadel and the museum are other attractions worth a quick visit. In honor of the Byzantine emperor Anastasius (r. 491-518), the city was once called Anastasiospolis. It was also called Makri, a Greek name the Turks mispronounced as Meğri. Finally, Fethi Bey, a pilot and local war hero, became the source of inspiration for the town's current name.

The Lycians who lived around Fethiye spoke a language that is yet to be deciphered.

One of the most popular things to do in Fethiye is to join one of the daily tour boats that depart from the harbor and cruise round the twelve islands of the bay and out to Göcek.

Tlos, near Fethiye, was one of the most important cities of Lycia. Offering a fabulous view of the Xanthos valley, the city has a gymnasium (now used as a school), a church, a theater, and an agora (market place), all of them impressive. Tlos should be a must-see on any Turkish itinerary even though the locals sometimes call it "Kanlı Divane" (Bloody Lunatic), after Kanlı Ali Ağa who slew several people to protect his family's honor.

Heading further east, Saklıkent,

Gemiler Adası (St Nicholas Island)

Saffet Emre Tonguç

between Tlos and Patara, boasts a beautiful gorge, perfect if you are looking for an ice-cool place to hang-out and eat trout lunches over a river in the intense heat of the summer.

Xanthos on the Eşen River is thought to have been the capital of Lycia. Most of the artifacts found in this area were carried off to the British Museum in the 19th century, so if you are ever in London, take a look at the Nereid Monument and try to imagine what the site would have looked like before they were removed. The Harpy Monument, the theater, a church with a mosaic floor, and a 2500-year-old column decorated with Lycian inscriptions are some of the remains that can still be seen in situ.

Fethiye and the surrounding area are often included on Blue Voyage itineraries.

Saffet Emre Tonguç

WHERE TO **STAY?**

Hillside Beach Club
Phone: (0252) 614 83 60
www.hillside.com.tr
Located in a spectacular bay, this is one of Turkey's most popular holiday resorts. It offers extraordinarily good food and service, coupled with a great spa and sports activities.

Atapark Hotel
Phone: (0252) 612 40 81
www.atahotels.com
An inviting town-center hotel with a good wine cellar and some rooms offering sea views.

Ece Saray
Phone: (0252) 612 50 05
A great hotel offering 5-star comforts right in Fethiye Marina.

WHERE TO **EAT?**

The fishermen who supply the Fethiye fish market convert their shops into small restaurants in the evening. It's a great place to come for a cheap bite to eat.

Meğri Restaurant
Phone: (0252) 614 40 46
www.megrirestaurant.com
The best restaurant in the area with two branches in the bazaar; try the one at Çarşı Caddesi No. 13 first. Here you can sample Turkey's most delicious cuisine, including mezes (appetizers) and kebabs. Leave room for dessert!

HOW TO **TRAVEL?**

Fethiye is 50 kilometers from Dalaman airport and 15 kilometers from Ölüdeniz, with frequent dolmuşes linking the two.

Göcek

A GHOST TOWN
057 Kayaköy

Fatih TÜRKMENOĞLU

Kayaköy is a fabulously beautiful village full of derelict stone houses near Fethiye city center. But behind the beauty of the narrow streets, the abandoned churches and the lovely views lies a traumatic story of forced population exchange recently brought vividly to life in Louis de Bernières' wonderful novel, *Birds Without Wings*.

Kayaköy is only 5 kilometers from Fethiye city center.
Refik Ongan

Although the exact date of its establishment is not known, it is possible to trace the settlement of Kayaköy back to the 14th century. Built over the site of the ancient city of Karmylassos, the town was called Levissi in the days before 1923 when its population was predominantly Ottoman Greek. Even then, however, sources suggest that the village kept close ties with the neighboring Muslim villages. After the population exchange between Greece and Turkey, the locals traded places with Turks from Greece. Some just picked up their bags and left, while others entrusted their houses to friends who stayed behind. All left with the hope that one day they would be able to return.

Unfortunately, after the ones, who left couldn't come back again, the once thriving village of 25,000 inhabitants was never the same. Instead of living in the abandoned houses, the Western Thracian Turks preferred to live in new ones that they built on the slopes. Famous for its schools, doctors, pharmacies, vineyards and olive groves before the population exchange, this once prosperous place was rediscovered by tourists in the '90s. By that time, however, most of the houses had been destroyed by treasure hunters and the roofs had mostly caved in. Eventually, the area was declared an archaeological site.

Each Kayaköy house was designed so that it did not block its neighbor's light. Today, more than 400 houses are under state protection.

It may look tough, but it's worth climbing to the top of the old village where the view will soon make you forget your aches and pains. It's also worth visiting the remains of the two churches (the Katapanagia and the Taxiarhis) which still await restoration.

If you want to stay here, there is only a handful of pensions and hotels, as well as the Kayaköy Art Camp. However, there are several restaurants offering great food and views.

A 45-minute walk with beautiful views will bring you to the sea near Soğuksu, where the ruins of a monastery stand astride a small off-shore island. There is also a (tough) five kilometer walking trail to Ölüdeniz.

As you wander the narrow streets of Kayaköy, you will encounter "villagers" with many different nationalities.
Mehmet Çabuk

HOW TO **TRAVEL?**

Dalaman airport is roughly 60 kilometers from Kayaköy. Havaş shuttle buses run to Fethiye where you can take a minibus from the town center.
For drivers, the most scenic route follows the coast road from Marmaris or Antalya.

WHERE TO **EAT?**

Kaya Wine House
Phone: (0252) 618 04 54
Restored stone house offering great food and wine with superb views of the ruins, which are especially beautiful when floodlit at night.

WHERE TO **STAY?**

Kaya Apart
Phone: (0252) 618 01 59

Selçuk Pansiyon
Phone: (0252) 618 01 48

WHAT **TO DO?**

Kayaköy Sanat Kampı (Art Camp)
Phone: (0252) 618 01 83
www.kayasanat.com
The camp offers photography, painting, percussion, weaving and drama workshops. Accommodation is available in stone houses or tents. Safari tours as well as land and sea excursions (including to Butterfly Valley) are also available. Weekly rates include full board, classes, and accommodation in a stone house or tent.

THE QUEEN OF BEACHES

058 Ölüdeniz

Saffet Emre TONGUÇ

Almost too beautiful for its own good, Ölüdeniz is one of the places that has made a huge contribution to Turkey's tourism industry. Posters, books, postcards, and billboards almost always include a photograph of Ölüdeniz, where a glorious lagoon sits alongside a spectacular stretch of sand at the foot of a steep hill.

Boats at the entrance to Ölüdeniz.

Saffet Emre Tonguç

Although Belcekiz beach is open to everyone free of charge, there is an admission fee to visit the protected lagoon of Ölüdeniz ("Dead Sea"), which offers a fabulous view of the sea, meeting and mingling with the lagoon as soon as you step through the gate. A pebble beach fading gently out into a sea that is every shade of blue promises a tranquility that could bring time to a standstill - surely heaven on earth. Try to avoid the weekends, however, when the crowds can quickly turn heaven into noisy hell.

You can walk through pine trees and beautiful scenery from Kayaköy to Ölüdeniz.

For sports enthusiasts, Ölüdeniz is a great and safe choice for canoeing. Paragliders also use the adjoining mountain, the 2000-meter Babadağı (Mt Baba), as a launchpad for flying down to the beach after soaring over the lovely view.

(Sky Sports Phone: (0252) 617 05 11)

Nearby are several beautiful bays and the ruins of some Byzantine churches and monasteries. Since it boasts a 7th-century monastery dedicated to St Nicholas, Gemiler Adası, which is a popular anchoring place for Blue Voyagers, is also known as St Nicholas Island. The island's summit is accessible via a long vaulted tunnel. Once up at the top, you can inspect the church's floor mosaics and enjoy the beautiful scenery.

Kelebek Vadisi (Butterfly Valley) takes its name from the hundreds of butterflies that colonize a nearby valley. There is a popular small beach here and a steep but potentially dangerous path up from the back of the valley to lovely Faralya. You can get to Butterfly Valley on a daily boat tour from Ölüdeniz.

© Saffet Emre Tonguç

WHERE TO **STAY?**

Paradise Garden Hotel
Phone: (0252) 617 05 45
www.paradisegardenhotel.com
The hotel is right on the hill that descends to Ölüdeniz, so the view is fantastic, as are the large secluded pools and the gardens.

Montana Pine Resort
Phone: (0252) 616 71 08
www.montanapine.com
One of the best hotels in the region.

Hotel Meri
Phone: (0252) 617 00 01
www.hotelmeri.com
Close to the Ölüdeniz lagoon, this venerable hotel leans gently into the pine trees. Most of the rooms have lovely views that can be enjoyed from the balconies.

You can also stay in Ovacık or Hisarönü near Ölüdeniz, although both places are over-developed.

HOW TO **TRAVEL?**

Regular minibuses link Ölüdeniz with Fethiye town center.

You can still enjoy the tranquility of Ölüdeniz out of season, although the tourist hordes are starting to take their toll on this fabulous natural paradise during the summer months.

Bünyad Dinç

"KALKANBOROUGH" OR JUST PLAIN…
059 Kalkan

Fatih TÜRKMENOĞLU

There are so many Brits living in Kalkan that soon the name will have to be changed to "Kalkanborough"! The quaint little village of the past has metamorphosed into a beautiful and expensive tourist center. From lovely wooden houses to super-chic restaurants, you can find almost anything you want in Kalkan. *The Independent* newspaper even selected it as the "most romantic vacation spot in Europe".

Kalkan is a favorite among Eudopeans, especially British.
Saffet Emre Tonguç

Kalkan boasts one of the most attractive locations along this part of the coast. Until the 1920s, it was a tiny fishing village named "Kalamaki," which means "small fishing rod" in Greek. The church of the old village is now used as one of the town's two mosques. What was once a small fishing village has expanded inland towards the mountains, but although it has grown enormously, much of the old character, along with many of the lovely old houses, has somehow been preserved. Start exploring with the bazaar in the town center. As you go, look at all the old houses with their quaint wooden balconies, many of them now turned into pensions, restaurants or giftshops.

The British discover Kalkan

Until 1984, access to Kalkan was only by boat and what is now a small town was a tiny village, popular with a limited number of hardy tourists. The locals had little interaction with the outside world. They would welcome strangers into their homes and to their dinner tables. But of course money changes everything. After the road from Kalkan to Fethiye was asphalted in 1984, Kalkan quickly became better known, and today hundreds of luxurious homes are being built and sold at relatively high prices to foreigners. Nearly half of the current population is British. There are even two English newspapers: the Kalkan Times and Kalkan Post.

The Independent newspaper dubbed Kalkan "The most romantic holiday destination in Europe".

This is such a picturesque place that you can easily get used to the leisurely Mediterranean way of living. Should you so choose, you can shoot the breeze, swim for an hour or so in the morning, sleep for a couple of hours in the afternoon, and then sip your drinks beneath the moonlight. You can pick up a philosophy book and reflect on the meaning of life. Or you can take advantage of its position and use Kalkan as a base for exploring the surrounding area. You are right in the middle of Lycia with all the ruined cities of Antiquity close at hand and waiting to be discovered.

The local beach is pebble, but the long sandy beach of Patara is only three kilometers away. Midway between Kalkan and Kaş lies tiny Kaputaş Beach. Other, better beaches are accessible on local boat tours. The lovely Güvercinlik (Pigeon House) Sea Cave, two kilometers away, is also reached by boat.

Serhan Güngör

WHERE TO **STAY?**

There are some great hotels in town.

Kalkan Han
Phone: (0242) 844 31 51
Strongly recommended

Balıkçıhan Pansiyon
Phone: (0242) 844 30 75

Villa Mahal
Phone: (0242) 844 32 68
An outstanding boutique hotel with a fantastic view.

Owlsland
Phone: (0242) 837 52 14
Traditionally decorated village-style pension in sleepy Bezirgan.

WHERE TO **EAT?**

Gironda
Phone: (0242) 844 31 36
A fabulous restaurant and bar with an enchanting colonial atmosphere.

Aubergine Restaurant
Phone: (0242) 844 33 32
Right on the beach and serving great food.

WHAT **TO DO?**

Inland from Kalkan is the sprawling village of Bezirgan. A 15-minute walk will bring you to the ruins of Pirha, the ancient Bezirgan. İnbaş Mağarası (cave) near Bezirgan village is also worth exploring.

The ruins of ancient Xanthos-Letoon, Patara, Kekova-Simena, Tlos, Pınara, and Arsada are all nearby, as are those of less well-known Pydnai or Kydnai which the locals call "Gavur Ağılı" (infidel Barn).

Kaputaş Beach

Saffet Emre Tonguç

DIVING IN COOL WATERS
060 Kaş

Fatih TÜRKMENOĞLU

The endless Mediterranean awaits you, tranquil, blue and infinite… Ahead, two fish are frolicking and a diver is heading towards a cave deep below the water. The waters around the pretty harbor town of Kaş are perfect for diving but also for boat trips out to nearby Kekova with its romantic Lycian ruins. Kaş is one of Turkey's finest small resorts, with some great restaurants and distinctly upscale shopping opportunities within easy reach of several truly wonderful archaeological sites.

Port of Kaş

Wrapped around a pretty harbour, Kaş is one of Turkey's most inviting small resorts, with some lovely shops in Uzun Çarşı, a picture-postcard cobbled street lined with old houses draped in bougainvillea. This was once the Lycian city of Antiphellus and as you wander around town you will bump into huge, ancient sarcophagi on many street corners. The lovely old theatre, which dates back to Hellenistic times, is sometimes used to stage performances in summer.

One of the ancient names for Kaş was Abessos. Another was Antiphellus, meaning "across from Phellus", which is another ancient city high in the hills at nearby Çukurbağ. Until the early years of the Republic, the surrounding area was referred to as "Andfili", a name derived from Antiphellus.

Diver's delight

Kaş is one of the 50 best spots for diving in the world and by far the best in Turkey. At least 15 diving schools try to tempt

Kaş Theater
Serhan Güngör

the passers-by. I walked into Nautilius, the first one that crossed my path. “We can go right away,” they said. “OK” I replied meekly.

Fearing that I might back out at any second, I longed for the boat to leave as soon as possible. On the way, my instructors and I sipped some tea and chatted. When the boat stopped the instructors taught me what to do and, more importantly, what NOT to do. They showed me the signs for things like “problem,” “no problem,” and “my ears are ringing”. Then they described how I should make my ears pop as I dived more deeply. Finally I put on the gear, which felt as if it weighed a ton, and dived in.

No problem, the bottom of the sea is perfect!

The instructor waited for me to get used to breathing calmly before going any deeper. He checked my pulse to see that everything was normal and signed “no problem”. I signed

Experiened divers enjoy the waters of Kaş and Kekova. The area is perfect for diving; the sea flora and the plethora of sea creatures make it a worthwhile experience

Bünyad Dinç

Kaleköy

Bünyad Dinç

it back. He signed "do you want to go deeper?", and at once my fears vanished. Gently fluttering my fins, I started to follow him.

Oh, the wonders I have seen...

Caves, rocks, fish, tires housing schools of fish, amphorae that change color with the rays of the sun, shipwrecks, octopi...

I must have dived down to six meters without encountering any problems; on the contrary, the sea was so blue, so clear that I was overcome by a sense of infinite peace. According to my instructor, the visibility was about 40 meters. It was all so exciting that I decided to join a five-day training course and qualify as a single-star diver.

A boat tour around Kaş will give you the opportunity to vist some gorgeous bays.

Diving instruction

To take a diving course, you need a health report, that indicates that you have no physical handicaps to prevent you from diving. Over the summer, new courses start almost every day. The training lasts five days. Theoretical education is backed up with visual material. Most beginners need training to use the equipment and this is given in shallow water. You take 10 dives and then, if you pass the written exam, you get your license.

Uzunçarşı, (Long Bazaar) is one of the loveliest streets in Turkey.
Saffet Emre Tonguç

◡HAT TO DO?

ly boat trips take in ◡aryum Bay, Simena, ◡ova and Üçağız village, ◡ the chance to swim ◡ve Lycian ruins and ◡n visit beautiful Kaleköy ◡age with its castle and ◡ian necropolis.

◡ makes an excellent ◡e for visiting the Lycian ◡s at Xanthos-Letoon ◡ Patara. There are also ◡rs to the basilica of St ◡holas in Demre, and to ◡ Saklıkent Gorge, with ◡ice-cold water. A few ◡rs also travel inland to ◡t the Green Lake and ◡ old Ottoman town of ◡alı.
◡other popular excursion ◡eekdays only) is to the ◡eek island of Kastellorizo ◡eis in Turkish) which is ◡arly visible offshore. ◡ats stop long enough for ◡ to eat a fish lunch, ◡lore the lovely old ◡uses along the harbor ◡ do a spot of shopping ◡th euros, of course!). ◡e your passport to the ◡at captain the night ◡ore you want to go.

WHERE TO STAY?

Hotel Club Phellos
Phone: (0242) 836 19 53
www.hotelclubphellos.com.tr
Right in the heart of Kaş, the decoration is very '80s, the pool is inviting, and the staff are friendly.

Villa Kurt
Phone: (0242) 836 16 31
www.turqueria.com
Attractively decorated 4-bedroom villa in a lovely garden with pool.

Sardunya
Phone: (0242) 836 30 80

Gardenya
Phone: (0242) 836 23 68

Linda Beach
Phone: (0242) 836 13 28

Çakıl Pansiyon
Phone: (0242) 836 15 32

Aqua Princess
Phone: (0242) 836 20 26

Hadrian Hotel
Phone: (0242) 836 28 56

HOW TO TRAVEL?

The Antalya-Kaş highway has one of the most splendid views in the country. Kaş is 210 kilometers from Antalya airport and 160 kilometers from Dalaman. If you are driving from Antalya, you can reach Kaş via Kemer, Kumluca and Finike. If you prefer to take a bus, there are plenty of services from Antalya.

WHERE TO EAT?

Blue House
Phone: (0242) 836 21 71

İkbal
Phone: (0242) 836 37 93
Good service in a beautiful garden.

Bahçe'de Balık
Phone: (0242) 836 27 79
Excellent fish restaurant in an inviting garden.

Smiley's
Phone: (0242) 836 28 12
Long-lived favorite fish restaurant.

Hideaway Café & Bar
Phone: (0242) 836 33 69
Famous for its cocktails, desserts, and Sunday brunches.

Efendi, Barselona, Déjà Vu and **Echo** are all excellent bars.

THE SUBMERGED CITY

061 Aperlae

Saffet Emre TONGUÇ

Aperlae is a half-submerged ancient city which was inhabited as early as the 5th century BC. While diving is not allowed in Kekova, here you can grab your snorkel and flippers, and explore the historic underwater site to your heart's content. Walls, columns, terracotta-covered floors, and earthenware fragments smile up at you from the bottom of the Mediterranean.

The Mediterranean coast of Turkey has played a pivotal role in maritime trade throughout history. The ancients regarded the Mediterranean as the center of the world, hence its name which means simply the "middle of the earth".

In Roman times, Aperlae was the capital of a settlement consisting of the neighboring towns of Simena (Kaleköy), İsinda (Belenli) and Apollonia; the inhabitants of this region were called Aperlites. Today, the remains of Aperlae include the Roman walls, which start by the sea and ascend the hill, occasionally supported by bastions, and a necropolis (literally, a "city of the dead", the term now refers to a graveyard).

Located between Kaş and Kekova, Aperlae makes an ideal stop for Blue Voyagers.

The area also boasts the ruins of several churches and chapels. Pilgrims to Jerusalem sometimes traveled by boat, establishing settlements along the coast as they went. Consequently, these shores were studded with minor Christian sites, and the remains of churches and monasteries can often be seen even in places with no proper settlement.

Those early ships cruised along with only oars and sails to help them. The mariners would spend each night in a different port, but sometimes fell victim to harsh weather conditions. No small wonder, then, that the seas of Turkey are full of cultural treasures. Ancient shipwrecks are often discovered by sponge fishermen and then dredged up from the sea. What is regarded as the oldest shipwreck in the world was found at Uluburun, near Aperlae; it contained numerous artifacts that shed light on the ways of the maritime past. Today the astounding remains of that shipwreck can be seen in the Bodrum Castle, the world's largest underwater archaeology museum.

Kaleköy is located near Aperlae.
Bünyad Dinç

HOW TO **TRAVEL?**

Although it is between Kaş and Kekova, Aperlae is difficult to access by land and is therefore a jewel best known to Blue Voyagers. To get there by land, you leave Üçağız Village, and walk along part of the Lycian Way. In this way, you can experience nature at its most sublime and arrive eventually in Aperlae.

If you buy a copy of Kate Clow's *The Lycian Way*, it will guide you to the other historic sites along this magnificent 509-kilometer-long trail.

Saffet Emre Tonguç

THE START OF THE CHRISTMAS TRADITION

062 Myra (Demre)

Saffet Emre TONGUÇ

Now known as Demre, ancient Myra was one of the most beautiful of the ancient Lycian cities. After passing endless greenhouses and orange groves, you reach a magnificent Greco-Roman theater built by the Greeks, and restored and expanded by the Romans. Nearby are some very picturesque tombs carved into the rock, and back in the town centre stand the remains of a Byzantine basilica, mysteriously associated with the story of Santa Claus.

House tombs near the theater

Saffet Emre Tonguç

Even if you think you've seen enough ancient theaters, the Greco-Roman version at Myra is particularly spectacular. Staircases on both sides of the structure lead up to seats for the audience. First, you should climb these to get an overview of the site. Below, at the back of the semi-circular section called the orchestra, you will see some theatrical masks carved into the stage.

The theater in Myra bears a bas-relief of Tyche, the goddess of fortune, and an inscription that reads: "May the city's history be filled with glory and fortune."

Near the theater are several so-called "house tombs" carved into the rock. If you climb up to take a closer look, you'll find that some of them have distinctive bas-reliefs; for example, of a death scene or a warrior.

A celebrated local figure, Saint Nicholas was born in Patara and became the bishop of Myra (modern Kale/Demre). He was also a participant at the First Council of Nicaea in 325. After he died, Saint Nicholas was buried in one of the sarcophagi in Myra church; however, his relics were stolen by Italian sailors in 1087 and reburied in a church in Bari, Italy. On 6 December - Saint Nicholas Day - many visitors come here to join in the festivities. The 4th-century church was partially destroyed by the Arabs in the 9th century, but was restored and rebuilt by Saint Nicholas' namesake, the Russian Czar Nicholas I. The synthronon (semicircular bench seat for the clergy in the apse) still survives from Byzantine times. Ecclesiastical history enthusiasts may also like to visit the Ala and Sion churches,

Myra Theater

near Kale, too.

The historic port of Myra at Andriake (modern Çayağzı) sits beside the coast road to Kaş. Nearby stand the remains of one of the Roman Empire's most important grain depots. Built in 139 AD, during the reign of Emperor Hadrian, the building is still in good condition.

There are daily boats from Çayağzı to Kekova, Kaleköy and the surrounding area. In just 45 minutes, you can find yourself admiring a submerged city deep beneath the waters of the Mediterranean near beautiful Kaleköy, a village where time really does stand still - there are still no more than 25 houses here. The mediaeval castle that gives the village its name is a magnificent structure that gazes down on the Mediterranean from the hill. Behind it, an extraordinary collection of Lycian sarcophagi lie scattered and forgotten.

WHERE TO **STAY?**

Ankh Pansiyon, Kaleköy
Phone: (0242) 874 21 71
Right on the waterfront. The rooms may be ordinary but they offer a view of Kekova and Kaleköy itself that is breathtaking. The owners do the best they can. If you are hungry, they pile the tables with food. Most people arrive by boat. You get yourself to Üçağız and then the owners pick you up.

THE STORY OF SANTA CLAUS

There are many different stories about Santa Claus (or Noel Baba, as he is known in Turkish). According to one, a poor man had three daughters, who were about to come of age. But as he was unable to pay their dowries, the girls faced either staying single or becoming prostitutes or slaves. To help out, Saint Nicholas threw three bags of gold down the chimney, this saving the girls from a wretched future.

Saint Nicholas is also the patron of sailors. Before setting sail, Christian sailors used to pray: "O Saint Nicholas, provide us with a safe journey." When they returned safely, they would offer a small model ship as a gift to any church dedicated to St Nicholas. Next time you're in İstanbul, visit the Hagia Nikola church on the Haliç (Golden Horn) and check out the model ships for yourself.

Saffet Emre Tonguç

Both ancient Myra and the Church of Saint Nicholas are very popular destinations with Russian day trippers from Antalya. The restaurants and souvenirs on offer are average at best. A bronze statue of Saint Nicholas by the Russian sculptor Gregory Pototsky used to stand in the square in front of the church but the local mayor acceded to popular demand and replaced it with a plastic Santa Claus clad in his red suit, an image created by Coca Cola in the 1930s, after the Great Depression. The authorities later placed Pototsky's original statue near the entrance to the church.

Ironically, it has never snowed in the birthplace of Saint Nicholas! It seems that in today's world image really is everything; the rest is simply history.

TREE-HOUSE VACATIONING

063 Olympos

Fatih TÜRKMENOĞLU

For many years Olympos has been famous for its tree-houses which are particularly popular with younger holidaymakers. The fame of the tree-houses sometimes risks swamping that of Olympos itself, a gorgeous, wooded river valley in the shadow of the soaring Bey Mountains. A lovely beach is a short walk from the tree-houses; to reach it you must pass through the romantic remains of ancient Olympos, a Lycian city that later fell to the Romans.

The Olympos coast is one of the rare places, where Caretta caretta (loggerhead turtles) leave their eggs to be hatched.

Saffet Emre Tonguç

There may be plenty of other accommodation at Olympos, but Kadir's Tree-houses has always been a particular favorite. Not only were they the first set of tree-houses to spring up in the valley, but for years they were by far the most original of all the places to stay. There are hundreds of references to Kadir on the internet, and Kadir himself is probably better known abroad than in Turkey. This is the sort of place where people arrive planning to stay for three days and end up staying a month.

Some guests spend the whole day lounging in the shade, while others play sports during the day and barely make it to bed. In the evenings, the staff build a campfire in the courtyard and guests sit and sing songs around it. Come midnight, the whole valley descends into a profound silence, although, for those who want to prolong the fun, the Öküz (ox) and Ahır (barn) bars stay open after-hours.

Kadir himself is an interesting guy, a French teacher by profession, who later picked up English. When he first established this place, there were no roads, so he had to carry bread in on his back every morning. "I offer my guests the kind of life that I like to live myself," he says.

At the other end of the beach is Çıralı, a small but fast-growing resort much favored by those of an alternative disposition, who prefer hotels and pensions to the more basic tree-house experience.

According to Kadir, his rooms sometimes sell for more than those in five-star hotels. Needless to say, they're always full in summer. For those who ask, "Is there a TV in the room or a pool in the garden?" his standard response is, "Don't bother coming here, you'll be bored." He still brings in fresh produce from the Antalya market and the food is delicious, as are the omelettes he makes for breakfast.

The ruins of Olympos

The ruins of ancient Olympos can't hope to match up in drama to those of Ephesus or even nearby Phaselis. However, half-buried amid fragrant bushes and trees, they are wonderfully romantic. The stretches of wall near the beach date from a much later period when the Genoese used Olympos as a trading centre.

Beydağları (Bey Mountains) Olympos National Park is perfect for keen mountaineers.

Saffet Emre Tonguç

Legends of Çıralı/Olympos

According to legend, an army arrived here to conquer the city in ancient times but failed to achieve its goal. On a second attempt, the soldiers attached burning firewood to the horns of goats and sent them towards the city. Thinking that a huge army was approaching, the inhabitants speedily surrendered. Since then, the place has been called "Çıralı" (with firewood).

Perhaps the most famous attraction at Çıralı/Olympos is the Chimaera, called the Yanartaş (Flaming Rock) in Turkish. In mythology, the Chimaera was a gigantic monster, part lioness, part goat, and part serpent that lived on the slopes of the mountain and was eventually killed by the hero Bellerophon who flew over it on his winged horse Pegasus and poured molten lead into its mouth to suffocate it.

In reality the Chimaera is a natural gas supply deep inside the mountain which causes inextinguishable flames to burn on the mountainside. Ancient mariners used the flames as a simple lighthouse. Today they are much less powerful but none the less impressive, especially under a moonlit sky.

HOW TO **TRAVEL?**

Non-drivers should take a Kumluca dolmuş (shared taxi) from Antalya bus station and get off at the Olympos dolmuş stop; from there, you can take one of the dolmuşes heading down to Olympos. Drivers should take the highway from Antalya towards Kemer, and once past Çıralı follow the signs for Olympos.

Temple

WHERE TO **STAY?**

Kadir's Tree-houses
Phone: (0242) 892 12 50

Türkmen Tree-houses
Phone: (0242) 892 14 02

Olympos Lodge
Phone: (0242) 825 71 71
www.olymposlodge.com.tr
Stunning hotel right behind a lovely stretch of beach. Statues and peacocks grace the garden.

Arkadia
Phone: (0242) 825 73 40
Four inviting bungalows amid the orange groves of Çıralı.

Sarcophagus

WHAT **TO DO?**

Four-day gulet trips to Fethiye are available from Olympos.

Two-day and one-star diving courses are also available. Or you can go rock climbing in the company of experienced instructors.

At nearby Adrasan there are several excellent restaurants with tables set up on decks over the river. Best of the bunch is the Paradise Café & River Garden (Phone: (0242) 883 12 67).

WHERE TO **EAT?**

Kayalar Restaurant
Phone: (0242) 825 00 10
Tuck into fresh trout beneath the shade of huge plane trees in Ulupınar, before you get to Olympos.

ENCHANTING MOUNTAINS AND THE MEDITERRANEAN SEA

064 Termessos and Phaselis

Saffet Emre TONGUÇ

Located inside the Güllük Dağı National Park, Termessos is one of Turkey's most outstanding archaeological sites. It reminds me of Machu Picchu in Peru, except that to reach Termessos only requires a 20-minute climb to the top of Mount Güllük. Phaselis, on the other hand, is one of Turkey's most romantic archaeological sites. Founded by natives of Rhodes in 690 BC, Phaselis is so enchanting that, according to legend, Alexander the Great was persuaded to spend an entire winter here.

The theater of Termessos is one of the world's most magnificent historic sites.

Saffet Emre Tonguç

The city on top of the world: Termessos

At a height of nearly 1000 meters, Termessos was once called Solimi by its inhabitants who named it after Mount Solymus (present-day Güllük Dağı). Termesossians controlled several trade routes and were known for their warrior spirit - so much so, in fact, that even Alexander the Great was intimidated! Having conquered approximately 90 percent of the known world in his lifetime, he was actually discouraged from attacking Termessos (partly because of the city's natural defenses) and continued on his way without touching it.

The Termessos theater has a seating capacity of 5000 and is absolutely breathtaking, the kind of place to leave you in complete awe of the ingenuity needed to create it in such a location. As you walk around the ruins and then continue uphill you come across the necropolis and find hundreds of sarcophagi scattered around, in complete harmony with nature. At the end of the road stands the custodian's watchtower, and

There is a spectacular view of Mount Tahtalı from Phaselis harbor.

Saffet Emre Tonguç

below the spectacular Pamphylian valley.

Beautiful Phaselis

After descending from Termessos, follow the road towards Kemer via Antalya's Konyaaltı Beach. It takes about an hour to bypass the hundreds of holiday villages and arrive at Phaselis. The city's strategic location on the main maritime trade routes and the fact that it had three ports and a large supply of timber from the forest lying behind it ensured it an important role in history. Nevertheless, the money-consciousness of the locals – who sold their citizenship for 100 drachmae – was legendary. Apparently Phaselians also favored a special kind of hair-do, called a "sisoe", which was not popular with the Christians; if you flip through the Bible, you will come across a verse that reads: "Ye shall not make a sisoe of the hair of your heads"!

Once Phaselis passed from the Byzantines to the Seljuks in 1158, it lost its importance as a harbor. Today, however, it hosts thousands of visitors who arrive on boats, blasting out music, every day. Behind the site's small theater, Mount Tahtalı rises up in all its majesty, resembling the backdrop to a stage. Remember the logo of the film company Tristar which depicts the winged horse Pegasus? According to Greek mythology, the hero Bellerophon tried to ride Pegasus to the top of Mount Tahtalı after he had killed the monster Chimaera on Mount Olympos. However, enraged at his impertinence, Zeus sent a gadfly to sting the horse and Bellerophon crashed back down to earth.

Don't be surprised if you are enchanted by Phaselis; she has made a habit of working her magic for centuries.

WHERE TO **EAT?**

Keptur
Phone: (0242) 251 05 74
Located near Termessos, it offers an extremely peaceful atmosphere to take a break and enjoy some food.

The ancient theater of Phaselis is a little slice of paradise surrounded by shady trees.

Saffet Emre Tonguç

THE CITY WITH IT ALL – HISTORY, NATURE, CULTURE AND SKIING

065 Antalya

Saffet Emre TONGUÇ

Commanding the Mediterranean from sheer cliffs rising out of the sea and backed by the Bey Mountains, Antalya has one of the most beautiful geographical locations in the world. It is also a vibrant modern city, grown up around a fascinating old inner city full of reminders of the past from Roman times right through to the Ottomans.

The Old Harbor at Antalya Kaleiçi (Old Town)

Saffet Emre Tonguç

Antalya was founded by the Pergamum King Attalos II in the 2nd century BC. Legend has it that Attalos instructed his soldiers to find "heaven on earth" and that after a long and tedious search across the world, his men offered the king this city, which he named Attaleia. Today, Attalos' statue stands across from the Clock Tower. The magnificent Hadrian's Gate, on the other hand, is named after the Roman Emperor Hadrian, who visited the city in 130 BC.

Antalya was an important harbor during the Crusades and served as a base for soldiers on their way to the Holy Land.

Conquered by the Ottomans during Sultan Bayezid's reign, Antalya was briefly seized by the Italians in 1918. It's a city that has attracted travelers throughout history and Ibn Battuta, who visited in the 14th century, wrote that the Egyptians called lemons "Adalia" because so many were exported from Antalya. Having traversed the area in 1671, Evliya Çelebi noted that the city walls were 4400m in length, and had 80 bastions, and that the 200 fountains received their water from the Düden Creek.

Famous for the Kaleiçi (Old Town) with its lovely old Ottoman houses, the Yivli Minare (Fluted Minaret) and the beaches along the coast, Antalya also has a wonderful museum.

After İstanbul, Antalya has the country's second busiest airport.

Antalya Museum

The statue of a dancer in Antalya Museum

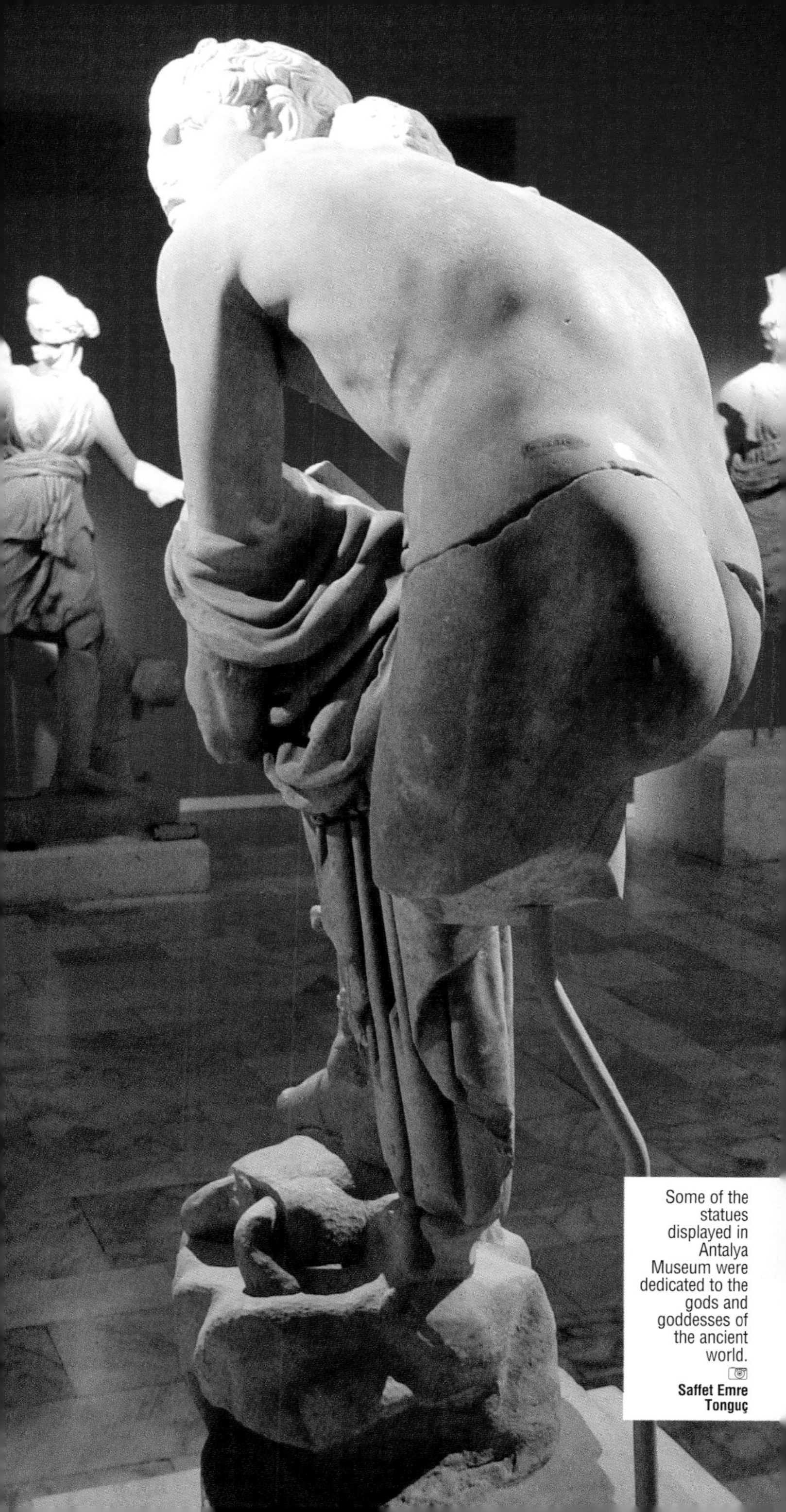

Some of the statues displayed in Antalya Museum were dedicated to the gods and goddesses of the ancient world.

Saffet Emre Tonguç

Hadrian's Gate
Saffet Emre Tonguç

An incredible collection spans a wide time frame with exhibits from the Stone Age to the Ottoman period. The most outstanding pieces are from the Roman era; the statuary alone would be enough to rank the museum among the top five in Turkey. In ancient times, Antalya was surrounded by Pisidia in the north, Pamphylia ("the land of all tribes") in the east, and Lycia in the west.

Because of its position at the crossroads of all the most important transport routes, the city acquired an incredible historical heritage, and the museum doesn't have enough space to accommodate all the finds from local archaeological sites.

Fluted Minaret
Bünyad Dinç

There are many things to do in Antalya and its environs: ski in Saklıkent in the winter, go to the ancient city of Selge near Köprüçay (which is perfect for rafting), visit Sillyum, see Side, get some rest in Manavgat, discover the ruins of Olympos, and wander amid the cedar trees in the ancient city of Idebessos on the northern slopes of Aykırca Creek. With time to venture a bit further, you can also admire one of the most beautiful Greek theaters in the world at Arycanda near Finike, and enjoy some trout at one of the many local fish farms.

Konyaaltı Beach

Mehmet Çabuk

WHERE TO **STAY?**

Hillside Su Hotel
Phone: (0242) 249 07 25
www.hillside.com.tr
One of Turkey's finest "designer hotels", it has a particularly impressive lobby and aquariums in the bedrooms. The food is delicious; they probably have the longest open-buffet table in Turkey. Because everything in the hotel is white, you just might get the feeling that you are in a hospital!

Minyon Otel
Phone: (0242) 247 11 47
www.minyonhotel.com
As the name implies ("minyon" is derived from the French "mignon" meaning small), the hotel is small and tremendously charming. The service is good and the staff very friendly; you feel as if you are vacationing in a luxury villa. Located in the historic Kaleiçi (Old Town), this well-kept secret hideaway is familiar only to connoisseurs. The small but tasteful rooms are complemented by a heavenly garden with a pool and pebble-stoned floors.

The Marmara Antalya
Phone: (0242) 249 36 00
www.themarmarahotels.com
Well-known as the world's first rotating hotel, this establishment offers fabulous views. The decoration of the rooms and the choice of colors enhance the unconventional style. The "rahle" (low reading bookstand) and "nalıns" (Ottoman bath slippers) in the bathrooms are interesting touches, and the open-buffet is extremely generous.

Hillside Su Otel

WHERE TO **EAT?**

Parlak Restaurant
Phone: (0242) 241 91 60
Both the home-cooked meals and the kebaps are delicious.

Mermerli Restaurant
Phone: (0242) 248 54 84
Located in Kaleiçi (Old Town) and overlooking the sea, this restaurant excels at seafood and mezes.

During the summer, Antalya's center of activity shifts to **Beach Park**, where numerous cafés play music and provide cabins, sunbeds and showers. Several good bars and nightclubs are also open throughout the summer. The Park hosts such restaurants as **Alara**, **Vedat Bey** and **Gaziantep**, where you can enjoy delicious dinners with the swishing sound of the waves below as a soothing accompaniment.
The view across from Atatürk Park to the Old Harbor is nothing short of spectacular.

Alternatively, you can try **7 Mehmet**, **Develi**, **Şişçi Ramazan**, **Urcan Balıkçısı**, **Hasır Kebapçısı**, **Gizli Bahçe**, **Beydağı Lokantası** and **Kral Sofrası** in the town center.

If you are interested in buying pickles, lokum (Turkish delight), jams, or marmalades, they are all on sale at **Yenigün**, which was established in 1914.

THE MAGNIFICENCE OF PERGE AND ASPENDOS

066 Tale of two beautiful Greco-Roman cities

Saffet Emre TONGUÇ

Legend has it that the Greeks established Perge on the banks of the Aksu River after the Trojan War. A typical ancient city, Perge had a beautiful theater and a 12,000-seater stadium; the arcades beneath the seats were once used as shops. Nearby Aspendos is famous for its spectacular Roman theater which was restored by Atatürk and is still used during the annual Aspendos Festival.

Hellenistic Gate in Perge.
Saffet Emre Tonguç

Perge has one of the largest Roman bath complexes in the entire Mediterranean region. If you use your imagination, you can easily visualize the bath as it was in its glory days when it would have been resplendent with marble columns and statues. Near the entrance to the structure is a huge sports stadium called a Palaestra. After working up a sweat here, the Romans would jump into the cool waters of the bath and enjoy themselves. The baths served women in the mornings and men in the afternoons.

The heart of ancient Perge was the Agora (market place) where mosaic-covered floors, shop doorways, a hook indicating the location of the butcher and a bas-relief in the shape of a knife all survive intact. In the middle of the main street stands a fountain that boasted a constant flow of water in ancient times. This not only beautified the city but also served as a pool for those who wanted to cool off on long, hot summer days. The main street used to feature four columns with bas-reliefs of gods; unfortunately, one of these bas-reliefs was stolen recently.

In the Agora (market place) a council called the Agoranomos used to supervise pricing.

From Apollonius to Saint Paul...

The famous mathematician Apollonius, whose

theories were utilized years later by the equally famous astronomer Kepler, was born in Perge. The Bible reveals that Saint Paul and Barnabas also visited this city. One of the most outstanding historians and geographers of the ancient world, Strabo of Amaseia (present-day Amasya), mentions Perge in his masterpiece, the 17-volume *Geographica*; in it he reveals that a special festival was held in Perge every year to honor Artemis (Diana), the virgin goddess of the hunt. Perge's most celebrated local name was that of Magna Plancia. As her family made sizable contributions to the city coffers, statues of her were erected all around town.

Colonnaded street in Perge

Some of the shops in the arches underneath the stadium contained boards with the names of their proprietors written on them.

Saffet Emre Tonguç

HOW TO **TRAVEL?**

Perge is 20 kilometers and Aspendos 60 kilometers east of Antalya.

On your way to Aspendos, you will pass through Serik.

WHERE TO **EAT?**

Belkıs Restaurant
Phone: (0242) 735 70 73
As you enjoy your lunch overlooking Aspendos, you can feed the ducks in the river.

A magnificent theater

The Roman Emperor Marcus Aurelius (r. 161-180 AD) commissioned the architect Zenon to build Aspendos Theater, near Antalya, which has a seating capacity of over 15,000. Above its entrance look out for this line written by the Curtius brothers, who sponsored its construction: "To the Gods of the Nation and the Imperial Family."

As one of the best-preserved theaters to have survived from Antiquity, Aspendos inevitably inspired its own legend. Apparently, the emperor proclaimed that he would marry his daughter to the architect who created the most beautiful structure in his city. In the end, two magnificent works of art emerged: the theater and the aqueduct. Unable to choose between them, the emperor summoned both architects and told them that since there were two monumental works and just one girl, he would be obliged to split his daughter in half. The architect of the theater immediately declared that he would withdraw from the competition. Realizing that it was Zenon, who was truly in love with his daughter, the emperor married her to him in a story that recalls that of King Solomon and the baby. In that story, when the King declared that he would cut the baby in two halves for the two women who claimed to be the mother, he knew that the woman who immediately renounced her claim was the real mother. This is what the saying "history repeats itself" must be all about!

With its 40 rows of marble seats, the theatre is extremely elegant. Over the carved niches for statues there stands a bas-relief of Dionysus, the Greek god of wine and the theater.

A little way away from the theater, which was used as a caravanserai by the Seljuks, stands a lovely Seljuk bridge over the Köprüçay creek (the ancient Eurymedon).

While in Aspendos, do inspect the remains of the Roman aqueduct and enjoy some freshly-squeezed orange juice at a nearby café.

Every summer an opera and ballet festival is held at Aspendos Theater

Saffet Emre Tonguç

The aqueduct that carried water from the Taurus Mountains to Aspendos is one of the most beautiful surviving examples of Roman architecture.

Saffet Emre Tonguç

A CITY FOR ALL SEASONS

067 Side

Fatih TÜRKMENOĞLU

One of the best things about Side is the way that the ancient ruins overlap and intertwine with the modern city. The theater, the museum, and the Temples of Apollo and Athena are all within easy walking distance of each other. The bazaar is extremely busy; as a melting pot for many different nationalities and languages, it generates an atmosphere that some find endearing and others find offputting.

Don't miss the spectacle of the Temple of Apollo.
Fatih Türkmenoğlu

The site of a famous love affair...

Some sources say that Side originally meant "pomegranate," and the pomegranate is the symbol of abundance and wealth. The city experienced its period of greatest prosperity in Roman times when it was a flourishing trade center with a large slave market. Some sources also suggest that it served as a love-nest for Cleopatra and Mark Anthony.

As you walk towards the bazaar from the bus station you will pass a beautiful, newly-excavated Roman fountain and then the remains of a colonnaded street once lined with ancient shops. The theater, which has a seating capacity of 15,000, is still used today. Side Museum is housed in what was once the old Roman bath-house; it has a delightful back garden full of stone sarcophagi. The Temples of Apollo and Athena overlooking the sea were built in the 2nd century AD. Few things could be nicer than sipping an evening drink at one of the cafés beside the temples. Protected by its land and sea walls, the ancient city of Side survived the Hellenistic and Roman periods. Unfortunately, the aesthetic beauty of the ancient buildings has not found echoes in many of the structures thrown up in recent years.

Originally one of the oldest settlements in Anatolia, Side is now a thriving modern resort

Side's historic sites are some walk from the bazaar in the heat, but the Municipality provides a Disneyesque tractor and trailer to get people from place to place in summer.

More local tourists

Traditionally, Side has been favored by the Germans and the Dutch, but ever since the five-star resorts lowered their prices for domestic tourists, the town has seen an increase in Turkish visitors.

Side Theater

Fatih Türkmenoğlu

·OW TO **TRAVEL?**

ide is about 80 ·ilometers from ·ntalya. The most ·omfortable way to get ·ere from İstanbul – ·specially now that ·rices are so low – is to ·y to Antalya and then ·ake a bus. Buses to ·ide leave from all the ·ajor bus terminals. ·ou can easily find ·inibuses for local ·xcursions, but car ·ental rates are also ·uite reasonable.

WHERE TO **STAY?**

Side is full of five-star hotels aimed at the package-holiday market. If you want something on a smaller scale, there are also many small hotels and pensions around the bazaar area.

Hotel Lale Park
Phone: (0242) 753 1131

Side Hotel
Phone: (0242) 753 3824

WHERE TO **EAT?**

Soundwaves Restaurant
Phone: (0242) 753 1607
A popular sea-facing restaurant with an international menu.

Aphrodite Restaurant
Phone: (0242) 753 1171
Long-lived steak and grill restaurant.

WHAT **TO DO?**

Manavgat is only 5 kilometers from Side. The Manavgat waterfalls on the Manavgat river make a popular day-trip destination in summer. From Manavgat you can also get to the little-visited ruins of Seleukia-in-Pamphylia, where the remains of an ancient bath-house and market place stand forgotten amid the pines.

Sorgun and Titreyengöl beaches are great.

If you are thinking about going rafting, you should head straight for the Köprülü Canyon. Many different companies sell rafting trips.

Antalya Balloons
Phone: (0242) 715 14 08
Soar above the glorious local scenery in a hot air balloon.

THE LATEST FAVORITE OF THE EUROPEANS

068 Alanya

Fatih TÜRKMENOĞLU

Alanya's ancient name "Korakos" meant "a place full of crows". The city was called "Kalonaros" (Beautiful Mountain) in the Middle Ages. When the Anatolian Seljuk Sultan Keykubat was enthroned, he took on the epithet "Alâeddin" (meaning "superior" or "sovereign") and Kalonaros became "Alaiye", or "the city of Ala". Eventually this was transformed into Alanya, the name the city goes by today.

Alanya was called "Kalonaros" (Beautiful Mountain) in the Middle Ages.

Bünyad Dinç

Modern Alanya is dominated by a huge plug of rock topped off with the remains of a Selcuk castle. This is by far the most interesting part of what is a predominantly modern city.
Make it easy on yourself by taking a bus or taxi up and then walking the three kilometers down again to take advantage of the wonderful sea views and to visit the other minor sites on the rock, including a fine Ottoman mosque and bedesten (covered market). Some lovely old Ottoman houses still cling to the hillside as well.
Of Alanya's several caves, the most famous is the Damlataş Mağarası (Dripping Stone Cave), whose humid atmosphere is supposedly good for asthmatics.

Alanya was offered to Cleopatra as a gift by Mark Anthony.

Some people will prefer the less crowded Dim Mağarası (Cave), known as the "Gavur İni" (Cave of the Infidel) to the locals.
Being the seaside resort it is, Alanya offers a great choice of daily boat tours which visit the Korsanlar, Aşıklar, and Fosforlu Caves, as well as the Cleopatra and Ulaş beaches.
The local museum contains small but interesting archaeological and ethnological collections. The house in which Atatürk stayed overnight on 18 February 1935 is also open to the public.

Kızılkule is the symbol of the city

Although the city of Alanya dates back for many centuries, it never played a major role in history. However, when Alâeddin Keykubat commissioned a Syrian architect to build the aptly-named Kızılkule (the Red Tower) in 1226, he put the city on the world map. Eighty-seven steps lead to the top and a spectacular view out over the sea.
The Tersane is another local attraction. Also commissioned by Keykubat, this dockyard, built in 1228, is the only example of its kind to survive from the Seljuk period. The tower next to it is known to have been used as an armory.

It's a pleasure to get lost in the streets of Alanya or to photograph an old mosque.

Bünyad Dinç

HOW TO **TRAVEL?**

Alanya is 115 kilometers from Antalya. There are frequent dolmuş (shared taxi) and bus services.

WHERE TO **STAY?**

There are many hotels and pensions. Apart from the five-star ones, I would recommend:

Kaptan Hotel
Phone: (0242) 513 49 00

Park Hotel
Phone: (0242) 513 16 75

Club Hotel Bedesten
Phone: (0242) 512 12 34
Housed in the old bedesten on the side of the rock that dominates Alanya, this hotel offers a rare historic atmosphere in a largely modern town.

WHAT **TO DO?**

Sinek Kalesi ("Fly Castle") in Elikesik village is a castle, which can be found only by asking around. It's worth making the effort as the view is fantastic and the local houses extremely interesting.

An old Seljuk caravanserai, **Şarapsa Hanı**, is 13 kilometers away.

WHERE TO **EAT?**

Ottoman House Restaurant
Phone: (0242) 511 1421
Wonderful Turkish cuisine including vegetable dishes cooked in olive oil, kebabs and beğendi (eggplant puree).

Aydoğan Kafe and **Muhtar'ın Yeri**, on the road, leading up to the citadel are great places for snacks with a view.

TWIN SEATS OF CHRISTIANITY

069 Antakya and Tarsus

Saffet Emre TONGUÇ

The famous Antioch of the past has become the less well-known Antakya of the present. This was the first city in which Christians are known to have referred to themselves as such, and three major religions still have representation in the city. Turkey's only surviving Armenian village, Vakıflı, is also very close to Antakya. To top even that, the city of Tarsus, world famous as the place, where Saint Paul was born, is not far away.

There is a Roman bridge at the entrance to the Tunnel of Titus Vespasianus.
Saffet Emre Tonguç

One of the world's most outstanding mosaic museums, the Church of Saint Peter, the restaurant-filled suburb of Harbiye and the extraordinary Tunnel of Titus Vespasianus are just a few of the things to be seen in and around Antakya.

Antakya was founded on the banks of the River Orontes (the present-day Asi) and in the shadow of Mount Silipus in the 4th century BC. The city became the capital of the Seleucid Kingdom after the death of Seleucus Nicator and during the reign of his son Antiochus Soter (r. 281-261 BC). As the third largest and most important Roman city after Rome and Alexandria, ancient Antioch held enormous historic significance. Even though the city was devastated by earthquakes in the 6th century, it still retains a few reminders of its venerable past. A beautiful Roman Bridge over the Orontes (Asi) River survived until the 1970s when it was knocked down to make way for a wider road.

The Antakya Museum was built, while the city was under French rule (1918-1939), and houses a plethora of mosaics, most of them depicting mythological scenes. What is now the Harbiye suburb was once the ancient Daphne, where, according to mythology, the nymph Daphne fled from the god Apollo and was changed into a laurel tree. During the Roman period, the area was full of magnificent Roman villas, almost all of which have been replaced by restaurants today. The majority of the mosaics in the museum were taken from the banquet halls and floors of these villas, as well as from the ancient city of Seleucia-ad-Piera in nearby Çelvik.

The church in Tarsus is still used for religious ceremonies.

Getting lost in the back streets of Antakya is very enjoyable; the old houses, with their French-style shutters and balconies, are beautiful even though most of them are rather dilapidated. The Orthodox and Catholic Churches bear witness

Orthodox Church of Antakya
Saffet Emre Tonguç

to the city's tradition of religious tolerance, and there is also a synagogue, although the current Jewish population of the city is less than a hundred.

The Habib Neccar Mosque, near the synagogue, stands on the site of the former Orthodox cathedral. The grave of Habib Neccar underneath the mosque is considered sacred by Muslims and Christians alike.

Located in the outskirts of the city, the Church of St Peter was built inside a cave and is thought to have been one of the earliest churches in the world. Just as he did with the Church of the Virgin Mary in Ephesus, Pope Paul VI declared the Church of St Peter a pilgrimage site for Catholics in 1967.

Saint Paul of Tarsus

Tarsus was the birthplace of Saint Paul the Apostle who lived in this area between 10 and 67 AD. Etymologically, the word "apostle" means "the chosen one". Although Saint Paul was not one of the original Twelve Apostles chosen by Christ, one day he had an epiphany on the Via Recta ("the Street Called Straight") in Damascus when he saw a vision of Jesus Christ and converted to Christianity. Until then, as Saul of Tarsus he had taken a near fanatical stand against Christ. Jesus had been born a Jew and this is why depictions of the crucified Christ often include the letters

Antakya Mosaic Museum
Saffet Emre Tonguç

INRI (IESVS NAZARENVS REX IVDAEORVM), which means "Jesus of Nazareth, King of the Jews."

Paul was later recognized as one of the most important apostles, because he was instrumental in spreading Christianity along the Mediterranean and across Anatolia through his travels.

Cleopatra and Mark Anthony

Queen Cleopatra of Egypt is said to have met Mark Anthony in Tarsus in 41 BC, and it's worth looking for the so-called Cleopatra Gate, which commemorates the event. Before leaving Tarsus, you may also want to hang out in some of the cafés inside newly-renovated stone houses; have a drink of water from St Paul's well; and take a look at the buildings of the Tarsus American College, which was founded by American missionaries in 1888. Nusrat, the famous battleship from the Gallipoli Campaign, is preserved in the local park. The waterfall in Tarsus is also perfect for avoiding the summer heat.

BETWEEN ADANA AND ANTAKYA

There are numerous historic sites and citadels between Adana and Antakya. Anavarza is a fascinating Roman city with a fantastic view from its mountaintop citadel. As you pass Toprakkale and proceed towards Karatepe, you will come to the site of Hierapolis Castabala, with Roman columns and a medieval castle to the rear.

Karatepe, also known as Aslantaş is the most beautiful Hittite site in Turkey; the archaeological remains hidden on a woody hill, and the view of the lake below make Karatepe truly outstanding. The 2800-year-old city of Adana(wa) was originally built by King Asitawandas, and the surviving bas-reliefs and sphinxes are very impressive.

The ancient city of Aslantaş
Saffet Emre Tonguç

St. Peter Church
Saffet Emre Tonguç

Tarsus Church

WHERE TO STAY?

Savon Hotel
Phone: (0326) 214 63 55
www.savonhotel.com.tr
An old soap factory converted into a beautiful boutique hotel where you can sample tasty local dishes in the restaurant.

Antakya houses

Antik Beyazıt Hotel
Phone: (0326) 216 29 00
www.antikbeyazitoteli.com
Right in the heart of the city, the hotel is in an old but restored Antakya house.

WHERE TO EAT?

Anadolu Restaurant
Phone: (0326) 215 33 35
One of the best in town. Both the cold mezes (appetizers) and the main dishes are great. They serve the usual kebabs, but you can also sample home-cooked dishes as well. The garden is lovely in summer. Treat yourself to künefe (shredded baklava stuffed with cheese).

Hidro Restaurant–Harbiye
Phone: (0326) 231 40 06
The tables are piled high with stuffed eggplants, large red peppers, içli köfte (similar to falafel) and humus.

Kral Künefe Salonu
Phone: (0326) 214 75 17
The best künefe in town.

Sultan Sofrası
Phone: (0326) 213 87 59
www.sultansofrasi.com
Try the local delicacies.

Café Atilla–Tarsus
Phone: (0324) 624 78 31

The well of Saint Paul

WHAT TO DO?

Antakya's bazaar is fun and interesting to explore; look out, in particular, for colorful woven trays that look as if they have strayed from South America. You can watch the creation of künefe in local pastry shops.

Dedicating his life to religion, Saint Simeon the Stylite retreated to live on top of a column. **Samandağ**, a mountain near Antakya, takes its name from the Arabic version of his name, Cebel Saman, which is similar to "Gibraltar" (Cebel-i Tarık) and derived from the name of the Commander Tarık Bin Ziyyad. The monastery and the column still survive near Samandağ.

The Tunnel of Titus Vespasianus in **Çevlik** is very interesting. Legend has it that rioting Jews were brought from Jerusalem and made to dig it as punishment. In so doing they protected the ancient city below from floods. Beşikli Mağara (Cave), further on, resembles the caves of Cappadocia. Çevlik's untidy beach gets quite busy in summer. There are even a few fish restaurants around.

14 MUST-SEE PLACES
IN THE CENTRAL ANATOLIA REGION

THE CENTRAL ANATOLIA REGION

THE TOWN OF 1,000 PIPES
070 Eskişehir

Fatih TÜRKMENOĞLU

Turkey's fifth biggest town, Eskişehir was built over a hot spring in an area which boasts some of the world's largest reserves of meerschaum. The university has brought a new liveliness to the town, which has also been improved by the provision of new monuments, fountains, and trees. A flashy new tram has made it much easier to get about too. From cafés to Chinese and Italian restaurants, from thermal baths to museums, mosques and ancient ruins, there is much to see and do in and around town.

A town of many bridges.

A thriving modern town

Originally called Dorylaeon by the Greeks and Dorileaum by the Romans, Eskişehir was probably established near an old Phrygian settlement on the banks of the Porsuk River. Famed for its thermal baths, the city prospered through trade and acquired city status in 1925. Through trade and manufacturing, it has always been a prosperous city; it was also the cradle of civil aviation in Turkey and is home to the Anadolu University, one of the country's biggest institutions of higher learning. After years of hard work, Eskişehir's star is once again in the ascendant, the new tram ("the Estram") a symbol of its go-ahead outlook.

Eskişehir has always been a prosperous town.

Eskişehir may be an "old town" in name, but there's not a great deal left to see of its past in the town center which was badly damaged during the Turkish War of Independence. Recently, the surviving 19th-century pastel-colored houses in the Odunpazarı (Wood Market) neighborhood have been given a makeover, making it one of the most enjoyable areas to explore.

It's worth taking a stroll along bustling, pedestrian Hamamyolu Caddesi, where every other shop seems to sell sweets. The large 16th-century Kurşunlu and Haznedar Camii (Mosques) are also worth a visit; the former might be a work of the famous architect Sinan. Spare some time, too, for the museums: the Archaeological Museum, which contains some of the finds from Dorileaum; the Atatürk and Culture Museum; and the Beylerbeyi Konağı, an Ottoman House which is sporadically open to the public.

Don't leave town without taking a dip in one of the thermal baths. Public baths can be found at the junction of Hamamyolu and Savtekin Caddesis (street), or you can book into a hotel which boasts its own thermal waters.

Meerschaum country

Eskişehir is famous for its light, white meerschaum stone, a substance which is not common elsewhere in the world. It has been mined and processed here for nearly 5,000 years, and many beautiful pipes and other astonishingly elaborate objects made from meerschaum (which means "sea foam" in German) are on display in the small Lületaşı Müzesi (Meerschaum Museum).

Odunpazarı – new look "old" houses.

HOW TO **TRAVEL?**

Eskişehir is 330km from İstanbul and 230km from Ankara. If you think you can manage without a car, it's enjoyable getting there by train. There are about 10 rail services daily from İstanbul.

Eskişehir Train Station
Phone: (0222) 225 55 55

İstanbul Haydarpaşa Train Station/Reservations
Phone: (0216) 337 87 24

WHERE TO **STAY?**

Has Hotel Termal
Phone: (0222) 221 40 30
Pleasant small business hotel in the town center with thermal water in the bathrooms.

WHERE TO **EAT?**

Try the haşhaşlı ekmek (poppy-seed bread) and the simits (rings of crispy bread covered with sesame seeds) of the best local bakeries; ask the locals for advice.
Eskişehir has lots of köftecis (meatball eateries), including Köfteci Ahmet and Tatlıdil Köftecisi. The Chinese restaurant actually has Chinese staff and the ingredients are imported from China. The Italian restaurant Sempre is also quite popular. If you're looking for a cozy place to eat, Sıcacık is good. Since there are many Tatars in Eskişehir, the Tatar cuisine is much in demand. Çiğ Börek on Atatürk Boulevard is a must. Mazlumlar has been dishing up milk-based desserts for three generations.

WHAT **TO DO?**

You can watch the meerschaum-making process at Işık Pipo (Pipe) or at Burhan Yücel Pipo, which is right next door to the Büyük Hotel. You can also visit the meerschaum mines in nearby Sepetçi Köyü and Kozlubel.

At Seyitgazi, the Battalgazi Külliyesi (Mosque Complex), commissioned by the 13th-century Seljuk Sultan Alâeddin Keykubad I's mother Ümmühan Hatun, commemorates a hero of the 8th-century battles against Arab invaders.

The ruins of ancient Midas Şehri (City) are a real must-see. They nestle at the heart of the so-called Frig Vadisi (Phrygian Valley), some 90 kilometers out of the city, around Yazılıkaya (Inscribed Rock) village. The most obvious sight is a plug of rock into which a large relief has been carved with inscriptions in the Phrygian alphabet – the so-called Midas Tomb. As the religious center of the ancient Phrygians, the site also boasts rock tombs where offerings may have been made to the Mother Goddess Cybele. There are also the remains of an acropolis, tunnel and altar.

The famous witty story-teller Nasreddin Hoca may have been born at nearby Sivrihisar, where the flat-roofed 13th-century Ulu Cami (Mosque) is full of lovely old wooden columns.

Excavations are still underway at Pessinus in Balhisar village, near Sivrihisar, where the remains of a temple to Cybele have been uncovered.

CARROTS WITH EVERYTHING

071 Beypazarı

Fatih TÜRKMENOĞLU

With its beautiful 200-year-old houses, interesting local dress and inviting weekend market, Beypazarı is an extraordinary place which deserves to be much better known. It is also the carrot capital of Turkey, where a surprising number of things come with an orange tinge!

The houses of Beypazarı are almost as fine as those in better-known Safranbolu.
Fatih Türkmenoğlu

As recently as 10 years ago, Beypazarı was virtually forgotten, a small town just one hour's drive out of Ankara, but a world away from it in atmosphere. Then, under an imaginative local administration, the old town center was revived. Many of the lovely old Ottoman houses were restored, and some of them were turned into hotels and restaurants. Old handicrafts, such as cloth-weaving, were given a higher profile, and a determined effort was made to publicize what the town had to offer. The result was astonishing. These days, Beypazarı is a thriving small town, best visited on the weekend, when there is a lively street market. To date, almost 400 houses have been restored, and many more are on their way to recovery. One is open to the public as a small museum offering an opportunity to see the lavish interior fittings and the curious bathrooms tucked away inside cupboards.

Beypazarı is a thriving small town, best visited at the weekend when there is a lively street market

Lords of the Bazaar

Like most Anatolian towns, Beypazarı has a very long history. Its ancient name was Logania, and remains from the Hittite, Roman, Byzantine, Seljuk and Ottoman periods have been found in and around town. At one time, it was governed by the Germiyanoğlus, who also ruled nearby Kütahya in the period following the collapse of the Seljuk Empire. Villagers used to come into town from the surrounding area to sell their goods in the bazaar (pazar), hence the name Beypazarı which means "the Lord of the Bazaars"!

Even today, the bazaar is well worth a few hours of anybody's time. Small shops line narrow, vine-draped streets, where blacksmiths, silversmiths, and an excess number of quilt-makers live peacefully in the past. They will be quick to say "hoş geldiniz" (welcome) and offer you a glass of çay (tea). Life for them is tranquil, unpretentious, and seemingly happy.

On weekends the bazaar spills out into Alaeddin Sokağı, the main street, where women set up stalls and sell herbs such as blackthorn and basil, alongside bottled carrot juice, and carrot-flavored lokum (Turkish delight), a testament to Beypazarı's role as carrot capital of Turkey. Many of them wear colorful printed shawls (bürgü) that cover their head and shoulders but which also make excellent tablecloths!

Women in block-printed shawls sell local produce at the weekend market.

Fatih Türkmenoğlu

HOW TO **TRAVEL?**

Beypazarı is on the old İstanbul-Ankara road, 98km out of Ankara. There are regular minibuses from Ankara's small Etlik bus terminal.

WHAT **TO DO?**

If you walk up Hıdırlık Hill you will get a good view of the whole of Beypazarı.

Karagöl Yaylası, Cevizlibağ, Zindancık and Dostlar are all lovely picnic places/trout restaurants within three to five kilometers of town. For something more demanding, head north for the İnözü Vadisi (Valley), where there are rocks to climb and caves to explore.

WHERE TO **STAY?**

Meva'ların ("Corner of Paradise") Konağı
Phone: (0312) 762 36 98
www.mevalarinkonagi.com
Simple rooms above a large café, right in the town center.

Müftüzade Konağı
Phone: (0312) 763 31 30

Hacıbostan Konağı
Phone: (0312) 763 08 37

Nuri Efendi Konağı
Phone: (0312) 763 41 40

Saluhan Pansiyon
Phone: (0312) 763 30 34

WHERE TO **EAT?**

The spicy mumbar (membrane of sheep intestines filled with spicy rice) and a buttery type of bread-stick called Beypazarı kurusu are delicious. Look out for these and other delicacies on sale at the bazaar.

Konak Münsür
Phone: (0312) 763 3 763
www.munsur.com
Serves tasty tarhana soup, which is made with dried yogurt, curds, meat and lots of garlic.

Beypazarı is famous for its bottled spring water sold all over western Turkey.

THE ANCIENT PHRYGIAN CAPITAL
072 Gordion

Saffet Emre TONGUÇ

Initially settled during the Bronze Age, Gordion became famous both for the story of the Gordion Knot and for King Midas, who turned everything he touched into gold. Named after its founder, one of many King Gordiuses, the city was surrounded by the burial mounds of the Phrygian kings. It's easy to visit on a day trip from Ankara.

Gordion holds a special place in ancient Greek mythology, with several different stories attached to it. According to one, Silenus, the faithful companion of the wine-god Dionysus, became intoxicated on wine given to him by King Midas and was taken hostage. As a ransom, Midas demanded that Dionysus grant him the power to turn everything he touched into gold. Dionysus granted him his wish, but the king soon came to regret his power when everything he touched did indeed turn to gold, including his daughter. The wretched king beseeched Dionysus to save him, whereupon the god advised him to wash his hands in the River Pactolus (the present-day Sart River), which means bundle of money in Greek. Midas was finally cured of his problem when the riverbed turned to gold.

In another story that revolves around Midas, the king acted as the judge during a musical contest between the god Apollo and the satyr Marsyas. When he preferred Marsyas' flute-playing to Apollo's, the wrathful god turned Midas' ears into those of a donkey and had Marsyas skinned. Regretting his sudden rage, Apollo later turned Marsyas into the present-day Çine River. Is it just chance, then, that music played a significant role in Phrygian culture? The Phrygians are believed to have invented numerous instruments and were the first people to play the flute.

Once the capital of Phrygia, Gordion is 90 kilometers west of Ankara.

There are so many different tales to be told about Gordion. According to yet another, it was prophesied that the first person to untie the intricate Gordion Knot would become the ruler of Asia. It was Alexander the Great, who finally decided to slice the knot in half with his sword. Then he went on to conquer Asia, ensuring that the prophesy became true. Today, the double knot used in Turkish carpets is called the "Gördes Düğümü" (Gordion Knot), a term derived from this story.

Even today, the rustling ears of Anatolian wheat are said to murmur the words "Midas has ass's ears" as the wind blows.

A bit of background

Remains of the Lydian, Persian, Greek and Roman civilizations can be seen in Gordion. In the 1950s, American archaeologists opened a 60-meter tunnel through one of the burial mounds and discovered what was initially thought to have been the tomb of King Midas. Three hundred meters in diameter, the majestic tomb, from the eighth century BC. had remained undisturbed for more than two millennia and still guarded its secrets; the finds, including wooden tables, bronze bowls, and dress pins, are now on display in the Museum of Anatolian Civilizations in Ankara. Other artifacts can be seen in the Gordion Museum.

Gordion and the Midas Tombs

Şemsi Güner

BEYOND POLITICS, FORMALITY AND DIPLOMACY

073 Ankara

Saffet Emre TONGUÇ

It sometimes comes as a surprise to foreigners, when they discover that Ankara, rather than İstanbul, is the Turkish capital. But, in 1923, Mustafa Kemal Atatürk moved the capital to a location right in the heart of Anatolia, in the hope of forgetting the Ottoman past and getting the new Turkish Republic off to a fresh start. Today, this is where you will find all the foreign embassies and international delegations. It's not a beautiful city, but it does have its pockets of history, especially around Ulus and the hilltop Citadel (Kale). Parts of the city center are also lively and sophisticated, with some great restaurants and shops.

Some of the city's most chic hotels are in Kavaklıdere.
Saffet Emre Tonguç

When they first settled here in c. 1200 BC, the Hittites named Ankara Ankuwah. Later, the site was occupied by the Phrygians, Lydians and Persians. After "untying" the Gordion Knot by slicing through it with his sword, Alexander the Great arrived in Ankara (then Ankyra) in 333 BC; capturing it swiftly, he then pressed on to Cappadocia. As Angora, Ankara eventually became the capital of the Roman province of Galatia, and proceeded to profit from its location on the imperial trade routes.

Once famous for its silky-wooled Angora goats, modern Ankara is an important center for trade and politics.

The year 1402 marked an important date in the city's history. Having devastated Anatolia and defeated the Ottomans at the Battle of Ankara, Tamerlane imprisoned the Ottoman Sultan Bayezid I in a cage and paraded him around town.

Five hundred years later, with İstanbul still threatened with foreign occupation, Atatürk declared Ankara the capital of the new Turkish Republic on 13 October, 1923. At first the İstanbul embassies refused to relocate to an under-developed town full of mud-plastered homes without water or electricity. But, when they were offered free land, they soon began constructing new buildings. The German and Austrian architects who helped Atatürk dream up the city plan predicted that the population (which was 30,000 at the time) would eventually reach 800,000. Today, it's roughly 4.5 million.

Located inside the old Çengel Han caravanserai, the Rahmi M. Koç Museum is a newcomer to the city.

Saffet Emre Tonguç

A quick look at old Ankara

The best place to begin exploring Ankara is the historic Citadel (Hisar/Kale). Now surrounded by sturdy walls, this part of town was first settled in Roman times. On the hillside just outside the walls stands the hugely important Museum of Anatolian Civilizations, while the Rahmi M. Koç Museum is located nearby in the old Çengel Han caravanserai. The courtyard of the colorful Pirinç Hanı is filled with antique shops and cafés.

Although it was only a provincial town until 1923, Ankara began to expand rapidly after it replaced İstanbul as the capital, and many of the

THE MUSEUM OF ANATOLIAN CIVILIZATIONS

This museum – one of the most outstanding in the world - displays the rich history of Anatolia from the Stone Age to Classical Antiquity in a restored, 15th-century bedesten (a bazaar warehouse). The collection kicks off with finds from Çatalhöyük, one of the oldest known settlements from the Neolithic period. The houses excavated at Çatalhöyük bear a strong resemblance to those from Xian Banpo in China and to American Indian homes in southwestern USA, showing how people, who live thousands of miles apart may still have a lot in common.

Statues of the Earth Mother and goddess of fertility, Cybele, wink at visitors from the display-cases and whisper that she is the namesake of the famous US film star Cybill Shepherd and "Sibel" is a popular Turkish female name. The laws and commercial documents that the Assyrians squeezed onto tiny clay tablets prove just what a magnificent civilization they possessed. The letter that the Egyptian queen Nefertiti wrote to the Hittite queen Pudahepa reveals the relationship between these two historically important civilizations. Apart from housing the Phrygian and Urartian finds, the basement of the museum also holds interesting artifacts found during excavations in and around Ankara itself.

The Hacı Bayram Veli Mosque and the entrance to the Temple of Augustus and Rome

Saffet Emre Tonguç

monuments from this period are in Ulus, below the Citadel. The former Grand National Assembly building now houses the Museum of the War of Independence. Across from it is a huge statue of Atatürk (Heykel). It was built before Atatürk introduced the Turkish alphabet as part of his reforms, so the inscription is in Arabic. Ankara Palas, an elegant mansion which witnessed many events in the early years of the Republic, is also nearby.

The city was called Angora in Roman times and gained importance, when it became a regional capital.

Ulus also shelters the remains of the old Roman city, including the Column of Julian, which used to bear a statue of the young Roman Emperor Julian (r. 361-363 AD). Near it are the remains of a Roman bath complex. Beside the Hacı Bayram Veli Mosque, the Temple of Augustus is one of Ankara's most impressive Roman monuments. Ironically, this polytheistic structure and the neighboring mosque are connected to each other. The temple walls bear Greek and Latin inscriptions, chronicling important events in the life of the Emperor Augustus (r. 27 BC – 14 AD), as well as details of the imperial expenditure!

Basalt bas-relief of the goddess Kubaba, Kargamış, 9th century BC

Saffet Emre Tonguç

ANKARA CITADEL

Full of cobblestoned streets lined with wooden houses, Ankara's citadel was originally built 3,000 years ago by the Hittites, although what you see today are remnants of a later citadel built by the Byzantine Emperor Michael III (r. 842-867). From Ak Kale (White Castle) at the top, you get a wonderful view out over Ankara. The area immediately below you is where the famous Roman General Pompey the Great defeated the frightful King Mithridates of Pontus in 65 BC.

The Alâeddin Mosque, near the south gate, is a splendid, 12th-century Seljuk work of art. Also beautiful is the Seljuk Aslanhane Mosque, whose roof is supported with 24 wooden pillars. This is one of the most outstanding buildings in the city. If you go inside, take a look at the exquisite pulpit which dates back to 1209. The mosque's founder is buried in the garden, in the sole example of a Seljuk tomb in Ankara. The nearby Ahi Elvan Camii is overshadowed by the Aslanhane, but is still worth a quick look.

The Pirinç Hanı (Copper Bazaar), between these two mosques, was erected in the 18th century to provide accommodation for travelers. Used by the military during the Turkish War of Independence, the building now houses over 40 shops. On Çıkrıkçılar Yokuşu (Hill), near the museum, you will find copper, bric-à-brac, carpets, and antiques for sale.

View from Ankara citadel
Saffet Emre Tonguç

Ankara citadel from a distance
Saffet Emre Tonguç

Atakule is the city's tallest building and offers a panoramic view of Çankaya and the Botanic Gardens.

Saffet Emre Tonguç

Kızılay Square

Saffet Emre Tonguç

Among Ankara's oldest mosques, the Hacı Bayram Veli Mosque is still one of the city's most frequently visited sites, even though it lost some of its popularity to the much larger Kocatepe Mosque in Kızılay in 1987. Known as a patron of the poor and the needy, Hacı Bayram Veli, who also founded the Bayram order of dervishes, died and was buried here in 1430; part of the adjacent temple was reused to provide a madrasa (theological school) for the complex.

Nightlife and shopping

As you travel from Ulus to Kızılay, the town center, you will pass through Sıhhiye and see some fine examples of Republican architecture, as well as Gençlik Parkı (Youth Park), the Opera Building, Ankara University, the Hall of Justice and the Hatti Monument, which commemorates the Hattis who lived here before the Hittites. If you continue from Kızılay along Atatürk Boulevard, the Great National Assembly building will appear on your right, and then you will pass assorted embassy buildings and arrive at Kuğulu (Swan) Park. Take the first left here to find Tunalı Hilmi Caddesi, on the far side of the small park. This is one of the city's most upscale shopping areas. If you're interested in Turkish handicrafts, drop in on Çeşni (Phone: (0312) 426 57 87. www.cesniturk.com) on Tunalı Hilmi to see old Ottoman wedding dresses and dowry pieces that have been changed into exquisite decorative objects.

The Karum Shopping Center, between the Hilton and Sheraton Hotels, is a pleasant mall with lots of local and international brands. If you leave Karum and head towards Gaziosmanpaşa, you will reach Arjantin Caddesi, the capital's most chi-chi restaurant district. Like Bilkent University and its environs, Arjantin Caddesi is one of the city's main nightlife centers.

If you don't turn off at Kuğulu Park, but instead climb the steep Cinnah Caddesi, you will come to the 125-meter-high Atakule, which offers a panoramic view of the city. Here you can spend time browsing the shops, or treat yourself to a great meal at the revolving restaurant. "Kule" (Tower) is in posh Çankaya, which also houses the Presidential Mansion.

Aside from the Armada and Karum Shopping Malls, one of the best malls in the city is Ankamall, beside the Akköprü metro station.

Saffet Emre Tonguç

ANITKABİR – ATATÜRK'S MAUSOLEUM

The body of modern Turkey's founder, war hero and first president, who died in 1938, was laid to rest in a mausoleum in the city he had turned into a capital. The word for mausoleum was derived from the monumental tomb of King Mausolos, which stood in Bodrum, and was one of the Seven Wonders of the Ancient World. Called Anıtkabir (Monumental Tomb), Atatürk's mausoleum was constructed between 1944 and 1953. Once the work was completed, his body was brought here from its temporary resting place in the Museum of Ethnography. Inspired by the iconic Hittite lions, the Aslanlı Yol (Lion Road) leads you to a large courtyard. After you climb the stairs, you will arrive at a simple, yet splendid Neoclassical structure, decorated with beautiful mosaics and Anatolian motifs. In between bowls, which contain soil from all over Turkey lies the grave of Atatürk, where thousands of visitors pay their respects every day. In a hall near a giant Turkish flag are the cars used by Atatürk and the tomb of İsmet İnönü (1884-1973), Turkey's first Prime Minister. There is also a museum that displays Atatürk's personal possessions; a life-like wax model of Atatürk is especially popular with visitors. For history buffs, one section of the museum displays details of the Turkish War of Independence through 3D images.

Lion Road

Saffet Emre Tonguç

WHERE TO **STAY?**

Sheraton
Phone: (0312) 468 54 54
www.sheratonankara.com
The Italian L'Angoletto restaurant is one of the best in town. The hotel is also great for conferences.

Hilton
Phone: (0312) 455 00 00
www.hilton.com
The hotel's Green House restaurant is one of the best places in Ankara to sample international cuisine.

Angora House
Phone: (0312) 309 83 80
Housed in a beautifully restored building in the Citadel, this is an elegant and hospitable establishment with more character than most places in town.

Swissotel Ankara
Phone: (0312) 409 30 00
www.ankara.swissotel.com
Next to the Presidential Mansion, the hotel has 150 rooms. The Amrita Spa is perfect for relaxation.

Bilkent Hotel
Phone: (0312) 266 46 86
www.bilkentotel.com.tr
87 standard rooms plus 27 individually-decorated chambers called konaks.

Radisson Hotel
Phone: (0312) 310 48 48
The Loca Restaurant is excellent.

Gordion Hotel
Phone: (0312) 427 80 80
Elegantly decorated business hotel just off Tunalı Hilmi Caddesi.

Ambassador Hotel
Phone: (0312) 428 48 48

Metropol
Phone: (0312) 417 69 90

WHERE TO **EAT?**

Washington
Phone: (0312) 445 02 12
Both the view and the food are great in this Citadel restaurant.

Zenger Paşa Konağı
Phone: (0312) 311 70 70
Inside a restored house in the Citadel, this restaurant offers good mantı (ravioli), pide and gözleme (pancake) and even better views.

Çengelhan Divan Brasserie
Phone: (0312) 309 68 00
Classic, delicious Divan recipes, inside the new Rahmi M. Koç Museum.

Chez le Belge
Phone: (0312) 484 14 78
Away from the city hustle and bustle in Gölbaşı on the Konya road, this restaurant boasts fine French cuisine.

Trilye
Phone: (0312) 447 12 00
www.trilye.com.tr
The town's best fish restaurant, in a lovely garden. From the chef's seafood special to the lobster thermidor, the food is superb.

Mezzaluna
Phone: (0312) 467 58 18
The new Italian in town, with a view of Seğmenler Park.

Köşebaşı
Phone: (0312) 446 59 59
Ever since Bill & Hillary Clinton dined here, this has been one of Ankara's most famous kebab places. It certainly lives up to its reputation.

Cafemiz
Phone: (0312) 426 44 77
www.cafemiz.com.tr
One of the best cafés in town, with inviting decor.

Niki
Phone: (0312) 426 54 90
This small, clean İran Caddesi bistro promises good service. It is frequented by the Ankara foreign missions - make reservations in advance.

Kuki House
Phone: (0312) 427 14 00
www.kuki.com.tr
Ankara's best patisserie - try the waffles and desserts.

Budakaltı
Phone: (0312) 427 72 71
One of the best places on Arjantin Caddesi. Located inside a lovely villa, it's a favorite with the Ankara elite.

Kırmızı Rouge
Phone: (0312) 241 66 67
World cuisine in the Arcadium Shopping Mall on Çay Caddesi.

Ivy
Phone: (0312) 444 04 89
The best American food in Ankara.

Schnitzel
Phone: (0312) 468 54 00
Don't be fooled by the name of this restaurant inside the Mega Residence Hotel; it serves not only Austrian specialties, such as schnitzel and apple strudel, but also very good seafood.

Wok
Phone: (0312) 446 19 92
Don't miss the sushi bar and weekend parties.

Arpien las Chicas
Phone: (0312) 466 43 26
As the name suggests, Mexican burritos, fajitas, etc.

And Evi
Phone: (0312) 312 79 78
Delightful place for tea and a snack right on the walls of the Citadel.

Eski Kandil
Phone: (0312) 312 39 47
Small, cozy café tucked between the antique shops on Can Sokak, near the Citadel.

WHAT **TO DO?**

Ankara makes a good base for visiting the ruins of Hattuşaş, Yazılıkaya, Alacahöyük and Gordion. Beypazarı, roughly 100 kilometers west of the city, looks destined to become another must-see day-trip location too.

TREASURES OF THE PEOPLE OF
A THOUSAND GODS

074 Hattuşaş and Alacahöyük

Saffet Emre TONGUÇ

As the capital of one of the world's first large empires, the Hittite city of Hattuşaş was right beside what is now the modern village of Boğazkale. Because of its strategically central location, fertile land and abundant water supply, the area was very attractive first to the Hattis and then to the Hittites. Best known for their wars, laws, and successful trade relationships, the Hittites not only left their mark on history, but actually recorded it on clay tablets, shedding invaluable light on the distant past. Other Hittite remains can be seen at Yazılıkaya and Alacahöyük. Together, they make up one of Turkey's UNESCO-recognized World Heritage Sites.

Hattuşaş
Saffet Emre Tonguç

The thousands of clay tablets unearthed at Hattuşaş revealed important information about the history of the Hittites who first appeared on the world stage nearly 4,000 years ago and then disappeared again c. 1200 BC. The Hittite language was first deciphered by the Czech linguist Bedrich Hrozny - the first sentence he was able to read said "Eat the bread and drink the water".

The Hittites arrived in Anatolia from the west and were deeply influenced by the language and religion of the civilizations that preceded them. The Treaty of Kadesh, signed by the Hittites and the Egyptians in 1258 BC, is a remarkable historical document that continues to be one of the earliest known examples of an international peace treaty; it revealed a wealth of information about Hittite history and foreign relations. David, the author of most of the Biblical book of Psalms, was married to Bathsheba, a Hittite who bore him a son called Solomon. Solomon was credited as the architect of the First Temple of the Jews; the Wailing Wall in Jerusalem (the Kotel) is thought to be a remnant of this structure. The seal mentioned in the Turkish expression "He who possesses the seal is Solomon" (meaning, whoever has the authority also has the power) was probably the Seal of Solomon, which according to some sources, bore the Star of David, an age-old symbol of the Jewish tradition and of Israel.

According to the Old Testament, the word Hittite means "The Son of Heth," Heth being a descendant of Ham, the son of Noah.

According to legend, King Tutankhamen's widow planned to marry a Hittite prince, but when the intended groom was murdered on his way to Egypt, the chance for a union between the two nations was lost. The Hittites were also known for abolishing incest; for regarding their king as the first among equals, rather than as an absolute leader; and for declaring that if the king were to bring harm to his brothers, he was to be beheaded.

The sites

When you first enter the site from Boğazkale, you encounter the 3,200-year-old Great Temple (Büyük Mabet) built for the storm god Teshub. The temple contains a green stone, which was given to the Hittites as a gift by the Egyptian queen Nefertiti. As you circle around the city, you will see various points of entry into Hattuşaş, such as the Lion Gate, the Sphinx Gate, the King's Gate, etc. Compared to famous Roman archaeological sites like Ephesus and Bergama, the remains at Hattuşas may not seem that exciting at first, but when one recalls that they represent the remnants of a civilization stretching back 4,000 years, one may come to admire the Hittites all the more.

As the open-air temple of the Hittites - who were known as the "people of a thousand gods"- the rock-cut site of Yazılıkaya is simply mesmerizing. The gods' faces are incised into the rock in profile, although, like their Egyptian counterparts, they seem to be marching with their bodies twisted to face forwards.

Alacahöyük is a third, more remote Hittite site with carved sphinxes guarding its access. Further information on the Hittites is available from Kurt Bittel's book, sold at the ruins. Stone replicas of Hittite objects are also on sale at all the sites.

HOW TO **TRAVEL?**

Hattuşaş is a three-hour drive from Ankara - you'll see the Boğazkale exit after Elmadağ, Kırıkkale and Sungurlu. Once you take the exit, it's about 23km to Yazılıkaya and a little further to Hattuşas. Yazılıkaya and Hattuşas are 3 and 30 kilometers from Alacahöyük, respectively.

WHERE TO **EAT?** and WHERE TO **STAY?**

Aşıkoğlu Motel
Phone: (0364) 452 20 04

Hattuşaş Pension
Phone: (0364) 452 20 13
Pleasant pension with restaurant right in Boğazkale village.

Believed to have been the second most important Hittite city after Hattuşaş, Alacahöyük is entered via the Sphinx Gate.
Mehmet Çabuk

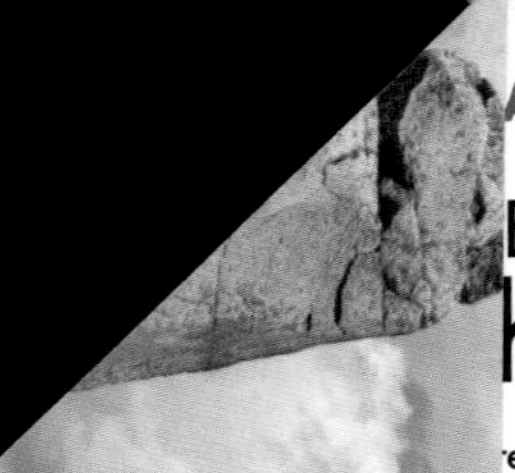

ERFECT PLACE TO END THE DAY
hisar

re TONGUÇ

For many people, the rock of Uçhisar - the "citadel on the edge" – will probably mark the highest point from which they manage to gaze out over Cappadocia. Looking curiously like an outsize snail, the rock "kale" (castle/citadel) can be seen for miles away, completely dominating views towards Nevşehir from neighboring Göreme. Climb up to the top towards the end of the day. As the setting sun plays light games with the extraordinary natural rock formations beneath you, you can raise a glass of Cappadocian wine and salute the beauty of life.

Evil eye tree!
Saffet Emre Tonguç

Most people who fly to Cappadocia actually land in Kayseri even though there is a more central airport at Nevşehir! A fast new road whisks visitors straight from Kayseri to Cappadocia, bypassing the much-restored Selçuk-era Sarıhan (Yellow Han), which was completed in 1249. These days, the Sarıhan (www.sarihan1249.com) hosts Mevlevi whirling dervish ceremonies in the evening, so you may want to come back again later.
The road then skirts Avanos and enters the magical landscape of Cappadocia, which is frequently compared to the surface of the moon – always assuming that the moon came with peri bacaları (literally, "fairy chimneys"- actually conical rocky outcrops). If it's springtime, stop at the Avcılar viewpoint and look down at Göreme - carpeted with violets and lilies, the valley is a vision from heaven.

Once a primitive "apartment block" where many people lived, Uçhisar Castle is now a museum.

However, if you are coming to Cappadocia from Nevşehir, it will be Uçhisar in all its rocky splendor that welcomes you first.

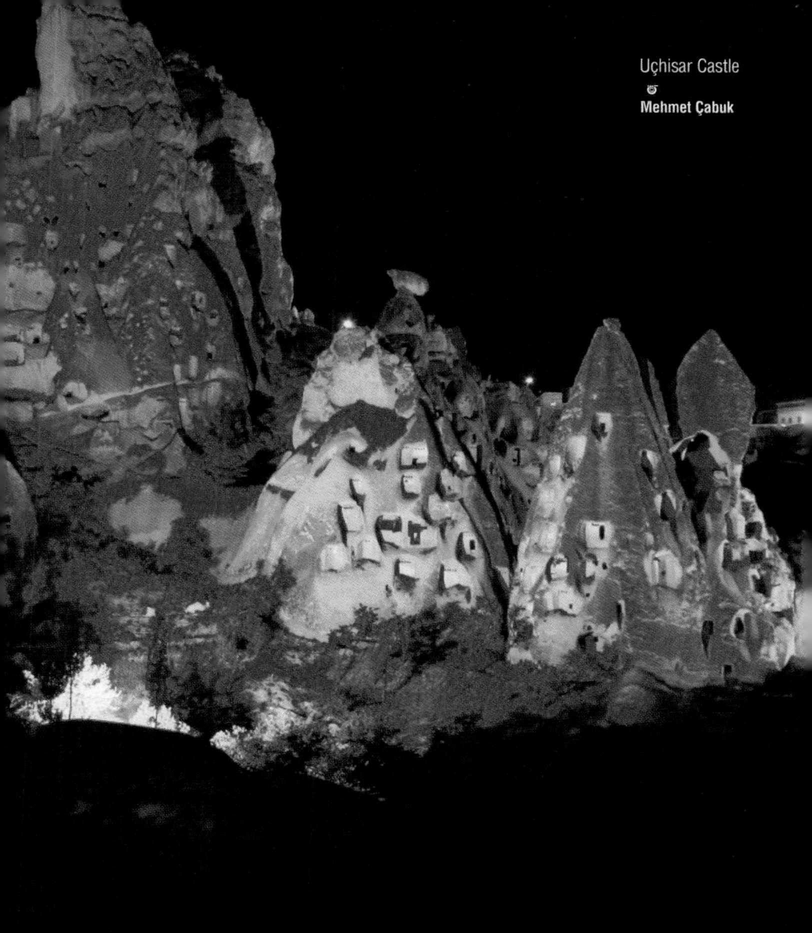

Uçhisar Castle
Mehmet Çabuk

WHERE TO **STAY?**

Les Maisons de Cappadoce
Phone: (0384) 219 2813
Glorious collection of self-catering apartments with unbeatable views, lovely gardens and matchless French style.

Lykia Lodge
Phone: (0384) 213 99 45
www.lykialodge.com
One of the oldest hotels in the area, it's a classic offering a great open buffet.

Karlık Evi (House)
Phone: (0384) 219 2995
www.karlikevi.com
With 20 rooms, this cozy hotel has a lovely view towards the castle. The owners host art camps here every year. Don't leave without tasting their "bulgur (cracked wheat) soup en cocotte" which takes the chef six hours to prepare.

Hotel Lale Saray
Phone: (0384) 219 23 33
www.lalesaray.com
Tastefully decorated rooms and a fantastic view - you get to see the entire region from on high.

WHERE TO **EAT?**

Elai Restaurant
Phone: (0384) 219 31 81
www.elairestaurant.com
An old Cappadocian house with great food and Mt Erciyes and the rock-cut history as the backdrop. If you would like to spend the night somewhere special, you can also rent one of the restaurant's inviting rooms.

Some of the peri bacaları (literally, "fairy chimneys") that ring Uçhisar were used as tombs during the Roman period. Most of the tombs had west-facing entrances and contained stone tables upon which bodies were laid to rest.

THE ROCKY HEART OF CAPPADOCIA
076 Göreme

Saffet Emre TONGUÇ

The village of Göreme is the bustling heart of Cappadocia. Hotels, pensions, restaurants, shops - you name it, Göreme has it. Because of its proximity to the Göreme Open-Air Museum (a UNESCO World Heritage Site), the village has developed rapidly since the 1980s although it still retains much of its charm, especially in the back streets.

Striking rock formations around Göreme.
Saffet Emre Tonguç

Many early Christian hermits, who wanted to lead a life of seclusion and asceticism, chose to settle in Cappadocia, where they hollowed out hundreds of rock formations to create astonishing churches, chapels and monasteries. Today, there are still perhaps 600 such churches in the area, some of them with superb frescoes on the walls. The frescoes range in date from the 7th through to the 14th centuries, although most were painted after the Iconoclastic period (730-87), when the Church forbade the creation of images. Anatolian Greek Christians continued to live in this area until the 1923 population exchange between Turkey and Greece, and the remains of 19th-century churches built to serve their congregation are also scattered across Cappadocia.

If you visit Göreme Open-Air Museum in the afternoon, you might manage to avoid the crowds.

The Cappadocian saints

Cappadocia has served as home to some of the Christian world's most important saints. For example, St Basil (Vassileios), an important figure in Orthodox Christianity, was born in Kayseri, the ancient Caesarea; the 1st and 2nd of January are kept as St Basil's Day for the Orthodox and Catholic faiths, respectively. It was St Basil who drew up the rules of monastic life for eastern Christianity. "What you possess is not yours to keep," is one of his best-remembered sayings.

The patron saint of England, Moscow, and Catalonia, St George (Ayios Yeorgios) was supposedly born in

Elmalı (Apple) Church

The Karanlık (Dark) Church inside Göreme Open-Air Museum
Saffet Emre Tonguç

Cappadocia, where he is usually depicted fighting a dragon. In fact, a real St George may not have existed. The stories told about him show signs of having been lifted from ancient mythology, with George represented as a strong hero, vaguely reminiscent of Heracles.

St Barbara, who has a church named after her inside the Göreme Open-Air Museum, was born in Nicomedia (present-day İzmit). Her father was a pagan aristocrat, who condemned his beautiful daughter to death because of her Christian faith. Later, the reward for her suffering was sainthood.

Göreme Open-Air Museum

The museum is situated on what is thought to have been the site of the original Göreme, then called Corama. As you enter it, you will notice small rock-cut cells once occupied by monks and nuns. The most important structures to look out for are the Elmalı (Apple), St Barbara, Yılanlı (Snake) and Çarıklı (Sandal) churches, although the Karanlık (Dark) church has the most magnificent frescoes, as bright today as when they were painted in the 11th century.

Another of the most outstanding churches is the 10th-century Tokalı Church, which stands across the road from the main part of the museum. The ceiling of the older section is decorated with scenes from the life of Christ. As you walk further inside, you will see other striking frescoes adorning the walls.

A balloon ride is a must in Cappadocia.
Saffet Emre Tonguç

On your way to the museum, take the turning in front of the Turist Hotel that leads to the Aşk (Love) Valley where you can lose yourself amongst some of the most dramatic "peri bacaları" (fairy chimneys).

Local hoteliers are experts at converting the secrets of Göreme and its surroundings into incredible locations for events. Just something to bear in mind, if you are planning something special.

Some of the finest fairy-chimney rock formations can be seen in and around Göreme which also makes a great base for a walking holiday.

Cappadocia is one of Turkey's most popular centers for buying kilims and carpets.
Saffet Emre Tonguç

Mornings and evenings

Even if you're not normally an early bird, it's an unforgettable experience to look down on Cappadocia from the basket of a balloon at the crack of dawn. Even in winter, the white blanket of snow is very becoming; from Mt Erciyes in the east, to Mt Hasan in the west, the whole area is rendered a magical mystery land.

In the evening, try and catch the whirling dervishes performing their rituals in an underground cave. As they leave the stage to the more conventional folk dancers, you will be left wondering: "Is all this for real?"

Kapadokya Balloons
Phone: (0384) 271 24 42
www.kapadokyaballoons.com

Yaşar Baba
Phone: (0384) 219 28 70

ANATOLIAN HOUSES - CAPPADOCIA'S MOST BEAUTIFUL HOTEL

The many beautiful hotels created inside old cave complexes make Cappadocia all the more attractive. The superb Anatolian Houses Hotel consists of 19 individually-decorated suites (some of them 70 square meters in size), including five inside "peri bacaları" (fairy chimneys). The suites offer plasma TVs, large jacuzzis, double sinks and showers, and silk carpets displayed in spot-lit showcases. Some of the suites have four separate rooms, and in some cases the Jacuzzi is placed right inside the "peri bacası," creating an amazing ambience.

Outside in the garden, wine flows from a fountain. There is also an indoor and outdoor swimming pool and a spa. The food is fantastic. This is a real hedonist's heaven, although the private meeting rooms mean that the hotel is also perfect for business meetings.
Phone: (0384) 271 24 63
www.anatolianhouses.com

HOW TO **TRAVEL?**

If you are heading to Cappadocia from Ankara, the journey takes about five hours. There are two decent places to stop along the way. One is Baran Tesisleri (Phone: (0332) 657 62 24), which is approximately 100 kilometers from Ankara. As you approach Aksaray, you will see the lovely Ağaçlı Tesisleri (Phone: (0382) 215 24 00), right beside the Nevşehir turn. From there, Cappadocia is only another 80 kilometers away.

WHERE TO **EAT?**

Alaturca Restaurant
Phone: (0384) 271 28 82
Try the zeytinyağlılar (vegetables cooked in olive oil) and the beğendili kebap (kebab with eggplant puree), as you sip your wine and admire the view.

WHERE TO **STAY?**

Kelebek Hotel and Pension
Phone: (0384) 271 25 31
www.kelebekhotel.com
Lovely hotel and pension combination, built around two fairy chimneys in the historic, older part of Göreme. Offers wonderful views.

Fairy Chimney Inn
Phone: (0384) 271 26 55
www.fairychimney.com
Beautiful hotel inside a "peri bacası" (fairy chimney) owned by a German anthropologist. The views are spectacular.

Göreme House
Phone: (0384) 271 20 60
www.goremehouse.com
A cozy, home-like establishment with 13 rooms. The view is lovely and the breakfast excellent.

Colors
Mehmet Çabuk

A LAND OF POTTERY Avanos

Saffet Emre TONGUÇ

The clay that the Kızılırmak (Red River) deposits in Avanos has been used to make pottery since Hittite times. It's a tradition that is still alive and well today, as the whole town is dotted with pottery workshops.

A pottery tree! Saffet Emre Tonguç

In Hittite and Phrygian records, Avanos crops up as an enchanting, fairy-tale-like place created by the god of volcanoes. Standing at the junction of many trade routes, it was called Vanessa in Roman times. During the Seljuk period its name was changed to commemorate the Seljuk commander Evranos Bey; later this was corrupted to Avanos. The 1st-century geographer Strabo tells us that Venassa was the third most important town in the Kingdom of Cappadocia, after Kayseri and Kemerhisar, a now all-but-forgotten settlement near Niğde.

The clay that gives the Kızılırmak its color is the basis for pottery-making, a handcraft for which Avanos is particularly famous. Passed down from generation to generation, from father to son, it's a handicraft that hasn't changed much since Hittite times. Some of the local potters provide information for tourists and put on demonstrations of pottery-making. Chez Galip (Phone: (0384) 511 42 40) and Güray (Phone: (0384) 511 23 74, www.gurayseramik.com.tr) are two places, where you can watch mud being given artistic life. The Fırça workshop (Phone: (0384) 511 36 86) is inside a mini underground city where, as you walk through the interconnecting caves, you discover a whole subterranean world of ceramics and tiles.

The Hittites, who learnt pottery-making from the Assyrians, referred to Avanos as Zu-Winasa.

Another source of income in this little town, as elsewhere in Cappadocia, is viticulture. The local grapes are good not just for eating but also for wine production.

Artists create pieces of art in the numerous pottery workshops in Avanos

Saffet Emre Tonguç

If you have time to spare, do visit the 2nd-century Yamanlı Church, two kilometers from the center of Avanos. The Özkonak underground city near Avanos is also perfect for avoiding the crowds who descend on the Derinkuyu and Kaymaklı underground cities at the height of summer. It is thought that tunnels connected local houses to these underground cities that could accommodate thousands of people for months at a time, whenever enemies were around.

On the way from Avanos to Göreme you can make a side visit to Paşabağı (the former Keşişler Vadisi - Valley of the Monks). It is filled with interesting "peri bacaları" (fairy chimneys), some of them clumped together like asparagus spears. It's a great place to come in early evening as the sun starts to set. Further down the road, the Zelve Open-Air Museum fills three valleys which were inhabited until the 1950s. Here you can visit the Direkli (Pillar), Balıklı (Fish), Üzümlü (Grape) and Geyikli (Deer) churches, as well as a small rock-cut mosque.

A little closer to Göreme, you pass through Çavuşin, where the 10th-century Church of St John (AKA the Great Pigeon House) is right by the main road, with some of its beautiful frescoes exposed to the air. Inland, in Old Çavuşin, the 5th-century Church of St John the Baptist boasts cathedral-like proportions. If you walk to Kızıl Çukur from Çavuşin, you will find all kinds of forgotten churches scattered among the gardens and vineyards.

WHERE TO **STAY?**

Kirkit Pension

Phone: (0384) 511 31 48

Lovely pension in a pair of restored houses, with a large rock-cut dining room and a tradition of live folk music nightly.

WHERE TO **EAT?**

Enjoy the gözleme (pancakes) and pickles of Hayriye Teyze as you leave Fırça, the pottery workshop.

Hanedan

Phone: (0384) 511 50 06

Built to resemble a caravanserai, the restaurant offers lovely decoration and good food.

APPADOCIA'S LARGEST SETTLEMENT

Jrgüp

Saffet Emre TONGUÇ

Until the 1923 population exchange between Turkey and Greece, Ürgüp – the old Prokopi - was predominantly inhabited by Greeks. The city boasts many beautiful stone houses, some of them now used as hotels. Other empty cave dwellings are currently being restored.

There ar numerous smal fields scattere between th natural roc formations o Cappadocia

Saffet Emr Tongu

Created by volcanic eruptions some 30 million years ago, Cappadocia meant “the land of beautiful horses” according to the Greek historian Herodotus. Whether it's the land of beautiful horses or the land of the beautiful rock formations created by nature would be difficult to say. The volcanic tuff, shaped and eroded by sun, wind, snow, frost, time, and human hands, has made this area particularly fertile and provided it with an income from viticulture and agriculture. Today, many delicious wines are produced in Ürgüp; you can tour the Turasan wine factory and taste different vintages at several shops around town.

Historically, Ürgüp was bigger and richer than Göreme with which it competes today for the tourist dollar. As a result the houses here were larger and more elaborate. You will see many fine stone buildings lining the road heading out of town towards Göreme. One of the churches used by the Greeks until the 1923 population exchange now houses Ürgüp's hamam (Turkish bath).

Ürgüp acquired a more modern kind of fame recently during the filming of the popular Turkish television series "Asmalı Konak" (The Vine-Shaded Mansion). A monument to this epochal event stands near the Turasan winery.

On the way from Ürgüp to Avanos, the Dervent Valley is filled with thought-provoking rock formations; the one resembling a camel is the most

frequently photographed, but everyone will have their own particular favorite. It's also worth dropping in on Ortahisar, which is clustered around a rock-cut castle like Uçhisar's, and boasts fine old houses and a small museum.

Fairy chimneys at Paşabağı
Aydın Kudu

WHERE TO **STAY?**

Serinn
Phone: (0384) 341 60 76
www.serinnhouse.com
Perhaps the most extraordinary hotel in Cappadocia, this ancient stone structure is decorated with extremely modern furniture. The owner Mrs. Eren's refined taste is reflected everywhere.

Sacred House
Phone: (0384) 341 71 02
www.sacred-house.com
An incredible combination of Cappadocian architecture and medieval castle. If you want to spoil yourself, this is the right place to come.

Esbelli Evi
Phone: (0384) 341 33 95
www.esbelli.com
A cluster of tastefully-decorated old houses carved out of the rock, with some very beautiful suites. The view from the terrace is magnificent.

4-Oda Cave House
Phone: (0384) 341 60 80
www.4oda.com
A cozy place where you feel immediately at home.

WHERE TO **EAT?**

Şömine Restaurant
Phone: (0384) 341 84 42
One of the best local restaurants with good service and very reasonable prices. Testi kebabı (stew cooked inside a clay pot) is the specialty of the restaurant and the region.

Ehlikeyf
Phone: (0384) 341 61 00
www.ehlikeyf.info
This restaurant serves both international and Turkish cuisine, including testi kebabı.

Ziggy's Café
Phone: (0384) 341 71 07
The place to come to experience contemporary Cappadocia. Not at all touristy, the café feels like something you'd find in a stylish İstanbul neighborhood, but without the attitude to go with it. The one dessert on the menu must be tasted to be believed – it's spectacular!

WHAT **TO DO?**

Argeus
Phone: (0384) 341 46 88
www.argeus.com.tr and **Peerless**
Phone: (0384) 271 30 10
www.peerlesstravel.com.tr.
If you need a good travel agency to organize your Cappadocia trip, these are thoroughly reliable companies with long experience in the business.

Saffet Emre Tonguç

DEEP BELOW THE EARTH
079 Underground Cities

Saffet Emre TONGUÇ

Some of Cappadocia's most astonishing sights are the underground cities which were dug many layers deep into the soil. Archaeological finds suggest that the Hittites may have been the first to think of this idea. Later, the expanded "cities" became home to Christians seeking refuge from the Arab invaders. What an awful surprise it must have been for the enemy to arrive and find no one to fight with or convert after long days of traveling!

Women at the entrance of Derinkuyu underground city
Saffet Emre Tonguç

Tatlarin underground city

Actually, the term "underground city" is a bit of a misnomer. Although these extraordinary places came equipped with kitchens, bedrooms, schools, churches, stables, store-rooms, wine-presses, ventilation shafts and wells, they were probably only ever inhabited for short periods at a time. In other words, they were emergency accommodations only. Some of the "cities" (and more than 30 of them have been identified) may have been connected to each other via tunnels, which meant that, in case of enemy attack, people could move easily from one to the other.

If you stick your head into one of the ventilation shafts, you will realize just how far beneath the surface you are, which should certainly fill you with admiration for the skill involved in creating the cities. Since smoke would have given their location away, the ventilation shafts were made very long and the smoke was released from different chimneys to confuse attackers. Massive circular rocks could be rolled across the passageways to seal them off in case of an attack.

There are interesting, little-known underground cities in Tatlarin, Güzelyurt and Mazıköy.

Today, the underground cities are well lit and signed, but just imagine having to struggle through the tunnels by candlelight without knowing your way around. Some of these tunnels are quite narrow, so if you are claustrophobic or have difficulty walking bent double, it's probably best to stick with the upper levels or visit one of the cities that are not so deep.

The most visited underground cities are at Kaymaklı and Derinkuyu (Deep Well).

Kaymaklı is just nine kilometers from Nevşehir, but Derinkuyu is the larger site. It has eight levels, is 55 meters deep, and extends over some 1,500 square meters.

Kaymaklı underground city

© Şemsi Güner

·appadocia's Little-Known Secrets

Saffet Emre TONGUÇ

Cappadocia is like nowhere else in the world. Both the striking rock formations and the never-ending layers of history turn it into a dream place; to get the best out of the area, though, you have to spread your wings beyond the busy Ürgüp-Göreme-Avanos triangle. Places like Mustafapaşa, Soğanlı and Güzelyurt are just as interesting to visit, if much less crowded. A walk through the Ihlara Valley is a winner, no matter what the time of year.

Old Greek House Hotel
Saffet Emre Tonguç

Mustafapaşa, Ortahisar and Niğde

Mustafapaşa (the old Sinassos) is a short drive south of Ürgüp. The tasty home-cooked meals dished up at the Old Greek House Hotel are extremely popular. They are served in a building which became famous thanks to a Turkish television series and which used to belong to the richest of the Greek families who lived here before the 1923 population exchange between Turkey and Greece. Don't be surprised to spot a fresco on an upstairs wall, which might remind you of a painting on display in New York's Metropolitan Museum of Art!

Take a leisurely stroll along the streets and inspect the 18th-century Ayios Konstantinos and Ayia Eleni Kilisesi (Church), which was dedicated to Constantine, the founder of Constantinople, and his mother Helena. The Ayios Vassilios Kilisesi boasts beautiful 20th-century frescoes. There is also a graceful madrasa in the town center that now forms part of the local university.

Buses from Nevşehir also run to Niğde, the ancient Nahita, where there is a pleasant hotel. Treat yourself to a good meal at one of the restaurants in town, then climb up to the castle and tour the mosques and churches. The wood-carvings of the Ilkhanate-era Sungur Bey Mosque are impressive. The doors may be locked but the old Greek church also shows off its blue frescoes to anyone who cares to stick their head through the windows.

Aqueduct at Kemerhisar
Saffet Emre Tonguç

Eski Gümüşler Monastery near Niğde is a well-kept secret. Here, you will see a smiling Virgin Mary depicted in one of the frescoes. You might be told that this is the only example of its kind, but the truth is that Mary was made to smile by one of the less-careful restorers during the renovation of the church! Nearby is Tyana (Kemerhisar), where an ancient aqueduct connected to a 3rd-century Roman pool has survived largely intact. Apollonius, a celebrated Greek philosopher and teacher, was born in Tyana in 1 AD. If you're looking for the cozy atmosphere of a village home, the Tyana Guest House might make a good place to spend the night.

The Ihlara Valley and Soğanlı

The 16-kilometer-long Ihlara Valley, with the River Melendiz running along the bottom of it, makes a magnificent place to visit, no matter what the time of year. It offers a fairly straightforward walk, with several frescoed churches to explore along the way. Just as you're starting to get tired, you can stop for lunch in Belisırma, roughly halfway along the valley. Then, at the end, you can visit a truly spectacular rock-cut monastery at Selime. Ignore those people, who tell you it was used in the filming of Star Wars - it wasn't, which doesn't make it any the less worth visiting!

As its name suggests, Güzelyurt (Beautiful Land) is a lovely, historic town although it goes largely overlooked, perhaps because it is less easy to reach by public transport than more central parts of Cappadocia. Here, the former Karballa Monastery is currently in use as a hotel and outdoor activities centre. Saint Gregory of Nazianzus, one of the most important saints of the Greek Orthodox Church, grew up here. The church where his body was once buried is now a mosque. In the town center you can visit a small underground city and an unusual rock-cut mosque, while on the outskirts the Monastery Valley resembles a mini Ihlara without the river.

Soğanlı is another corner of Cappadocia that is still waiting to be discovered. The sides of its twin valleys are pierced with medieval frescoed churches and high up on the valley walls there are hundreds of old pigeon houses, their entrances ringed with whitewash so that they resemble an outdoor shooting gallery. In the village square, local women compete to sell dolls with stiff skirts and high hats that are said to symbolize fertility.

Niğde Market

Saffet Emre Tonguç

WHERE TO **STAY?**

Gül Konakları
Phone: (0384) 353 54 86
Delightful luxury hotel set round a walled garden with several rooms set up to show aspects of life as it was lived in the Cappadocian past.

Tyana Guest House, Kemerhisar
Phone: (0388) 329 30 65
www.tyanaguesthouse.com

Grand Hotel, Niğde
Phone: (0388) 232 70 00
www.grandhotelnigde.com

Halil Pansiyon, Güzelyurt
Phone: (0382) 451 27 07
www.halilpension.com
A spotless pension run by Mrs. Fatma and her daughter Hafize.

Karballa Hotel, Güzelyurt
Phone: (0382) 451 21 03
www.kirkit.com

WHERE TO **EAT?**

Belisırma Restaurant
Phone: (0382) 457 30 57
As you walk along the river in the Ihlara Valley, you will come to Belisırma village. How would you like to dip your feet in the Melendiz River as you enjoy a lunch of oven-baked trout? Bliss.

Old Greek House Hotel
Phone: (0384)353 53 06
www.oldgreekhouse.com
In Mustafapaşa (Sinassos), near Ürgüp, this hotel also has a popular restaurant. Sitting at one of the floor tables on the first floor, you will feel as if you are traveling back in time.

Saruhan Restaurant, Niğde
Phone: (0388) 232 21 72

Interior of Greek Orthodox Church in Niğde

Saffet Emre Tonguç

081 Skiing on Mt Erciyes

Fatih TÜRKMENOĞLU

Imagine a mountainside, where the local kids come sliding by on their skis. On one side, picnickers surround a barbecue, on the other are majestic mountains, glitzy hotels - and toddlers on their sledges. The ski resort at Mt Erciyes, just outside Kayseri, is neither expensive, nor pretentious. And it is absolutely beautiful.

Skiing and winter sports are a vital part of the Erciyes way of life.

İsmail Keremoğlu

The sound of "arabesque" on the road to Mt Erciyes

It's very easy to get to Mt Erciyes by minibus and the journey might well become part of the adventure. Chances are that you will find half the town packed in beside you, especially if you visit on the weekend. With all the seats taken, some people may be sitting on stools, and the radio will probably be churning out the popular "arabesque" music (oriental-style music that comes with heart-wrenching lyrics). As you climb the mountain road, all the windows will probably be shut tight. Catching a cold seems to be the biggest national fear!

The conservative Kayseri of the recent past is changing rapidly. This is a town that has been dubbed an "Anatolian tiger".

Once you reach the resort area, at 2,200 meters, you may be surprised by the crowds. It can sometimes seem as if all the local children are up here skiing. Toddlers will be being dragged around on sledges. People will be gathered around a barbecue, waiting for their share of the mouth-watering sucuk (garlic sausage), tomatoes, green peppers and bread. The atmosphere will be warm and welcoming. You won't find any high-society types strutting their stuff in fancy aprés-ski gear up here.

Beach fun on a mountainside

Erciyes is FUN. With jet-skis for hire, sledges available for kids, and tea for a pittance, Erciyes offers the mountain version of Turkish-style beach entertainment. That's all very well, but of course the combination of skiers and sledge-riders on the same slopes can occasionally lead to chaos. The director of the Dedeman Hotel thinks that things will change soon. An Austrian company has been asked to come up with a master plan for reorganizing the slopes. Once it is implemented, the skiers will be separated from the more casual visitors.

Erciyes has three ski-runs. The long and fairly horizontal one is aimed at beginners, while a second, higher ski-run is reserved for more experienced skiers.

Most of the skiers are locals, but visitors also pop up from the south coast and from elsewhere in Cappadocia (just 45 minutes away), as well as from İstanbul and Ankara. Fans say that they love Erciyes' powder snow and the sheer pleasure of skiing with only a t-shirt in the scorching April sun.

After spending some time on the mountain, don't forget to drop in on Kayseri. The city is much more interesting than first appearances might suggest.

The summit of Erciyes is at 3,916 meters and reachable by climbers via Şeytan Boğazı and Hörgüç Kaya.

The view of Mt Erciyes from Kayseri.
Saffet Emre Tonguç

HOW TO **TRAVEL?**

Kayseri is extremely central. It is five hours drive from Ankara and two hours from Adana and Mersin. The Erciyes ski resort is also readily accessible. Minibuses depart from the Talas bus terminal in Kayseri town center and run you up the 24-kilometer road in 30 minutes.

If you're coming from İstanbul or Ankara there are regular daily flights to Kayseri. If you don't have too much luggage, you can head straight into the town center and take a minibus from there.

WHERE TO **EAT?**

Compared to Uludağ, the fare offered in Erciyes cafés is relatively inexpensive.

On the way back, drop in on Elmacıoğlu İskender in Kayseri; the service is good and the kebabs delicious. Don't leave without sampling some Kayseri mantısı (Turkish ravioli), yaprak sarma (stuffed vine leaves), and pastırma (spicy cured beef).

İskender Kebap Salonu
Phone: (0352) 222 69 65
Long-lived and very popular place to eat – İskender kebab, of course!

WHERE TO **STAY?**

Dedeman Hotel
Phone: (0352) 342 21 16

Ace Hotel
Phone: (0352) 342 20 53
Small boutique hotel which includes cost of skiing in room rates.

Bülent Hotel
Phone: (0352) 342 20 12
Discounts on weekdays.

Grand Eras Hotel
Phone: (0352) 342 21 28

WHAT **TO DO?**

Set aside some time to explore Kayseri town center. Most of what is worth seeing is inside or close to the hefty old city walls. Look out, in particular, for the lovely Güpgüpoğlu Konağı, a beautifully preserved 18th-century mansion; the 12th-century Çifte Medrese, which houses a small medical museum; the 12th-century Ulu Cami; and the 16th-century Kurşunlu Cami, the design of which may have been influenced by the famous Sinan, a local boy from a nearby village. The covered bazaar is also fun to wander around. Dotted about town there are also many conical tombs, called kümbets, that date back to Seljuk times. The 13th-century hamam (Turkish bath) in the Hunat Hatun mosque complex is a great place to go for a scrub after all the skiing.

ANATOLIA'S LARGEST AND
MOST IMPRESSIVE CARAVANSERAIS

082 Sultanhanı and Obruk Han

Saffet Emre TONGUÇ

Built by the Seljuk Sultan Alâeddin Keykubat in 1229, Sultanhanı was Anatolia's largest caravanserai. The entrance is still magnificent and carries faint echoes of Byzantine architecture. Obruk Han is equally impressive, if considerably less well known.

The Seljuks built nearly 100 caravanserais along the Silk Road, which started in Xian in China, traversed Anatolia and ended in İstanbul. These structures were sited using a rough calculation that camels could cover about 30 to 40 kilometers a day. The Sarıhan on the Avanos-Kayseri road and the Ağzıkarahan on the Aksaray-Nevşehir road are beautiful examples of the caravanserais typical of this region.

To encourage trade in Seljuk times, camel caravans were accommodated free for three days.

The huge Sultanhanı is still in extremely good condition. As you enter, there is a market area to the immediate right, and accommodation, and kitchens and bathrooms on the left. The beautiful stable, with its majestic entrance, is

Sultanhanı, which was built by the Seljuk Sultan Alâeddin Keykubat.

Saffet Emre Tonguç, Mehmet Çabuk

reminiscent of a Gothic cathedral. A masjid (Muslim chapel) stands in the middle of the courtyard.

Perhaps the most impressive of all Anatolian caravanserais is the ruined 13th-century Obruk Han on the road from Sultanhanı to Konya; thirty-six kilometers from Sultanhanı, take a rough road on the right and you will enter a world of surprises. The carevanserai was built using materials from an old Byzantine church and the walls are covered with crosses and Greek inscriptions. It has unusual crenellations over its otherwise plain entrance. There is a breath-taking 30-meter-deep crater lake to the rear.

For a brief moment, you feel as if you have stepped into a surrealist painting; then suddenly you hear the call to prayer from the mosque nearby. Obruk Hanı is a symbol of timelessness. As I was leaving, two sisters, Hatice and Zeynep looked straight into my camera. I did what I had to and froze time again by capturing their stare…

Views of Obruk Han, the most impressive caravanserai in Anatolia

Saffet Emre Tonguç

Crater lake behind Obruk Han

LAST RESTING PLACE OF MEVLÂNA
083 Konya

Saffet Emre TONGUÇ

A fast-growing city in the centre of Anatolia, Konya is a place in which the old blends with the new and the traditional coexists with the modern. It is world-famous as the burial place of Celaleddin Rumi, better known as Mevlâna, whose tomb is a revered place of pilgrimage even today. It was Mevlâna who dreamed up the idea of the whirling dervishes which means that Konya is also strongly associated with them as well.

Mevlâna Celaleddin Rumi's father Bahaeddin Veled's grave is next to his son's. It is in an unusual position, vertical rather than horizontal, apparently to illustrate the respect the father felt for his son.
Saffet Emre Tonguç

Konya was called Kuwanna by the Hittites 4,000 years ago, and then Iconium (the city of icons) by the Greeks; the Turks seem to have combined the two to come up with Konya. Visited by St Paul and St Barnabas on their travels, Konya is recognized, as the birthplace of St Thecla, a female follower of St Paul. Its proximity to Çatalhöyük (once believed to be the oldest settlement in the world), and its role as the capital of the Seljuk Empire and as the site of Mevlâna's tomb ensure that tourists flock to Konya.

Mevlâna's tomb is one of Turkey's most frequently visited sites.

Probably, the first thing that springs to mind, when thinking about Konya is the tomb of Mevlâna. Mevlâna's wonderful words, "Come, come whoever you are", not only reflect his philosophy of universal love and tolerance, but also seem to summon people to come and visit his tomb, which is crowded at all times. The complex that houses the tomb is topped off with a superb turquoise-tiled dome. It includes a masjid (Muslim chapel) and a "semahane" where whirling dervish rituals used to take place. Used as a museum today, the complex also features chambers, where the dervishes once lived. Right next door to the tomb is the Selimiye Mosque, which was commissioned by Sultan Selim II in 1567, while he was governor of Konya.

About Mevlâna

The great poet and religious leader Mevlâna Celaleddin Rumi was born in 1207 in what is now Afghanistan. Later, his family fled the Mongolian invasion and settled in Konya. Mevlâna means "our guide" or "our master", while Celaleddin means "majesty of religion" in Arabic. Mevlâna wrote most of his poetry in Persian, but also penned some verses in Turkish, Arabic and even Greek. His life took an unexpected turn when he met Şemseddin Tabrizi, who became his spiritual guide and companion. Şems vanished unexpectedly, believed murdered by Rumi's disciples who could not stand his influence over the Sufi master. After Şems' disappearance, Mevlâna retreated further into the world of Sufism and began writing his 25,000-verse masterpiece, the Mesnevi. For him, death was merely reunion with God and so a cause for celebration. Thus, 17 December, the date of his death (or his "nuptial night", as it is referred to) is celebrated with semas (ceremonies) at which Mevlevi dervishes perform their famous whirling dance. With their wide white skirts and conical headdresses symbolizing the ego's shroud and tomb respectively, the dervishes slowly revolve, passing divine energy from the Creator to his creations.

ANATOLIAN SUFISM

Although the word "Tasavvuf" (Sufism) often refers to Islamic mysticism in general, it is also the specific name given to Turco-Islamic mysticism, which was instrumental in the expansion of Islam. Hoca Ahmet Yesevi set up the first Turkic tariqah (dervish sect), and he was followed by Mevlâna, Hacı Bektaş Veli and Yunus Emre, who all chose Anatolia as a base from which to try and create a synthesis between Islam and older Turkish customs. While preserving the culture and traditions that existed before the coming of Islam, they managed to create something that harmonized with the basic principles of Islam and was based on love, rather than fear of God; on embracing people and society, rather than avoiding them. Mevlâna developed notions of time and space limited by mystical notions of self-annihilation and the renunciation of the world, thus revealing a different aspect of the Islamic faith. He was concerned that progress in the physical and mystical sciences should be free of the restrictions created by rules, lodges, sects, authorities, and possessions. Never severing their ties with daily life and the world, Anatolian Sufis pride themselves on being "passive in malevolence and active in beneficence". Thus they embrace the idea that "it is not enough to save only yourself - you must share, what you discover with everyone else". The Anatolian Sufis showed the world that every place and every occasion had its own individual decorum.

Whirling Dervishes

Saffet Emre Tonguç

Tomb of Mevlana
© Serhan Güngör

WHERE TO **STAY?**

Hotel Rumi
Phone: (0332) 353 11 21
www.rumihotel.com
11 km. from Konya Airport, the hotel offers a view of the Mevlâna Museum.

Hotel Ulusan
Phone: (0332) 351 50 04
Right behind the PTT (post office) and ideal for tight budgets. The rooms are spotless, but some of the bathrooms are shared.

Konya Rixos
Phone: (0332) 221 50 00
www.rixos.com
Lovely views, high standards, but a long way from the center.

Özkaymak Hotel
Phone: (0332) 237 87 20
www.ozkaymak.com.tr

WHERE TO **EAT?**

Köşk Konya Mutfağı
Phone: (0332) 352 85 47
In this restored Konya mansion you can eat traditionally at a table on the floor. The kitchen boasts excellent tandır kebabı (kebab baked in a clay oven), gözleme (pancake), and bamya (okra) dishes. Try the höşmerim dessert decorated with pistachio nuts.

Şifa Restaurant
Phone: (0332) 352 05 19
Serves Konya's two specialties - fırın kebabı (oven-baked kebab), and etli ekmek (pizza-like bread topped with minced meat). If you have a sweet tooth, try the saç arası or Mevlâna sarması dessert made by mixing dough with kaymak (heavy cream).

© Asude Akınlı

WHAT **TO DO?**

The former Karatay Medresesi (Seminary) built by the Seljuk vizier (minister) Emir Celâleddin Karatay in 1250-51 is now a museum. As you walk through the rooms in which students were once taught, feast your eyes on the wonderful Seljuk tiles and ceramics. You will not be able to take them off the predominantly blue tiles brought from the 13th-century Kubadabad Palace near Lake Beyşehir.

Study the wood and stone reliefs in the İnce Minare, built in 1264 and later partially destroyed by lightning. A Byzantine symbol, the double-headed eagle, crops up again here, this time in use as a Seljuk motif! The 13th-century Sırçalı Medrese also houses a small collection of tombstones.

Visit the magnificent, Arab-influenced 13th-century Alaeddin Mosque on Alaettin Hill. It was largely created out of reused Roman and Byzantine stonework.

Get a good scrub at the ancient Mahkeme Hamamı (Court Bath) behind the Şerafettin Mosque.

ÇATALHÖYÜK

Rediscovered by James Mellaart in 1958, Çatalhöyük marked a turning point in the history of mankind as one of the first settlements created after humans abandoned caves and began living in urban settings. If you are not interested in archaeology, the few remaining wall fragments may be disappointing, but others will think it worth the trip to witness a settlement dating back 9,000 years. Made from a blend of straw and sun-dried bricks, a few of the houses are still intact after thousands of years. It is thought that the double-roomed houses were built right next to one another as protection against marauding wild animals. The inhabitants also seem to have preferred to enter their homes via the roofs, rather than through conventional doors. The finds from the excavations, including bas reliefs, statuettes of goddesses and objects made from obsidian are on display in the Museum of Anatolian Civilizations in Ankara.

Çatalhöyük is one of the oldest Neolithic settlements so far uncovered.

Seated figurine of the Mother Goddess, Çatalhöyük, first half of 6th millennium BC, Museum of Anatolian Civilizations.

Black stone figurine of Mother Goddess, Çatalhöyük, first half of 6th millennium BC, Museum of Anatolian Civilizations.

KAPTAN

7 MUST-SEE PLACES
IN THE BLACK SEA REGION

THE BLACK SEA REGION

'N OF A THOUSAND)DEN SPOONS

raklı

Fatih TÜRKMENOĞLU

A small town to the south-west of Sakarya (Adapazarı), Taraklı, with its graceful wooden houses and narrow streets, still retains an authentically Ottoman atmosphere but is completely off the beaten track as regards to visitors.

Taraklı looks like a film set.

Bünyad Dinç

To arrive in Taraklı is to feel as if you are stepping onto the set of a TV soap opera set in the first years of the Republic. This is a place, whose small shops and red-tiled wooden houses clinging to a hillside rival those in Safranbolu and Şirince for beauty, but whereas Safranbolu and Şirince are overrun with visitors, Taraklı receives almost no attention. White-bearded grandpas amble about streets, where people never think to lock their doors. Flowers are still planted in old vegetable oil cans and the grocers seem to hail from another century.

Taraklı still follows the norms of Ottoman provincial town life. Doors stand wide open, hearts are pure.

Originally called "Dablar" and then "Bytinia", Taraklı has a history stretching back for 2,000 years. It was one of the first places conquered by Osman Bey (the founder of the Ottoman dynasty after whom the Empire was named), a fact mentioned by the Austrian orientalist Joseph Von Hammer in his *Geschichte des Osmanischen Reiches (History of the Ottoman Empire)*. The 17th-century travel writer Evliya Çelebi wrote: "They call this place Taraklı (with combs), because everybody makes spoons and combs". The Taraklı dialect is very distinct. Instead of "tavuk" (chicken, normally pronounced as tah-vook), for example, they say "toğuk" (toe-wook). Each family has a nickname and the locals use these to refer to each other.

Houses, mosques and wooden spoons

Eighty-one of the old houses are designated historic monuments, and restoration work has already started on a few of them. Some are absolutely enormous and boast stained-glass windows and elegant top-floor balconies ("cumbas"). Look out in particular for the graceful Fenerli Evi and the old Belediye (Municipality) building.

The lovely Kurşunlu Camii (Leaded Mosque, also known as the Yunus Paşa Camii) was commissioned by Sultan Selim I for Yunus Paşa in the 16th century. It houses some beautiful wood carvings. The local Kültür Evi (Cultural House) offers an opportunity to familiarize yourself with Taraklı handicrafts, particularly the art of making painted wooden spoons, which still plays a big part in town life. Locals also continue to make the wooden bread baskets and trays that you find on sale at service stations.

Fest Travel Archives

HOW TO **TRAVEL?**

Taraklı is 200km from İstanbul, 270km from Ankara and 68 km from Sakarya/Adapazarı. If you are driving, take the Bilecik exit from Sakarya/Adapazarı and follow the Geyve and Taraklı signs.

The last 30 kilometers is particularly beautiful, with plenty of quinçe trees lining the road.

If you are traveling by public transport, take a bus to Sakarya/Adapazarı. There are local buses from Sakarya/Adapazarı to Taraklı.

Bünyad Dinç

WHERE TO **EAT?**

A specialty of the area, "köpük helvası" (bubble halva) is light and delicious. Made entirely of wheat flour, "uhud" is another local delicacy that is sold in the market.

At the town's single restaurant, the Park Lokantası, try the keşkek, a tasty dish made from mutton and coarse ground wheat. A few trout restaurants also dot the road into town.

WHERE TO **STAY?**

There is no accommodation in the town center. If you want to stay overnight, you can stay either at the nearby thermal hotel or in the small town of Göynük, 30 kilometers away.

Göynük Hotel
Phone: (0374) 451 62 78
Restored Ottoman mansion with 11 rooms.

Taraklı Kaplıcaları
Phone: (0264) 494 41 61

Fest Travel Archives

WHAT **TO DO?**

Walk up Hisar Hill to inspect the scant remains of two ancient cisterns.

Visit the Karagöl Valley, 20km away. It is full of picnickers on weekends, so try and come mid-week.

The thermal baths, some 15km away, are supposedly good for curing an assortment of ailments.

Like Taraklı, the small town of Göynük is full of wonderful old Ottoman houses that go unobserved by most visitors. It's 28km from Taraklı.

A FORGOTTEN LAKE,
AN OTTOMAN TOWN

085 Abant and Mudurnu

Fatih TÜRKMENOĞLU

Roughly 300 kilometers from İstanbul, glorious Lake Abant shelters in a national park full of pine trees near Bolu. It's a secluded place where, especially in the middle of the week, you might arrive to find no cars, no sounds and no people... Not far away is picturesque Mudurnu, where stunning Ottoman houses are slowly finding new life as hotels and restaurants.

Spare plenty of time for Abant – it's perfect for unwinding.
Asude Akınlı

Lake Abant Natural Park is enchanting in every way. An ancient crater lake surrounded by fir trees forms the centerpiece of the park where it's possible to stay in five-star luxury right beside the water. The two five-star hotels tend to fill up with conference guests mid-week, so it might be wise to phone ahead and make a reservation.

Abant is beautiful in every season, but perhaps most of all in the fall, when the leaves are changing color.

This is a place to come for complete relaxation. There's not a great deal to do except take long walks around the lake or perhaps rent a horse-drawn carriage to make the same circuit in more romantic style.

Ottoman splendor a short drive away

A mere 25 kilometers from Lake Abant is the sleepy small town of Mudurnu which offers many of the same attractions as Safranbolu but with none of the tourist crowds. A small vine-shaded bazaar still echoes to the sound of copper-beaters and tinsmiths at work, and the nearby Yıldırım Bayezid Hamamı (Turkish bath) dates back to 1374. A river winds through the town center and on its banks stand several stunning old wooden houses, including the Keyvanlar Konağı, now a hotel with a restaurant in its plane-tree-filled garden.

This is a town, like Safranbolu, where you can play at being an Ottoman in an authentically-restored hotel. Perhaps the best place for doing this is Hacı Abdullahlar Konağı, tucked in a side street in the town center and handy for the smaller lokantas (cafes).

A romantic horse-drawn carriage ride around the lake is a great way to appreciate the tranquility.
Asude Akınlı

WHERE TO **STAY?**

Apart from the hotels around the lake, there are many pensions and camp sites along the road.

Petro Club
Phone: (0374) 225 28 70
In a lovely location outside the grounds of the natural park.

Abant Palace & Abant Köşkü
Phone: (0374) 224 50 12
A 12-room boutique hotel supplements the five-star place on the other side of the lake.

Büyük Abant Hotel
Phone: (0374) 224 50 33

Abant Evleri
Phone: (0374) 224 51 78

Hacı Abdullahlar Konağı
Phone: (0374) 421 22 84
Ottoman-style rooms with attractive period décor.

Keyvanlar Konağı
Phone: (0374) 421 37 50
Lovely riverside location.

Yarışkaşı Konağı
Phone: (0374)421 36 04
Imitation Ottoman house on the outskirts of the town with large restaurant.

Değirmenyeri Dağ Evleri
Phone: (0374) 421 26 77
Delightful wooden cottages on a farm in Kilözü village near Mudurnu.

HOW TO **TRAVEL?**

From İstanbul to Bolu is 300km, from Ankara to Bolu is 191km and from Bolu to Abant is another 35 kilometers. If you are not driving, there are infrequent buses from Bolu to the lake and Mudurnu. There is an admission fee for taking a vehicle into the national park.

WHERE TO **EAT?**

An Abant excursion is never complete without trying tomato soup with kaşar cheese, and eating koru kebab or meatballs at Koru Hotel. The yayla soup (yogurt soup flavored with mint) and bread are especially delicious at Abant Köşkü. For fish lovers, several trout restaurants line the Abant road.
Pick up some sucuk (garlic sausage) and bread for the road back.

WHAT TO **BUY?**

At weekends stalls selling all sorts of local foods are set up at the entrance of the national park. Butter, honey and home-made jams are especially inviting. The strawberry jam sold at the Koru Hotel is heavenly.

Bünyad Dinç

WHAT **TO DO?**

Longer horse-drawn carriage tours clip-clop their way round the entire eight kilometers of shoreline; shorter tours manage about half of it.

You can borrow bikes to cycle around the lake from almost all the hotels. Alternatively, you can go mountain biking or trekking; it should take someone, who is fit about an hour to circle the lake on foot.

If you're interested in riding, you can rent a horse in the villages; if you don't feel confident enough to ride alone, a villager will accompany you. You can also rent horses by the hour for a tour around the lake.

There is an area suitable for paragliding four kilometers away from the hotels on the way to Mudurnu. If you have the necessary equipment and the weather conditions are right, you can camp out overnight and then go paragliding in the morning. The hotels should have all the details.

With a car, it might be fun to explore some of the villages on the way to Mudurnu. Çetmi is typical. The small houses made of wood and sun-dried bricks and the small tea-houses are certainly worth a few hours of anyone's time.

AN OFF-THE-BEATEN-TRACK SKI RESORT

086 Kartalkaya

Fatih TÜRKMENOĞLU

Kartalkaya, near Bolu, offers several well-maintained ski slopes and no queues for the lifts. There are no words to describe the spectacular view from the mountainside. You can come here to take advantage of some great walking trails.

If you really enjoy skiing, Kartalkaya will not disappoint you.

Closer to İstanbul than Uludağ, the Kartalkaya (Eagle Rock) ski resort is tucked inside the Köroğlu Mountains National Park at an altitude of 2,000 meters. It has 32 slopes, offering skiing suitable for everyone from complete novices to professionals. You reach the slopes via 19 ski lifts and two chairlifts. The resort makes a great alternative for people who are tired of the Bursa road and the Uludağ crowds.

"It is the song of a night longer than a thousand years,
The sound of snow expected to last for a thousand years."
(Yahya Kemal)

Far from the wild nightlife

In the not too distant past, not even mules made their way up these slopes and when Mazhar Murtezaoğlu, owner of the Kartal and Grand Kartal hotels, decided to tackle the mountain, the villagers thought he was mad. Now Murtezaoğlu is getting the last laugh because Kartalkaya has become one of Turkey's most popular ski resorts, second only to Uludağ.

The road to Kartalkaya is beautiful, and there's no need to wait for the skiing season to start planning a visit.

Kartalkaya has three hotels, one of them operating on an all-inclusive basis. Compared to Uludağ, a visit is relatively cheap which means that young people from all walks of life flock here to try out the snow. There are fewer show-offs and fewer brand names gracing the slopes. Nor is there any wild nightlife. Instead, Kartalkaya feels more in harmony with nature.

Aside from downhill skiing, the resort has facilities for Alpine and cross-country skiing, ski touring and snowboarding. You can hire equipment here and take ski lessons.

)W TO **TRAVEL?**

talkaya is 260 meters from İstanbul, kilometers from kara and 50 kilometers n Bolu; the road signs good. If you're driving, 't set out without tire ins, a wheel brace and a rope.

agers linger by the talkaya road to rent out ins or help you with your 1 – it's a newly invented fession! Tow trucks also t on stand-by.

ou prefer to use public nsport, you can reach the resort by bus or by using hotel shuttle services n Bolu.

WHERE TO **EAT?**

The hotel food is good - in particular, nothing beats the "sucuk-ekmek" (garlic sausage and bread) combo. İsmail'in Yeri is the best place for breakfast. There are several newly-opened restaurants along the road, including the Uçar Meat Restaurant. Afterwards you can sip gluhwein (mulled wine) or sahlep (a hot milk drink flavored with orchid roots) at the café on top of the mountain.

WHERE TO **STAY?**

Grand Kartal Hotel
Phone: (0374) 234 50 50

Kartal Hotel
Phone: (0374) 231 12 80

Dorukkaya Hotel
Phone: 444 52 92
All-inclusive meal arrangements.

WHAT **TO DO?**

If you are staying for a few days, nearby Bolu is a largely modern town with a few attractions, including a small museum and a lively market.

Alternatively, you can visit the lovely Lake Abant or Yedigöller (Seven Lakes, actually a collection of small ponds) national parks which are at their most beautiful in the fall.

Mengen, 58km from Bolu, is famous for its cookery school, where chefs used to be trained to work for the president and other government officials. Most Mengen-trained chefs quickly find work elsewhere (and not just in Turkey either), so actually there are disappointingly few restaurants in the town.

E OTTOMAN PAST REVISITED

afranbolu

Fatih TÜRKMENOĞLU

One of the most beautiful small towns in Turkey, Safranbolu appears on the list of UNESCO World Heritage Sites on account of its extraordinarily well preserved Ottoman townscape. This is a place to come not just to explore the wonderful old wooden houses of a bygone age but also to stay in them and play at being Ottoman for a day.

The beauty of Safranbolu houses is the product of a combination of refined architecture and exquisite taste.

Fatih Türkmenoğlu

Old Safranbolu is a magnificent town split into two separate parts, with the modern town sandwiched between them. The best-known and most immediately picturesque area is Çarşı (Market), the lower town, which nestles in a valley and was where the locals lived in winter. Up above the new town is Bağlar (Orchards) to which they would retreat in summer to take advantage of the cool breezes. Between them, these two areas contain literally hundreds of huge wooden houses, mainly dating back to the 19th century. Not only are these exquisite on the outside, but their interior design was perfectly adapted to a lifestyle that has now virtually disappeared.

Don't forget to remove your shoes, Turkish style, before going into any Safranbolu houses or hotels.

Fixtures and fittings

Several Safranbolu houses are open to the public, offering an opportunity to see the elaborately carved wooden interiors even if you are not staying in one of the Ottoman-style hotels. In Ottoman days, people used a lot less furniture than today. Instead they sat and slept on sedirs, bench seats that ran around the walls, folding up their bedding and storing it in cupboards in the wall during the day. Niches in the wall held all their household belongings. Every Safranbolu house is slightly different but details to look out for include tunnels running behind the storage units in the kitchen so that the scent of passing cats would keep mice at bay; and revolving cupboards that allowed hot food to be moved from one room to another easily.

In most of the houses, the animals lived on the ground-floor, in areas that have often been enclosed to provide living space today. A few houses have huge pools of water right inside the house. They look like swimming pools, but were actually built to cool the houses, and so that fountains could supply the constant tinkle of running water as a soothing backdrop.

Some of the houses also

contain stone "safebox" rooms; when the family moved from Çarşı to Bağlar for the summer, they would store all their valuables, including their corn in these fire-proof rooms for safety. Several hotels have converted these unique safes into bars or lounges.

Even Safranbolu's door knockers are interesting. The ones that give off a resounding thud identified male visitors, whereas those with a gentler timbre let people indoors know that there was a female visitor at the door.

Roaming the streets

When in Safranbolu, the best thing to do is just wander the streets, soaking up the details of the houses and the local life-style. This is one of those rare Turkish towns where you can still find metal-workers and saddle-makers hard at work. The arasta (bazaar) in the town center used to be home to the makers of leather slippers called yemenis. These days it's mainly a souvenir market where you should be able to pick up some attractive textiles. The small café in the arasta is regarded as one of the quaintest in the country, a great place to tuck into a gözleme (pancake) lunch washed down with a small cup of red mulberry syrup.

There are also a few specific monuments to look out for. These include the lovely Cinci Hamamı (Turkish bath; 1645), with separate sections for men and women, and the contemporary Cinci Hanı, a caravanserai which now houses a luxury hotel.

And that name...

Safranbolu took its name from the precious saffron harvested from crocuses that was one of the mainstays of the local economy in Ottoman times.

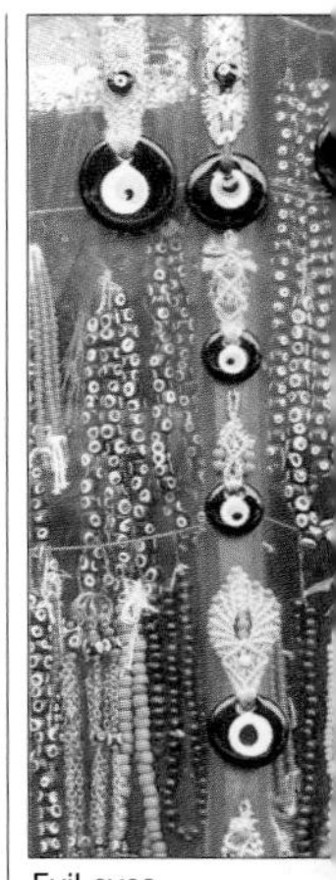

Evil eyes
Nil Yüzbaşıoğlu

)W TO **TRAVEL?**

ranbolu is 400)meters from anbul, 230 kilometers m Ankara and eight)meters from rabük. From the anbul-Ankara hway, take the Gerede t and head towards rabük.

ou prefer to use public nsport, there are quent buses from anbul and Ankara to rabük. Minibuses to ranbolu usually nect with arrivals at rabük. City buses nect Çarşı with Bağlar a regular basis.

/HERE TO **EAT?**

ring Havuzlu Konak
one: (0370) 725 28 83
e garden restaurant kes a very pleasant ce to while away an ening. Spinach nlama (a dish made h vegetable and eggs) d a special noodle up can be provided on quest.

e most famous local dish is the delectable kuyu kebab which is baked in an underground over. Try it at the Çevikköprü Tesisleri in the town center.

Safranbolu is renowned for its sweets which include safranlı zerde, a curious saffron and rice dessert. The yaprak helvası (chewy layers of white helva interspersed with ground walnuts) is delicious, as is the thick home-made baklava.

WHERE TO **STAY?**

Gülevi
Phone: 0-370-7254645
www.canbulat.com.tr
Ottoman style meets hip hotel. By far the most beautifully designed hotel in Safranbolu, its architect-owner has exquisite taste. Foreign visitors may be surprised to find the ground-floor rooms completely modernized although the bedrooms stick with Safranbolu's trademark Ottomania.

Turing Havuzlu Konak
Phone: (0370) 725 28 83
A great place for those who want to wallow in Ottoman nostalgia. You can sip your breakfast coffee around the gorgeous stone pool that graces a ground-floor room. The bedrooms have large brass beds and ottomans.

Selvili Köşk
Phone: (0370) 712 86 46
Bedrooms are a little overstuffed with furniture but there's a gorgeous first-floor lounge in this beautiful hotel.

Cinci Han
Phone: (0370) 712 06 80
Accommodation in a restored 17th-century caravanserai. Most rooms are quite small, although the top-floor Han Ağası Odası is magnificent.

Çeşmeli Konağı
Phone: (0370) 725 4455
One of Safranbolu's smaller and simpler Ottoman-style hotels with some very cozy rooms.

Gökçüoğlu Konağı
Phone: (0370) 712 63 72
Magnificent old mansion over in Bağlar. Everything about it is on a spacious and grand scale, even if the décor sometimes lets it down.

WHAT **TO DO?**

Climb up Hıdırlık Hill for a magnificent view over the town.

Buy Safranbolu-made lokum (Turkish delight) and small wooden models of the local houses as souvenirs.

Visit the Safrantat factory behind the petrol station in Kıranköy (the modern part of town) to see Turkish delight being made.

Tour neighboring Yörükköyü, an extraordinarily beautiful, half-abandoned village of old Ottoman houses with a great local museum.

Take a trip out to the 18th-century aqueduct that spans the Tokatlı Gorge at nearby İncekaya, or to the Bulak Mencilis Mağarası, an impressive cave complex 10km away.

AN ENCHANTING SEASIDE TOWN
088 Amasra

Fatih TÜRKMENOĞLU

Once you finally reach Amasra along the bumpy roads of the Western Black Sea, you will be amazed at the beauty of this town. The beach, the citadel and the sunset are enough to put anyone in the mood for a holiday - and that's before you sit down to a fish supper!

Amasra is the city that Homer called "Sesamus".

Serhan Güngör

Amasra was named after the Persian Princess Amastris and is one of the oldest settlements in Anatolia. In the course of history, the town passed through Pontic, Roman and Genoese hands. Then Sultan Mehmed II the Conqueror seized it in 1460. The largest church was converted into a mosque, and Amasra became one of the most beautiful Ottoman towns.

Not much remains of old Amasra, although the spectacular Kuşkaya (Bird Rock) monument at the entrance of the town dates back to the 1st century BC. You can also visit the remains of the Byzantine citadel astride a promontory with fine views out to sea.

The Amasra Museum contains exhibits from Roman, Byzantine and Ottoman times. The building served as a Marine Academy during the Ottoman period.

The two off-shore islands, Boztepe (Gray Hill) and Tavşan Adası (Rabbit Island), are accessible by boat. Alternatively, you can get to Boztepe by crossing the Kemere Bridge, which was built in Roman times. It's a good road with a wonderful view.

The town of Amasra, which has two islands, two bays and five hills, makes the perfect place for a holiday that combines history with nature.

A seaside film set

Amasra used to be thought of primarily as a summer resort for people from Ankara, but the locals have grown accustomed to an increasing number of visitors ever since their town was used as the set for a Turkish movie. In the summer, and especially on weekends, the hotels are frequently full.

Serhan Güngör

HOW TO **TRAVEL?**

Drive past Bolu, and turn left in the direction of Devrek after Yeniçağa; you reach Amasra via Çaycuma and Bartın.

If you prefer to use public transport, take a bus from İstanbul to Bartın. From the Bartın bus terminal, minibuses will run you the last 17km to Amasra in 20 minutes. The whole trip takes nearly seven hours.

WHERE TO **EAT?**

On weekends, home-made noodles, vegetables and lentils are sold in the market square.
There are several popular fish restaurants in town, including the Mustafa Amca'nın Yeri, Çınar, and Çesm-i Cihan.
Try turbot or red mullet with a large bowl of salad.
To round off your meal order some bananas dipped in honey and nuts and dilute the sweetness with some strong Turkish coffee.

WHERE TO **STAY?**

In high summer, Amasra is still a place, where you can pay for bed and breakfast in a family home. Ask around the harbor if you fancy doing this.

Timur Hotel
Phone: (0378) 315 25 89

Seymen Hotel
Phone: (0378) 315 34 86

Türkili Hotel
Phone: (0378) 315 37 50

Amastris Oteli
Phone: (0378) 315 17 22

WHAT **TO DO?**

Take a boat ride out to Tavşan Adası or along the coast from Büyük Limanı, the main harbor.

Watch the breathtaking sunsets over the harbor.

Shop for wooden plates, spoons and ornaments at the Çekiciler and Kaledibi bazaars.

Climb Boztepe hill for a spectacular view.

If you're staying in Amasra for a few days, Bartın and the lovely old Ottoman town of Safranbolu are short bus rides away.

Coat of arms in the walls of the castle.

Serhan Güngör

THE CITY ASTRIDE THE GREEN RIVER

089 Amasya

Fatih TÜRKMENOĞLU

Amasya is one of Turkey's most beautiful small cities. The Yeşilırmak (Green River) runs right through the center, with fabulous old wooden houses clinging to its banks. Looming above it are the spectacular tombs of the Pontic Kings. Dotted about town are some fine old Ottoman mosques and tombs. It makes a great place for a short break.

Amasya's name regularly crops up in stories about Alexander the Great.

Nil Yüzbaşıoğlu

It is impossible to visit Amasya and not fall in love with it. The riverside promenade and lovely old mansions alone would justify a visit, but this is a town, like Dalyan, where the nobility of old chose to have themselves entombed high above their erstwhile subjects. Today their tombs make a magnificent sight as you walk around town.

The capital of Pontus

Amasya was once a Hittite city. It was conquered by Alexander the Great, but went on to a period of its own greatness under King Mithridates II (r. 256-220 BC), who brought the town to the peak of its glory as the capital of the Pontic Kingdom. It was here that Strabo, one of the world's first geographers, was born in c. 63 BC. After a determined struggle against Mithridates VI (r. 120-63), the city was captured by the Romans and then subsumed into the Byzantine Empire, which left few traces here.

In 1075, Amasya was captured by the Seljuks and became a resting place for armies setting off on military expeditions to Persia. The town is rich in reminders of the Ottomans, who sent their sons here to learn statecraft. In the 19th century, it became an Islamic center with a total of 18 madrasas (seminaries) and more than 2,000 students.

On 12 June 1919, Mustafa Kemal Atatürk held one of the planning meetings that led to the Turkish War of Independence here, an event commemorated by a statue in the main square.

Many of the wonderful, but dilapidated Ottoman houses have recently been brought back to life and some accommodate delightful hotels, pensions and restaurants.

Amasya was called "The City of the Şehzades (Crown Princes)", because it was here that the Ottoman crown princes were readied for government.

Tombs of the kings

High above Amasya sit 18 tombs, which used to house the remains of the 4th-century BC Pontic kings. There are also traces of a Pontic palace reused by the Ottoman governors. One more tomb, the Aynalı Mağarası

(Mirrored Cave), is four kilometers away off the Samsun road. Unlike the others, this tomb bears a Greek inscription on the outside; fast-fading frescoes on the interior suggest that it was reused as a Byzantine church.

Seljuk and Ottoman Amasya

Amasya has a wealth of historic monuments scattered around town. Most date from Ottoman times, although there are a couple of earlier survivors including the Seljuk Gök Medrese Mosque, which was built in 1267, and the magnificent Gümüşlü Mosque, which was built in 1326, when the İlkhan Mongols held sway over Amasya.

The early Ottoman Mehmet Paşa Mosque was commissioned by Lala Mehmet Paşa in 1486. It incorporates a soup kitchen, a hospital, an inn, and a bath-house. The Beyazıt Paşa Mosque was built in 1419, and resembles the Yeşil Cami (Green Mosque) of Bursa. The octagonal Büyük Ağa Medresesi (Seminary) dates back to 1488 and is still in use as a Koranic school.

Most of Amasya's surviving Ottoman houses are in the Hatuniye neighborhood to the north of the river. Here, you will find the Hazeranlar Konağı (Mansion), built in 1865, which is open to the public and set up to show how people would have lived in the town's heyday.

Don't miss the Taş Han (Stone Inn), which dates back to 1758, and the 15th-century Vakıf Bedesten Kapalı Çarşı (Covered Bazaar), the latter still in use today.

Amasya's small museum on Atatürk Street contains some curious clay sarcophagi and a collection of Seljuk mummies, which are not always on show to visitors.

Romeo and Juliet of Amasya

According to a local legend, Ferhat was an artisan who fell in love with Princess Şirin and wanted to marry her. The Queen opposed the marriage, but asked Ferhat to dig through Apple Mountain to create a water channel for the city. Just as he was about to finish this task, he received a message that Şirin had died. Horrified, Ferhat threw his hammer into the air, whereupon it came down on his head and killed him. The story turned out to be a cruel hoax, and when Şirin arrived to find her lover's dead body she threw herself off the mountainside. Surprisingly, two kilometers of a six-kilometer-long early Roman water channel still survive on Ferhat/Apple Mountain.

OW TO **TRAVEL?**

ere are regular buses m Ankara to Amasya. ward connections to ranbolu are trickier hout a car; you will obably need to go via stamonu.

nasya is 130km from msun, 335km from kara and 685km from anbul. The roads are nerally good.

/HERE TO **EAT?**

nasya is famous for its oles; don't leave town hout sampling an apple ssert. Other must-tries lude Çılbır soup ached eggs in a egary soup mixed with yogurt); toyga (a soup made with yogurt, hazelnuts, rice, egg and mint); and stuffed fava beans

WHERE TO **STAY?**

İlk Pansiyon
Phone: (0358) 218 16 89
An old Armenian house from the Ottoman period has been restored with great attention to detail. The bathrooms may be simple, the absence of a radiator disappointing in winter, but the wide windows, ornate ceilings, and low floor beds are impressive. You feel as if you are playing the lead role in an Ottoman play.

Eylül Buğusu
(September Mist)
Phone: (0358) 212 14 05
Lovely small hotel with a courtyard and bar in the back streets of Amasya's historic Hatuniye neighborhood.

Emin Efendi Hotel
Phone: (0358) 212 08 52
Part old, part new hotel.

Haşena Hotel
Phone: (0358) 218 39 79
Another hotel with a mixed identity, part old and part new.
Overlooking the river and Pontic tombs in the Hatuniye neighborhood.

Apple Palace
Phone: (0358) 219 00 19
Hillside four-star hotel with views of the tombs. Shuttle buses ferry clients to and from town.

WHAT **TO DO?**

Brave the stiff hike up to the Pontic citadel for spectacular views of the city.

Visit nearby Kaleköy, where the crumbling citadel, wooden mosque, and bath-house are all interesting. Saraycık village is also worth a quick look, and there is a great trout restaurant in Yassıçal village.

A CITY CALLED "TABLE"

090 Trabzon

Saffet Emre TONGUÇ

At the far eastern end of the Black Sea coast, modern Trabzon is a busy port with an illustrious history; it was here that the remnants of the Byzantine Empire hung on for a last few desperate years after the conquest of İstanbul. Many people come to Trabzon to visit Sumela Monastery, which clings precariously to the hillside nearby. Others come to support one of Turkey's most popular football teams. It's a bustling town, with its eyes firmly fixed on neighboring Russia and the Caucasus.

Sumela Monastery is a monument to human perseverance – just think of the work needed to build it in such a perilous location.
Saffet Emre Tonguç

Trabzon started life as Trapezus (meaning "table" in Greek), a name it acquired because the town appeared from a distance to be sitting on a table of land. The history of the town dates right back to the 8th century BC. It languished under Roman and Byzantine rule and then grew in importance, because of its position on one of the branches of the Silk Road. Its golden age came between the 13th and 15th centuries, when there was a late flowering of Byzantine art and culture here, especially between 1204 and 1461 when a breakaway Byzantine court held sway at the far end of the Black Sea, as far away from Constantinople (İstanbul) as it could get.

Today, Trabzon is one of Turkey's most important cities in terms of trade. Since the collapse of the Soviet Union, its location, close to the border with Georgia and just across the water from Russia and the Ukraine, has ensured that it has acquired a distinct Slavic-Caucasian feel that expresses itself in the presence of Russian food and other goods in the shops and restaurants.

On the trail of the past

One of the first things that will strike visitors is the town's dynamism, which somehow manages to coexist with the traditional demeanor of the salesmen in the bazaar. It's in

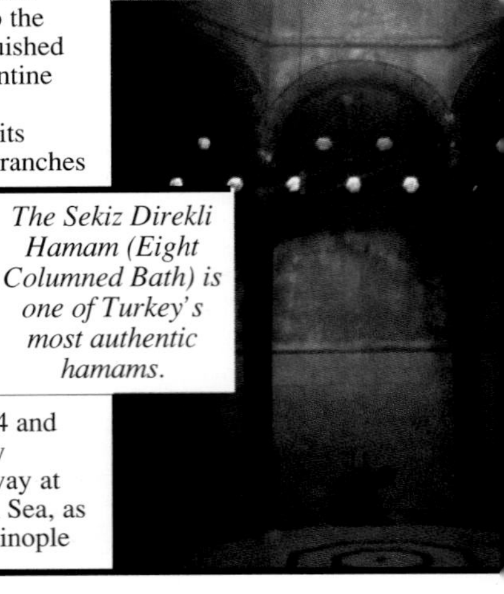

The Sekiz Direkli Hamam (Eight Columned Bath) is one of Turkey's most authentic hamams.

A fresco in Sumela Monastery that has stood the test of time.

Saffet Emre Tonguç

the bazaar that you will find some of the town's most interesting sights: the allegedly Seljuk Sekiz Direkli Hamamı (Eight Columned Bath); the Çarşı Camii, Trabzon's largest mosque; and the Bedesten (covered bazaar) inside a structure built by the Genoese in the 14th century. Here, a few jewelers still make the unique, hand-woven gold and silver Trabzon necklaces.

Elsewhere in town, the 9th-century Byzantine church of St Anne (Küçük Ayvasıl) and the early 20th-century Kostaki Konağı (Mansion), once the home of a Russian merchant of Greek descent and now a museum, are also worth a look. Across the Tabakhane Creek stand the 13th-century Yeni Cuma Camii (Mosque), which was once the Church of St Eugenius, the patron saint of Trabzon; the huge Fatih Camii which started life as the 10th-century Panagia Chrysocephalos ("Our Lady of the Golden Head") cathedral; and the Fatih Hamamı (Bath). In this part of town, a section of the old city walls still survives as silent witness to the splendor of the past.

The Atatürk Köşkü (Villa), built for a local banker between 1890 and 1903 and later used as a temporary home by Mustafa Kemal Atatürk, is set high on the hills, and contains reminders of the Turkish War of Independence and the ensuing years of revolution. Even further uphill, near a military compound, stand the remains of the 15th-century Kaymaklı Monastery, its walls covered with 17th-century frescoes. Unfortunately, the church is being used as a barn, so the priceless paintings are probably doomed.

Another Hagia Sophia

One of Trabzon's finest monuments is the 13th-century

WHAT WAS PONTUS?

The Ancient Greeks originally called the Black Sea the Axeinos Pontus ("the Inhospitable Sea"), then changed it to Euxeinos Pontus ("the Hospitable Sea").

Consequently, this part of the coast has often been called the Pontic coast, a name which passed first to the Pontic Kingdom, based around Amasya and then to a second Pontic Kingdom, which was created after the Crusaders expelled the Byzantine Emperor from Constantinople in 1204. Alexios Comnenus then set up a breakaway Byzantine state around what was called Trebizond at the far end of the Black/Pontic Sea. This statelet survived until 1461, when the Ottomans finally seized it.

Pontic Greeks continued to live here until the 1923 population exchange, and even today there are a few people still speaking a form of Greek in some of the remote Black Sea valleys.

Used as a mosque for centuries, the Church of Hagia Sophia became a museum in 1964. It is one of Trabzon's most precious treasures, and the frescoes covering the inside walls are among the finest examples of later Byzantine art.

Saffet Emre Tonguç

Atatürk's Villa
Asude Akınlı

church of Hagia Sophia, which stands on a headland overlooking Trabzon harbor; there are images of ships scratched into the exterior walls. The church has a detached bell-tower, but is best known for its beautifully-restored 13th-century frescoes which cover the walls and ceilings. In its grounds stands a serender, a very typically Black Sea-style of raised wooden granary.

Boztepe is an ideal spot to watch the city and the Black Sea at sunset.

The monastery clinging to the cliff

Most people come to Trabzon to visit Sumela Monastery, which clings to a cliff-face 46km south of town (Sumela means literally "Virgin Mary of the Black Mountain"). Recently restored in part, the monastery perches like an eagle's nest above the Altındere creek. Its walls are still covered in frescoed Bible stories, although these have suffered badly from vandalism over the years.

Joking in two languages

Greeks call the people who migrated from the Black Sea "Pontii", after Pontus, the name they gave to the Black Sea. Just as the Turks make unkind jokes about people from the Black Sea, so the Greeks make unkind jokes about the Pontii, just with the names of the main characters changed. So in the Greek version the Turkish Temel and İdris become Yiorikas (George) and Kostikas (Constantine) and Fadime is changed into Simela. Unfortunately, in both cases the point of the jokes is the same – to make the locals look stupid!

The pink Colchis flower that you can see in Uzungöl gave its name to Georgia. Jason and the Argonauts went to Colchis in search of the Golden Fleece.

© Saffet Emre Tonguç

HOW TO **TRAVEL?**

Since Trabzon is so remote, the best way to get there from the big cities is to fly. For Sumela Monastery and Uzungöl, you need to drive towards Rize and look for signs.

The entrance to Sumela Monastery is about 20 minutes from Maçka village. From there a steep path zig-zags up to the monastery, which looms over it at 1300 meters above sea level. If you are not up for the hike, you can always take the shuttle.

WHAT **TO DO?**

Not far from Trabzon is Uzungöl (Long Lake), where a beautiful expanse of water glitters amid the pine trees.

Some people will think there has been too much development in such a rustic spot. However, it's a great place to come for a walk or a picnic.

WHERE TO **EAT?**

Galanima Restaurant
Phone: (0462) 248 71 27
www.galanima.com
Ten kilometers from Trabzon and three kilometers from Akçaabat, this restaurant is located in a 130-year-old "konak" (mansion). The fish and meatballs are excellent.

Coşandere Turistik Tesisleri
Phone: (0462) 321 27 47
www.cosandere.com
Five kilometers from Sumela, the establishment is in a hotel. The local dishes and trout are very good. Sports facilities are available.

Sümela Restaurant
Phone: (0462) 531 12 07
Serves local dishes such as "kuymak", "kaygana", cabbage soup, and fresh trout.

Altındere Restaurant
Phone: (0462) 531 11 87

Yayla Lokantası, Hamsiköy
Phone: (0462) 542 62 78
Try the baked beans and meatballs with the sütlaç (rice pudding) to follow.

WHERE TO **STAY?**

Zorlu Grand Hotel
Phone: (0462) 326 84 00
www.zorlugrand.com
The only five-star hotel in town, it's in a very central location and has an indoor pool and top-floor gym. The restaurant serves some delicious local dishes.

İnan Hotel
Phone: (0462) 656 60 21
This Uzungöl hotel makes a great escape from the city. Even if you don't stay, it's still worth eating at the restaurant - absolutely the best near the lake.

Hotel Büyük Sümela,
Phone: (0462) 512 35 40
www.sumelaotel.com
This hotel is in Maçka, 25 kilometers from Trabzon and 13 kilometers from Sumela Monastery.

Usta Park Hotel
Phone: (0462) 326 57 00
Located in Trabzon town center.

5 MUST-SEE PLACES
IN THE EASTERN ANATOLIA REGION

THE EASTERN ANATOLIA REGION

THE TOWN ON THE SHORES OF TURKEY'S LARGEST LAKE

091 Van

Saffet Emre TONGUÇ

A white cat with mismatched eyes, a rock-cut citadel, and a lake big enough to be called a sea are just a few of the wonders to be found in the former Urartian capital of Van in remote Eastern Turkey. Van also makes a good base for exploring the surrounding area where you'll find a lovely medieval church alone on an island, an impressive waterfall, and a castle straight out of a fairy tale.

A tea-house in Van

Saffet Emre Tonguç

Turkey's largest lake, Lake Van, sprawls over an area of 3,750 square kilometers. It's a beautiful and mesmerizing place that retreats into silence once the sun goes down. On its shores stands the modern town of Van, which was probably founded by the Assyrian queen Semiramis, nearly 4,000 years ago.

Covering 3,750 square kilometers and with a depth of 451 meters, Lake Van is the world's largest saline lake.

The mosaic of civilizations that has created Turkey is very colorful. Wherever you go, you come across yet another all-but-forgotten civilization, or even several different civilizations piled on top of one another. Van is typical of these palimpsest locations, having played host to a wide range of ancient civilizations, from the Hurris to the Urartians, and from Alexander the Great to the Romans. The Urartians called Van, Tuşba, and made it their capital in 832 BC. Otherwise, very little is known about them, although they carved long cuneiform inscriptions into the walls of Van Castle.

In recent years, Van has had to cope with considerable migration from the surrounding countryside. It has also been enlivened by the creation of Yüzüncü Yıl University. If you arrive here by boat from Tatvan to the west, you will be amazed by the size of the modern city. The newer

Mahmudi was so thrilled with Hoşap Castle that he had the architect's hands cut off to ensure that he would never be able to build another one like it.

Kenan Tamer

suburbs are almost four kilometers further inland than the old lakeside town.

Right at the heart of Van, Cumhuriyet Caddesi serves an "all roads lead to Rome" function. From hotels to breakfast shops, from the museum to the main market, it all seems to be happening along Cumhuriyet Caddesi.

Van, Çavuştepe and Hoşap castles

If you are interested in history and archeology, you must visit Van Castle, which sits astride a hill with a wonderful view on the western outskirts of town. Built by the Urartian King Sardur I in 840 BC, the castle has reminders of all the various people, who have made use of it, including the Armenians and the Ottomans. As the sun sets, this is a magical place to come.

If you drive 28 kilometers south of Van, you will find the ruins of an Urartian palace at Çavuştepe. Several thousand-year-old barley depots, still with the remains of the barley inside them, several water channels, not to mention one of the world's oldest squat toilets, also survive to bear witness to the refinement of ancient Urartian civilization. Try and track down the sharp-witted Mehmet Kuşman, who kept guard here for years. Having spent lots of time with archaeologists, Kuşman eventually deciphered the Urartian alphabet and can read the ancient inscriptions fluently – one of the very few people in the world who can! Perhaps he's looking for clues to the ancestors he carries in his DNA.

On the northern shore of Lake Van, Ahlat boasts one of Turkey's most interesting cemeteries.

If you head out from Çavuştepe towards Hakkari, you will come to Hoşap Castle (Güzelsu Kalesi in Turkish), 55 kilometers away from Van. Commissioned by Sarı Süleyman Mahmudi in 1643, this castle resembles the serrated back of a dragon when viewed from a distance. Walking through the gateway, which is adorned with lion figures and a Persian inscription, you find yourself in a fairy-tale castle straight out of the mystical Orient. Hoşap Castle was once full of chambers, mosques, baths, fountains, dungeons and cisterns, now all in ruins. It will probably come as a complete surprise to you, but

The Church of the Holy Cross on Akdamar Island was nearly demolished in 1951. Renowned author Yaşar Kemal, a journalist at the time, was instrumental in getting it preserved.

Saffet Emre Tonguç

The Armenian Church on Akdamar Island was reopened to visitors in 2007 after thorough restoration.

Saffet Emre Tonguç

Ahlat Cemetery

Şemsi Güner

Detail of carving on the wall of the Church of the Holy Cross, Akdamar Island

this is one of the most wonderful aspects of traveling in Eastern Anatolia - that you can traverse the vast, empty terrain for kilometers and then stumble on something completely unexpected.

Akdamar Island and the Church of the Holy Cross

After leaving Van, you can head north towards the beautiful Muradiye Waterfall and then to Doğubayazıt, or west to Akdamar Island, to see a masterpiece of Armenian architecture. If you opt for Akdamar, don't be in too much of a rush – it's well worth pausing near the small jetty where boats wait to carry you to the island to enjoy a meal of pearl mullet cooked fresh from the lake.

Built for the Vaspurakan king Gagik I in around 920, the domed Church of the Holy Cross on Akdamar Island boasts beautiful bas-reliefs on its exterior walls. Look, in particular, for depictions of the Biblical stories of Noah's Ark, Adam and Eve, David and Goliath, and Jonah and the whale.

On your way back, ponder the story of the young man who swam across the lake from Gevaş to Akdamar every night to visit the beautiful young Tamara. Her father found out about this secret affair and changed the position of the light guiding the young man, thereby causing him to drown on a stormy night. The last words the young man muttered gave the island its name - "Ah, Tamara." A similar tale is told about the Dardanelles, only with Tamara's name changed to Hero. In times gone by, travelers passing the night at the Silk Road caravanserais would sit and swap tales; the names would be different but the stories were always the same. That is how the other Turkish tales like Kerem and Aslı, and Leyla and Mecnun emerged. Times may change, but romantic stories never do.

Akdamar Island from a distance

Saffet Emre Tonguç

Muradiye Waterfall

HOW TO **TRAVEL?**

There are daily flights to Van as well as bus services from all major towns. You can reach Akdamar Island by boat in 10 minutes. The jetty is 45 kilometers from Van.

WHERE TO **STAY?**

In Van, the stars shown on hotel signs may not always accurately represent what you'll find inside. For instance, **Grand Çağ Hotel** only has two stars, but it is far nicer than many of the four-star places. The rooms offer many perks, from Internet access to air-conditioning and 600-channel satellite TV.
Phone: (0432) 214 57 13
www.grandcag.com.tr

Büyük Urartu Hotel
Phone: (0432) 212 06 60
www.buyukurartuotel.com
Centrally located, with wild weddings on the roof in summer.

Büyük Asur Hoteli
Phone: (0432) 216 87 92
Efficiently managed. A popular hotel right in the town center.

Şahmaran Hotel
Phone: (0432) 312 30 60
On the shores of Lake Van, quite far from the city center.

Tuşba Hotel
Phone: (0432) 312 29 66
www.tusbaotel.com
The hotel offers a view of the lake, which the locals refer to as the "sea". In summer, you can jump straight into the water from the hotel's pier.

WHERE TO **EAT?**

Start the day with a hearty Van breakfast. Among the better places to do this are the Sütçü Feyzi Erol Kardeşler and Konak Kahvaltı Salonları (breakfast cafes) in the bazaar. A plate piled hight with kaymak (heavy/double cream), butter, Van honey, otlu peynir (a whole-milk cheese flavored with herbs) and a big hunk of freshly baked bread is the key to starting the day with a smile on your face. You can also buy otlu peynir, which contains herbs like thyme and wild garlic in the bazaar.
To buy honey, try Balcı Behçet, who delivers all over Turkey (Phone: (0432) 216 28 58, www.balcibehcet.com).

Besse Restaurant
Phone: (0432) 215 00 50
A comparatively elegant restaurant where meat dishes dominate the menu. Also serves trout and fresh pearl mullet. On a road parallel to Cumhuriyet Caddesi.

Anzaf Et Lokantası (Meat Restaurant)
Phone: (0432) 217 57 67
Delicious dishes on the table and Lake Van in the background. Taking its name from an ancient Urartian citadel, this restaurant is on the way to Gevaş. As so often in Van, no alcohol is served.

Merkez Et Lokantası
Phone: (0432) 216 97 01
Specializes in delicious kebabs.

WHAT **TO DO?**

Van Museum has some magnificent items on display. As you trace a historical journey that started around 9,000 BC, be sure to note the rare tombstones from Hakkari.

Pay a visit to Van University's Cat House to see the white Van cats, which are supposedly able to swim. Although they are famous for their mismatched eyes (one blue and one yellow), in some cases they have two blue eyes.

If you're interested in jewelry, keep an eye out for tula-work pieces with Urartian motifs that are made out of silver alloy. Atasoy Gümüş (Maraş Caddesi No 8; Phone: (0432) 216 12 34) is one of the best places to start looking.

Opposite Atasoy Gümüş is Saçı Beyaz, a lovely café where you can sit and watch local life drifting by. If you're after something more authentic, take a seat at one of the tea-houses with a sign reading in the window "Kaçak çay bulunur" (Smuggled tea available). Knowing that you're from out of town, the locals will be eager to offer you tea and kick off a conversation with "So, where do you come from, my brother?"

Driving from Tatvan to Bitlis, it's worth ascending the 'other' Mt Nemrut at the western end of Lake Van to see the spectacular crater lakes on its summit.

IS THIS WHERE 1001 NIGHTS BEGAN?

092 Doğubayazıt

Saffet Emre TONGUÇ

The first page of Bruce Feiler's New York Times best-seller, *Walking the Bible*, opens in Doğubayazıt, as does the first part of the Bible which tells the story of the Great Flood. For millions of people worldwide, Doğubayazıt will always be the town in the shadow of Mt Ararat, where Noah's Ark is believed to have come to rest. However, it is also home to the wonderful İshak Paşa Palace which stands on a hill just outside town.

Saffet Emre Tonguç

Just 35 kilometers from the Iranian border, Doğubayazıt stands near the foot of soaring Mt Ararat (5137m), where Noah's Ark is said to have come to rest after the Biblical flood. Supposedly there have been six other floods since that first one; the seventh is expected to herald the Apocalypse.

Doğubayazıt took its name from Sultan Bayazid of the Mongolian Jalayir tribe. "Doğu", meaning "east", was added later to avoid confusion in the mail. Although the town earns its living from agriculture, livestock husbandry and tourism, it is always full of trucks on their way to or from Iran. There are many shopping arcades which sell cheap imported alcohol and cigarettes, as well as electronic appliances and tea. Although they sell every conceivable household item, from porcelain to trinkets, and from thermos flasks to tablecloths, they also sell far too many of the sort of knick-knacks that you buy on a whim and then put away and never look at again.

The streets of Doğubayazıt are full of color and surprise.

The people of Eastern Turkey are very warm; everyone you talk to will offer you tea to sip in kıtlama style (a tooth-rotting way of drinking it which involves putting the sugar cube in your mouth and then sipping the tea so that it sweetens in the mouth).

Most of the locals complain that the town's tourist potential is not being properly exploited.

Refik Ongan

İSHAK PAŞA SARAYI

One of the most distinctive examples of 18th-century Ottoman architecture, the impressive İshak Paşa Sarayı (Palace) stands dramatically on a hillside, seven kilometers to the east of Doğubayazıt. Reminiscent of the palaces in the book of *One Thousand and One Nights*, the sprawling structure, which covers 7,600 square meters, is an amalgam of Seljuk, Ottoman, Georgian, Persian, and Armenian building styles. Construction was initiated in 1685 by Çolak Abdi Paşa and completed by his son İshak Paşa in 1784. A gold-plated portal that used to provide access to the palace's first courtyard was removed by the Russians – who invaded Doğubayazıt three times - and taken to the Hermitage Museum in St. Petersburg. Right beside the portal stood a fountain intended to offer refreshment to tired and thirsty visitors.

Access to the second courtyard, with its haremlik (women's quarters) and selamlık (men's quarters), was only granted to family members and special guests. The harem had a magnificent entrance and consisted of a kitchen, a hamam and numerous living rooms. Pipes visible in the ground were used for heating, sewage and water – all very progressive for their time! The most outstanding section of the harem was the ornate dining-room, which was decorated with stone flowers and elaborately carved columns. The selamlık consisted of a library, mosque and audience rooms. A structure which resembles a Seljuk kümbet (tomb topped by a dome) contains the remains of Çolak Abdi Paşa and his relatives.

The legendary love story of Kerem and Aslı is thought to have taken place in the Keşiş' in Bağı (Monk's Vineyard) on the way to the İshak Paşa Sarayı.

The Palace makes a great place to watch the sunset.

Just past the palace complex are a mosque and citadel that are believed to date back to the Urartian period.

The impressive İshak Paşa Sarayı resembles a palace straight out of the book of *One Thousand and One Nights.*

Saffet Emre Tonguç

The tomb of Ahmed-i Hani, the 17th-century philosopher and author of Mem-u Zin, is near İshak Paşa Sarayı.

Aydın Kudu

HOW TO **TRAVEL?**

Doğubayazıt is 51 kilometers from Iğdır, 95 from Ağrı, 285 from Erzurum and 1,210 from Ankara.

If you are driving from Doğubayazıt to Van, stop at the hill after half an hour to catch a beautiful view of Mt Ararat. Shortly afterwards you will drive through Çaldıran, where the Ottoman emperor Yavuz Sultan Selim defeated the Persians in 1514, and come to the Muradiye Waterfall. If you are heading from Kars to Doğubayazıt, you will pass through Iğdır after 138 kilometers. About an hour after you leave Kars, the road starts to follow the Armenian border and the Arpaçayı River turns into the Aras.

Night falls at least an hour earlier in Eastern than Western Anatolia, a fact to bear in mind when planning your trip.

WHERE TO **EAT?**

Doğuş Restaurant
Phone: (0472) 312 73 48
The best local restaurant, the Doğuş has a wide menu, with everything from soup-like dishes called "aşçı yemeği" (chef's dish) to lahmacun and kebabs. Dağ kebabı is a specialty.

Evin Restaurant
Phone: (0472) 312 60 73
Mostly serves kebabs, pizza and pide but also some soups and trout.

Gaziantep Sofrası
Phone: (0472) 312 07 02
Rotisserie chicken, grilled steak, and tripe and other kinds of soup.

WHAT **TO DO?**

Special permission is needed to climb Mt Ararat, which was closed to tourists for many years. If you are interested in climbing, get in touch with Buklamania Outdoor Sports who will obtain the necessary permits in advance.
Phone: (0212) 245 06 35, www.bukla.com.
Alternatively, contact Middle Earth Travel in Göreme in Cappadocia.
Phone: (0384) 271 25 59, www.middleearthtravel.com.

WHERE TO **STAY?**

In the past, terrorism has put an end to several attempts to revive local tourism. You should not, therefore, expect too much of the hotels.

Golden Hill Hotel
Phone: (0472) 312 87 17
This four-star hotel has 90 rooms, and is the newest and by far the best in the area. Some rooms offer mountain views but service tends to the amateurish.

Sim-er Hotel
Phone: (0472) 312 48 42
www.simerhotel.com
Far from the town center but close to the Iranian border, the hotel offers a lovely view of Mt Ararat.

Nuh Hotel
Phone: (0472) 312 72 32
www.hotel.nuh.8m.com
65 clean rooms in the town center. While dining at the roof-top restaurant, you can see Mt Ararat.

Derya Hotel
Phone: (0472) 312 75 31
Central location and 60 rooms, most with balconies.

093 Noah's Ark and Mt Ararat

Saffet Emre TONGUÇ

With its snowy peak smiling down on every corner of Doğubayazıt, Mt Ararat takes pride in being Turkey's highest mountain. A site so dramatic and conspicuous cou hardly fail to attract more than its fair share of stories, but far and away the most famous is that of Noah's Ark, which is said to have come to rest here after the Great Flood. Ararat stands a mere 16 kilometers away from the Armeni border. Not surprisingly, the Armenians also regard it with particular reverence.

The view of Mt Ararat from Iğdır.

Known as Koh-i Nuh (Noah's Mountain) to the Persians and Ararat to Westerners, Mt Ağrı (Mountain of Pain; 5,165m) is an extinct volcano, which is thought to have erupted for the last time nearly 10,000 years ago. Above 4,200 meters, it is dotted with beautiful glaciers. To the south-east stands Küçük Ağrı (Little Ararat, 3,896m); together the two mountains cover approximately 1,200 square kilometers of land. After the Great Flood, the Ark of the Prophet Noah, who had stocked it with a pair of each species of animal, is thought to have come to rest on Ararat. It is a story typical of Turkey, which is very rich in Biblical sites. Some sources claim, for example, that Adam and Eve's Garden of Eden was in the Aras Valley, to the north of Mt Ararat.

Such stories have always intrigued people who yearn to test their veracity. Some trace the original link between

© Saffet Emre Tonguç

Ararat and the Ark to the first-century historian Josephus, who wrote that the Ark had run aground on the mountain. Later, St Jacob is said to have begged God to show him the Ark. He then fell asleep on the mountain and awoke to find himself holding a piece of wood from the boat. Two Persian princes arrived in 1887 and claimed that they had seen the Ark's bow and stern, and that the mid-section was buried in snow. After two Russian pilots said that they had caught an aerial glimpse of the boat in 1916, Czar Nicholas sent nearly 150 men to photograph it. During the Bolshevik Revolution, which brought about the demise of the Czar and his family, the photographs were presumably lost, but rumors continued to circulate that the Czar's daughter Anastasia wore a cross made out of wood from the Ark around her neck. On their way to the Iranian Shah's New Year Party in 1977, the press claimed that former US President Jimmy Carter and his entourage had seen the vessel, and in 1989, CNN released a series of photographs taken by a pilot from Chicago who believed that they showed Noah's Ark. James Irwin, one of the first men to land on the moon, climbed Mt Ararat countless times in an attempt to find the Ark. However, Ararat still maintains its air of secrecy and beckons new adventurers.

While in Doğubayazıt, you should also visit a huge crater carved out by a meteor near the Iranian border, as well as a strange-shaped piece of earth, which is supposed to be part of the Ark.

Ararat, the Western name for Mt Ağrı, is the name used to refer to the land of Urartu in the Talmud.

Aydın Kudu

Aydın Kudu

GET READY FOR COLD WINTERS

094 Erzurum

Fatih TÜRKMENOĞLU

My mother grew up in Erzurum and my father-in-law spent his childhood there. They often reminisce about the open-minded Erzurum natives of old, about the snowed-in roads of winter, and about the tea always brewing on the samovar. When I finally visited Erzurum, I found a large modern city with a thriving university to go alongside its many historic monuments.

Fountain in the town center.
Saffet Emre Tonguç

With so much family history tied up with Erzurum, our house is never short of tel peynir (string cheese) and kıtlama sugar waiting to be softened with tea. Nor would any family gathering be complete without the singing of the folk song "Sarı Gelin". Although the exact lyrics would be meaningless in translation, suffice to say that the song is about a venerated bride-to-be and about Erzurum.

Ancient history

Erzurum's history dates back to around 4,000 BC and it has had many different occupiers. After the Hurrians, Urartians, Scythians, Medes, Persians, Sassanids, and Romans, the town was governed by the Byzantines, who called it Theodosiopolis, and then by the Arabs.

Following the Turkish conquest of Anatolia after the Battle of Malazgirt (Manzikert) in 1071, the town was given to Saltuk Bey, leader of the Saltukoğulları emirate, who made it his capital. Later, in the Seljuk and Ilkhanate periods, beautiful new buildings bestowed an architectural distinction on the town.
It became a part of the Ottoman Empire in the 16th century, during the reign of Yavuz Sultan Selim.

Erzurum today

There are countless sights to see in Erzurum. The best place to start is the citadel where you can climb up on the walls to get a bird's eye view over the Çifte Minareler and out to Palandöken. Work on the citadel is thought to have been started by the Byzantines in the 5th century. Don't miss the interesting old tower that contains a clock given to the Ottomans by Queen Victoria of England in 1877.

The 14th-century Yakutiye Medresesi is one of the last examples of a medrese

WHAT IS A DADAŞ?

According to various sources, a "dadaş" is a chivalrous, brave, straightforward, compassionate, honest young man who is true to his word. He is also an exemplary Erzurum gentleman - a noble soul.

Twin Minaret Seminary
Saffet Emre Tonguç

(seminary) with a closed courtyard; it currently houses the Museum of Turkish-Islamic Arts and Ethnography. The 16th-century Lala Mustafa Paşa mosque next to the museum is also worth a look.

During the construction of the 13th-century Çifte Minareli Medrese (Twin Minaret Seminary), stones were brought all the way from Khorasan in Persia. The tilework on both the Çifte Minareler and the Yakutiye Medresesi is breathtaking. Immediately behind the Çifte Minareli Medrese stand the Üç Kümbetler (Three Tombs), one bearing animal motifs that look like those on Chinese calendars.

The 12th-century Ulu Cami (Mosque) is said to have three separate mihrabs (niches indicating the direction of Mecca) because the Sultan wished to please all three madhabs (traditions of Islamic jurisprudence) at the same time.

The building in which the Erzurum Congress was held in 1919 now hosts the Atatürk Museum.

Skiing in Palandöken, rafting on the Çoruh

Although it may have been a burden in the past, today snow provides Erzurum with an important source of income. The nearby Palandöken ski resort, where the 2011 World Universiade Ski Olympics will be held, is very popular because the season runs for almost six months (from November to May), the snow is powdery, and the slopes are only 20 minutes from the town center. The 30 slopes cover 28 kilometers, and include some of the longest and steepest ski runs in the world; indeed, some people argue that Palandöken has the best natural ski runs in Europe. There are two separate runs for slalom and grand slalom, and nine ski lifts to carry enthusiasts to the top. It's a fantastic experience to ride up in the dragon ski lift and then enjoy some wine with “sucuk-ekmek” (garlic sausage and bread). A live feed from Palandöken (3185m) on the official website of the Erzurum Governor's office let's you check the snow conditions before setting out.

Not enough of a thrill for you? Then you can also head north from Erzurum to go white-water rafting on the River Çoruh, near Yusufeli. Although the river is threatened by dam-building projects, for the time being it is still possible to enjoy it, especially in May and June, before the summer heat gets into its stride.

Kids in front of Yakutiye Seminary

Saffet Emre Tonguç

HOW TO **TRAVEL?**

Erzurum is 880km from Ankara, 1,230km from İstanbul and 1,460km from Izmir. The İstanbul-Erzurum flight takes approximately 2 hours. You can also reach Erzurum after a long, slow train ride from Ankara or İstanbul. Erzurum airport is 15 kilometers from the Palendöken ski resort.

WHERE TO **STAY?**

Both the Polat Renaissance and Dedeman hotels have indoor swimming pools. The first has 224 rooms, while the latter has 186 rooms and 12 suites.

Ski Resort Dedeman
Phone: (0442) 316 24 14
www.dedemanhotels.com

Polat Renaissance
Phone: (0442) 232 00 10
www.polatrenaissance.com

Palan Hotel
Phone: (0442) 317 07 07

Kardelen Hotel
Phone: (0442) 316 68 51

Hotel standards in Erzurum town center are generally lower than those in Western Turkey.
You can try
Kral (Phone: (0442) 234 64 00) or Oral (Phone: (0442) 235 25 00).

WHAT **TO DO?**

The local Turkish baths are beautiful. Try the Kırk Çeşme (40 Fountains) and Erzurum hamams.

The Rüstem Paşa Hanı was built in 1561 and is also known as Taşhan. The little shops inside it sell jewelry made from a semi-precious stone called oltu taşı, a form of jet which is extensively mined around Erzurum.

Drive north from Erzurum towards Yusufeli, stopping off along the way to inspect the all-but-forgotten medieval churches of the so-called Georgian Valley. The best are at İşhan, Öşkvank and Bağbaşı (Haho).

WHERE TO **EAT?**

Emirşeyh Kebap Lokantası
Phone: (0442) 214 15 44
Try the meatballs, the yatık döner (horizontal döner) and beş beyaz (five whites) salad. The five "whites" of the salad are yogurt, mushrooms, egg whites, salt, and garlic. I'm not sure how they come up with that incredible taste!

Gel-Gör and **Koç Kebap** are the two best-known kebab restaurants. The secret of the local cağ kebab lies in marinating the meat with yogurt, salt, black pepper, and onions and then wrapping it in a thin, pitta-like bread called lavaş before eating it. "Cağ" is the name of the horizontal rotating spit. From a distance, it looks as if a regular döner spit has been turned on its side. Koç Kebap doubles up as a library. The owner is the author of books of poetry and aphorism.

Süreyya Hanım'ın Yemekçi'si in the Pelit Meydanı (Square) is superb. The kesme çorba (soup) and ekşili yaprak sarma (sour olive wraps) are to die for.
If you spot eşkin or çaşır on sale at a grocer's or street vendor's, buy some straightaway. After boiling them, you can eat either with olive oil and lemon juice.
You must try the kadayıf dolması (AKA the Viagra of the "Dadaş") for dessert. Look for **Muammer Usta**'s place.

At the **Hemşin Pastanesi** (patisserie) on Kuloğlu Street there are poems plastered on the walls and people drop by to play the saz. The su böreği (flaky pastry), künefe (shredded pastry stuffed with cheese) and sütlaç (rice pudding) are all wonderful, as is the breakfast. No carbonated drinks are permitted here - only fruit juice, milk, and fresh tea.

Güzelyurt Lokantası
Phone: (0442) 234 50 01
This immaculate restaurant, owned by a man from Çamlıhemşin, has been dishing up home-cooked meals and alcohol from opposite the Yakutiye Medrese since 1928.

Erzurum Evleri (Houses)
Phone: (0442) 213 83 72
In this complex of eight old houses decorated with authentic furniture you can enjoy typical Erzurum dishes. Be sure to remove your shoes before entering.

"SNOW" AND... 095 Kars

Saffet Emre TONGUÇ

Providing the background for Nobel prize-winning author Orhan Pamuk's novel *Kar (Snow)*, Kars is renowned for its heavy winter snowfall which makes the city look like a blushing bride in her wedding gown, or so the romantics say. In any case, Kars certainly looks most unlike the other cities of Eastern Anatolia; there is something more aristocratic, more noble about this town, perhaps because the solid stone buildings left behind from a short period of Russian occupation in the 19th century are so elegant.

The financial office in Kars is located in an old Russian building.

📷 **Saffet Emre Tonguç**

Kars is a town that reeks of the power it held in the past. Although it was under Russian occupation from 1878 to 1918, it's a place that has always managed to hold its head up high. With its wide streets laid out in a grid pattern and its elegant stone buildings, it can look particularly attractive on a sunny winter's day. Although there are plenty of specific attractions, perhaps the best thing to do here is to just stand and breathe in the scent of history emanating from the buildings.

Whenever I visit Kars, I start by climbing up to the citadel, which was built to dominate the city from above. Then I visit the tomb of Celal Baba, a mythical 14th-century hero who allegedly stuck his head under his arm and went back to war after being beheaded. It stands near the entrance to the citadel, and has been destroyed and rebuilt countless times following invasions.

Next, I inspect the 10th-century Church of the Holy Apostles, which carries bas-reliefs of the 12 apostles on its dome and was renamed the Kümbet (Rotunda) after it was converted into a mosque in 1579. As I cross the Taş Köprü (Stone Bridge) built over the Kars Creek by Sultan Murat III, I glance at Namık Kemal's house. Namık Kemal (1840-88) was a famous poet, who lived in Kars and developed ideas for

Declared the capital of the Armenian state in 961, Ani is thought to have had a population of close to 100,000 in the early 11th century.

An old Russian house

hen the
menian Church
the Holy
ostles in Kars
is converted into
mosque, it was
named the
mbet (Rotunda).

ffet Emre
nguç

The Ebul Menuçehr Cami is thought to have been the first Seljuk mosque built in Anatolia.

Saffet Emre Tonguç

modernizing the country that were to influence Atatürk. He died in exile on the Greek island of Chios.

Then I explore the museum, which has a beautiful collection of archaeological finds and a rich ethnographic section. Finally I turn my attention back to the houses with their thick greystone walls and occasional gardens. The Governor's Mansion, the Defterdarlık Building (the Finance Office), the Belediye building (Municipality/Town Hall) and the train station all survive from the period of the Russian occupation. The old Russian Orthodox Church, now the Fethiye Mosque, is by far the most magnificent building in town.

Exhausted, I wind up in a café, drinking tea brewed in a samovar, before stopping to buy tangy Kars cheese and the freshest of honey to take home with me.

Ani Ruins

On to Ani and Sarıkamış

The next day I head out to Ani, the abandoned capital of the 10th-century Bagratid Kingdom of Armenia, which is 45 kilometers from Kars. Here I contemplate the mysterious past and how it is that a place once so important can be laid so low. I take a long look at the 11th-century Church of the Redeemer and the Church of the True Cross (Haç Kar) and wonder whether the Kaçkar Mountains could have been named after the cross as I reflect on its interesting name. I enjoy the view of the Arpaçay (Barley River) from the first Seljuk mosque, the Ebul Menuçehr Cami. Most of all, I try to imagine Marco Polo passing through this old walled town that straddled the Silk Road.

From Kars, I travel another 55 kilometers to Sarıkamış. On the way there, I remember the tens of thousands of soldiers who froze to death in the Allahuekber Mountains in 1915, an event which serves as

Beaut
Çobande
Bridge star
beside the ro
on the w
from Erzur
to Ka

Saffet E
Ton

a reminder of Young Turk Enver Paşa's ambition. But the same snow that brought death then is now a source of pleasure, squashed flat beneath the weight of hundreds of skis. I remember stories of rides on horse-sledges with snowdrops, a vision of happy people, with flushed cheeks and fur over their knees, riding in horse-sledges. To make this dream come true I head out over Lake Çıldır with the snow falling incessantly… In the background a song is playing: "When all the people were friends and games were played, a long, long time ago…"

Kars Citadel
Saffet Emre Tonguç

WHERE TO **STAY?**

Kar's Hotel
Phone: (0474) 212 16 16
www.karsotel.com
Surprisingly stylish hotel housed in one of the beautiful stone houses built during the Russian occupation, with spacious rooms decorated in pastel colors. The basement restaurant is excellent.

Hotel Karabağ
Phone: (0474) 212 34 80
www.hotel-karabag.com

Sim-er Hotel
Phone: (0474) 212 72 41
www.simerhotel.com

Çamkar Hotel Sarıkamış
Phone: (0474) 413 65 65
www.camkar.com

Toprak Hotel Sarıkamış
Phone: (0474) 413 41 11
www.toprakhotels.com
Newer hotel with more stars than neighboring Çamkar.

WHERE TO **EAT?**

Ocakbaşı Restaurant
Phone: (0474) 212 00 56

Şirin Sultan Sofrası
Phone: (0474) 212 56 16

Festival in Ani
Saffet Emre Tonguç

Kars Museum

Ruins of the Church of the Redeemer in Ani

6 MUST-SEE PLACES
IN THE SOUTHEAST ANATOLIA REGION

THE SOUTHEAST ANATOLIA REGION

MOSAIC CITY

096 Gaziantep

Saffet Emre TONGUÇ

Famous for its pistachios and mouth-watering food, the city of Gaziantep has been one of the main beneficiaries of the Southeastern Anatolia irrigation project (GAP), intended to make life in Southeastern Turkey easier. Recent years have seen a lot of restoration work done on its fine old buildings. At the same time, the opening of the new mosaic museum to house the finds from nearby Zeugma has brought Gaziantep a lot of extra touristic attention.

Aphrodite mosaic in Zeugma Museum

Saffet Emre Tonguç

Over the centuries, the city of Gaziantep has been invaded by innumerable different groups, ranging from the Hittites to the Persians, and from the Romans to the Arabs. It took its name from the Arabic words "Ayn Teb", meaning "beautiful creek". The "Gazi" prefix, meaning "victorious warrior", was given to the city to commemorate its courageous resistance to an 11-month French siege during the Turkish War of Independence in 1920. Today's Gaziantep surpasses many other Anatolian cities in terms of efficient city-planning, and its wide boulevards take many visitors by surprise.

The diversity of civilizations that have passed through Gaziantep have left a rich heritage of architectural and historical monuments. Start your visit with a walk from the 36-bastioned, mainly Seljuk citadel down towards the Bakırcılar Çarşısı (Coppersmith Bazaar), and then wander around a picturesque market area filled with spice vendors, blacksmiths, and butchers. Next, take a look at the Jewish and Armenian quarters behind

The Gypsy Girl mosaic

Saffet Emre Tonguç

the Gül Palas Hotel, and stop by the Hasan Süzer Ethnographic Museum, situated amidst vast houses that resemble miniature castles. Don't miss the huge black-and-white striped building that started life as an Armenian cathedral and was converted first into a prison, and later into the Kurtuluş Camii (Mosque). You will love the dome that rises up above the Corinthian capitals.

Having worked up an appetite, prepare to satisfy it with a visit to one of the kebab restaurants that feature çiğ and içli köfte on their menu. After lunch, head straight for the Zeugma Museum, the second largest mosaic museum in the world after the Bardo in Tunisia. The story of Zeugma is a sadly familiar one, of archeological treasures snatched from the ground just before a new lake created by a dam drowned the site of a once wealthy Roman city forever. Luckily, the new museum is magnificent. As you stroll past the mosaics, think about the Sassanids ransacking the city in 252 BC, rather than about what has happened more recently. The exquisite works on display suggest that some of the people of the past had more sophisticated taste than our own! Don't miss the iconic Gypsy Girl mosaic which is in a room apart from the larger pieces. The museum also houses one of the world's largest collections of seal imprints with almost 100,000 pieces.

Yesemek - an outdoor sculpture workshop

The village of Yesemek, roughly 115 kilometers from Gaziantep, was once home to an open-air workshop for Hittite sculptors. Scattered across the ground lie hundreds of unfinished monuments just waiting for visitors to come and admire them. To get here, take the İslahiye road.

Yesemek

HOW TO **TRAVEL?**

The quickest and easiest way to get to Gaziantep is to fly, but there are also good bus services from most big towns, including Kayseri, Malatya and Şanlıurfa.

WHERE TO **STAY?**

Anadolu Evleri
(Anatolian Houses)
Phone: (0342) 220 95 25
www.anadoluevleri.com
The Anadolu Evleri are three old Gaziantep houses, which have been beautifully restored and decorated with period furniture. Breakfast in the black-and white striped stone courtyard of the hotel takes you on a journey straight back into the past.

Antik Belkıs Han
Phone: (0342) 231 10 84.
www.belkishan.com
If you're looking for an unconventional place to stay, this old Gaziantep house with its lovely courtyard has been converted into a chic boutique hotel.

Tilmen Hotel
Phone: (0342) 220 20 81
The hotel restaurant is popular with Gaziantep locals. Try the çiğ köfte (uncooked meatballs).

Grand Hotel
Phone: (0342) 325 65 65
www.gaziantepgrandhotel.com

Tuğcan Hotel
Phone: (0342) 220 43 23
www.tugcanhotel.com.tr

WHAT **TO DO?**

Hasan Süzer Ethnographic Museum.
Phone: (0342) 230 47 21
This old Gaziantep house has been restored to show the old-fashioned way of living in style.

Women can relax at the **Şıh Hamam** (Phone: (0342) 225 29 87), men can get a decent scrub at the **Yusuf Çelebi Hamam** (Phone: (0342) 225 29 87).

If you need a good travel agency to organize a tour of Southeastern Turkey, **Vipol Tourism** (Phone: (0342) 221 02 90; www.vipolturizm.com) arranges private tours in the region. They also do tours from Gaziantep to Syria.

WHERE TO **EAT?**

İmam Çağdaş Et Lokantası
Phone: (0342) 231 26 78
www.imamcagdas.com
One of Turkey's best kebab restaurants, this place has been open to discerning diners for 120 years. Green peppers, lemon and parsley and a cup of ayran, are brought to the table first. Why not try the lahmacun (a flat, pizza-like bread topped with meat) before your kebab? Make sure to round off the meal with some of the tasty baklava for which Antep is famous.

Çavuşoğlu Et Lokantası
Phone: (0342) 338 18 28

Şirvan Et Lokantası
Phone: (0342) 324 25 26

Papirüs Cafe
Phone: (0342) 220 32 79
This café is housed in an old Armenian house with high ceilings and delightful frescoes. You should try the zahter tea made from oregano.

Gaziantep Tahmis Café
Historic café which sells delicious menengiç coffee made from Antep pistachios.

CITY OF PROPHETS - AND PIGEONS!

097 Şanlıurfa

Saffet Emre TONGUÇ

Known as the City of the Prophets, Şanlıurfa is where the Prophet Abraham is thought to have been born, and where he was tossed from the citadel to the ground by wicked king Nimrod, only to land in a bed of roses near the Balıklı Göl. The Prophet Job also lived in a cave near Şanlıurfa, where he waited patiently for seven years for God to restore his health and wealth. This is a wonderfully exotic town, with a fascinating bazaar and a beautifully landscaped center. You should allow at least a full day to explore it.

The Minaret of the Ulu Cami
Saffet Emre Tonguç

The streets of Şanlıurfa still carry a sense of Eastern mystery about them. It feels as though the merchandise brought in by the old camel caravans - the aromatic spices, the colorful fabrics - are still spread out across the city. The best place to get the feel for Şanlıurfa is the sprawling bazaar in the town center. Each trade and craft used to have its own area, but today some exist in name only, as their artisans have not been able to keep up with the needs of a fast-changing world. The Bedesten (Kazzaz Han) shops are stuffed full of Middle Eastern and Iranian shawls, glittery dresses, colorful shirts, and tablecloths, while the Sipahi Çarşısı (Bazaar) carries a variety of goodies, ranging from kilims and blankets to carpets and felt. The sound of coppersmiths banging away on metal as they practice their craft still echoes across the Bakırcılar (Coppersmith) Bazaar.

Built in 1562, the old Gümrük Han, right in the heart of the bazaar, acts as the town's meeting place. Perched on small stools called kürsü, with kefiyes (light shawls) wrapped around their heads, men play chess or checkers, while smoking nargiles or drinking tea to relax at the end of the day. Others drink the painfully bitter mırra coffee, served in cups without handles, and puff away on cigarettes rolled from smuggled tobacco. Nearby is the İsot Bazaar. A by-product of the capsicum annum family, which includes bell peppers, chili peppers and jalapeños, isot is a spice resembling red pepper flakes and is a crucially important cooking ingredient for the Şanlıurfa locals – so much so, in fact, that they even make ice cream with it!

The Atatürk Dam is part of the GAP (Southeastern Anatolian Project)

The City of Prophets

Şanlıurfa has a history dating back nearly 11,000 years. The prophets Adam, Job, Abraham, Jethro and Elias are all believed to have lived here, when the surrounding area was still called Mesopotamia. A story also relates how Jesus wiped his face and then sent the imprint of it on a handkerchief to King Abgar of Edessa (Şanlıurfa), thus causing him to make a miraculous recovery from near death. As a result of this miracle, Şanlıurfa (then Edessa) became one of the first towns to embrace Christianity.

But the most famous story connected to Şanlıurfa tells how the Prophet Abraham was born in a cave here. Later, he offended the Assyrian king Nimrod, who had him burned on a pyre, and then thrown from the citadel. God stepped in and turned the fire into water and the coals into fish. Abraham landed safely in a bed of roses. All of this is commemorated in the town center, where a rose garden spreads out in front of the cave where he was born, and where fat sacred carp live a life of luxury in the nearby Balıklı Göl (Fish Lake).

Literally "the night of one's turn", the sıra gecesi is regarded as a social support network. Around 10 friends get together, and, as the name suggests, take turns to host each other.

One of 50 fabulous places to see in the world

Until the Ottomans took over in 1561, Şanlıurfa was tossed from one government to another. Amongst its many rulers were the Hittites, the Persians and the Romans. When Alexander the Great arrived in the city, he named it Edessa, after a town in his homeland Macedonia. The name "Şanlıurfa" is thought to be of Arabic origin and derived from "Al Ruha", meaning "with plentiful waters". After it was relieved from a French siege in 1920, the city was granted the prefix "Şanlı" (Glorious) in recognition of its role in the resistance.

Göbeklitepe near Şanlıurfa, was designated one of "50 Fabulous Places to See in the World" by Condé Nast, one of the world's most respected travel magazines.

Balıklı Göl with the Rizvaniye Mosque behind it.

Saffet Emre Tonguç

Asude Akınlı

The birds of Mesopotamia

Pigeons provide a great source of entertainment for the men of Urfa. During the traditional "Karışma (Mixing)" event, which is usually held in winter, hundreds of pigeons are released into the sky, where they meet and mingle, creating a spectacular visual feast.

On your way from Şanlıurfa to Gaziantep, stop to visit the bald ibis breeding farm in Birecik, on the banks of the Fırat (Euphrates) river. Unfortunately, these ugly birds are virtually extinct in the wild. Birecik is worth seeing for its castles and houses. Here you can also take a boat tour to Halfeti which was flooded by the waters of the Birecik Dam. Half an hour away from Halfeti by boat, Rumkale (Greek Castle) is extraordinarily beautiful and still bears traces of the Romans, Byzantines and Crusaders who made use of it; the foremost spiritual leaders of the Armenians also lived here in the 13th century. Rumkale looks almost surreal - you find yourself rubbing your eyes to make sure what you're seeing is real.

Serhan Güngör

A ŞANLIURFA **SECRET**

If you would like to buy traditional Şanlıurfa handicrafts, call Yasemin Bilici at (0543) 591 67 98. Ms. Bilici has brought together a group of unemployed housewives with limited resources who create beautiful objects such as felt Christmas decorations for her, while also supporting themselves. Her shop can be found in the El Ruha Hotel.

HOW TO **TRAVEL?**

Coming from İstanbul or Ankara, it is probably best to fly to Urfa. There are bus services from most big towns.

WHERE TO **EAT?**

Çardaklı Köşk
Phone: (0414) 217 10 80
One of the best local restaurants, it is, like most places in Şanlıurfa, alcohol-free.

Kahraman Urfa Kebap Salonu
Phone: (0414) 215 21 30
Open since 1937 in the Köroğlu Çarşısı. Hurray for meat-lovers - it's a kebab-fest!

Halil İbrahim Sofrası
Phone: (0414) 216 84 44
The restaurant's name is perfect for Urfa - the mythological figure Halil İbrahim's table was famous for its never-ending supply of delicious food. The restaurant, which has a view of Balıklı Lake, serves kebab specialties.

Urfa Sofrası
Phone: (0414) 315 61 30
Opposite the Harran Hotel. Try the Urfa tabağı, borani and içli köfte (meatballs wrapped in bulgur).

WHERE TO **STAY?**

Hotel El-Ruha
Phone: (0414) 215 44 11
www.hotelelruha.com
The newest and most popular hotel in town. The lobby chips away one of its five stars, but the natural caves they use for their sıra geceleri add a certain charm to this 80-room establishment. Proximity to the Balıklı Lake is an advantage. No alcohol is served.

Harran Hotel
Phone: (0414) 215 44 11
In the town center. Good service, plus a bonus – alcohol is served.

Gülizar Konuk Evi (Guest House)
Phone: (0414) 215 44 11
www.gulizarkonukevi.com
An old Urfa dwelling transformed into a pleasant guesthouse. You can try local dishes in the restaurant.

Beyzade Konak (Mansion)
Phone: (0414) 215 44 11
www.beyzade.com
A beautiful example of Urfa's marvelous stonework, although the furnishings are a bit idiosyncratic.

Cevahir Konuk Evi
Phone: (0414) 215 44 11
www.cevahirkonukevi.com
An old konak converted into a boutique hotel. You will love the restaurant.

Kilim Hotel
Phone: (0414) 215 44 11
www.urfakilimotel.com
Right in the town center, it is one of the nicest and least pretentious places to stay.

Yıldız Sarayı Konuk Evi
Phone: (0414) 216 94 94
Newly-opened hotel in the back streets of Urfa, featuring traditionally-decorated rooms where you sleep on floor beds, alongside more conventional ones.

A TOWN OF BEEHIVE HOUSES

098 Harran

Saffet Emre TONGUÇ

Just south of Urfa, Harran is well-known for its beehive-shaped houses. At one time the Prophet Abraham lived here with his wife Sarah. The town was the site of one of the earliest known universities. It was also the place where the Roman emperor Caracalla was murdered in 217.

Saffet Emre Tonguç

Ishmael, the first-born son of Abraham by Hagar, is considered to be the ancestor of the Arabs, whereas Isaac, the second son of Abraham by his wife Sarah, is regarded as the father of the people of Israel. Abraham's readiness to sacrifice his son Ishmael to prove his faith is commemorated during Kurban Bayramı (the Feast of the Sacrifice, or Eid al-Adha). The fact that both the Jewish and Muslim faiths recognize the same story of the nearly sacrificed son shows that, despite their endless conflict, the Jews and the Arabs are actually closely related to each other.

Harran is thought to mean "crossroads" or "junction" in Sumerian. The town was regarded as a center of idolatry and home to the Sabians, who had a profound knowledge of astrology; its residents worshipped the moon, the sun, and the planets. Present-day Harranites, who claim that their ancestors came from Iraq, are eager to take advantage of the benefits of tourism, regardless of their age. You will find children joining your party to sell souvenirs made from harmal seeds (resembling a chickpea), or to offer their services as guides.

Harran is famous for its mud-brick houses which resemble the domed structures in Avignon, France, and Alberobello, Italy, and around Aleppo, in northern Syria. With their natural air-conditioning, they keep their inhabitants cool in summer and comfortably warm in winter. Called Kümbets, these houses are shaped like European beehives. Today, many are used as barns.

The town still boasts the remains of an Ulu Camii (Mosque) dating back to the Ummayad period, and an 11th-century citadel. It was host to one of the world's first universities, dating back to the 8th or 9th century, which was destroyed by the Mongols. Virtually all that remains now are the names and works of its scholars. The celebrated chemist and physicist Jabir ibn Hayyan (721-815; AKA Geber in the West) wrote his theories on the division of matter and the generation of energy through splitting the atom here.

Newly fertile land

Thanks to the irrigation channels connected to the Atatürk Lake as a result of the Southeastern Anatolia Project (GAP), Harran's erstwhile arid soil now sprouts endless cotton fields.

While in the area, you may want to travel an extra 40 kilometers to visit the village of Şuayip, where the Prophet Şuayip (Jethro), is believed to have lived. Mysterious Soğmater, which once boasted temples to the sun, the moon, and the planets, is only 55 kilometers from Harran.

While having a cold drink at Harran Evi, you can try on the local costumes.

Saffet Emre Tonguç

HOW TO **TRAVEL?**

There are direct buses from Şanlıurfa to the modern part of Harran, whence it's 10 minutes' walk to the beehive houses.

WHERE TO **STAY?**

Harran Evi

Phone: (0414) 441 20 20

Try out life in a beehive house for yourself, sleeping inside on the floor, or outside, on one of the "tahts" (thrones) that the locals use to escape the summer heat.

STONE HEADS ON A MOUNTAINSIDE

099 Mt Nemrut and the Gods

Saffet Emre TONGUÇ

By the time you reach the tomb-sanctuary of the self-proclaimed god, King Antiochus of Commagene, on the summit of Mt Nemrut, you will probably be short of breath, partly because of the hike but even more because of the wonders unfolding in front of your eyes…

The statues on Mt. Nemrut
Saffet Emre Tonguç

The famous stone heads on a mountainside, that appear on so many advertisements for Turkey, are to be found on top of Mt Nemrut (2,150m), which is near the oil-rich town of Adıyaman and the village of Kahta.
On the way from Kahta to Nemrut there are a few extraordinary places to visit in between the oil wells. Karakuş, nine kilometers to the north, houses the tomb of Antiochus I's wife. Another nine kilometers brings you to Cendere, which has an 1,800-year-old Roman bridge. There used to be four columns on the bridge, but one is now missing. Apparently, when Emperor Caracalla (r. 211-217) had his brother Geta killed, the column bearing his name was removed. Now there are only three columns which were erected for Caracalla himself, for his father, Septimius Severus, and mother, Julia Domna. One day, while Carcalla was relieving himself behind the bushes during a visit to the Temple of Sin in Harran, he was assassinated by a resentful officer who had demanded a promotion. What goes around comes around!
If you hit the road early in the morning, you can visit the ruined citadel in Old Kahta, as well as the remains of an ancient Commagene palace at Arsameia, on your way to the summit. If you're arriving from Şanlıurfa, pause to take a look at the Atatürk Dam on the Euphrates (Fırat), the heart of Turkey's largest irrigation project GAP (Southeastern Anatolia Project).

On to the summit

King Antiochus (r. 70-38 BC) regarded himself as the descendant of both, the Persian Emperor Darius and of his arch-rival, Alexander the Great. As a symbol of his power, he erected – in the middle of nowhere – several colossal statues of the ancient gods. The mound which covers his grave is 50 meters high but, despite modern technology, it has still not been penetrated. On the terraces over the mound's eastern and western facades, nine statues stand in a single row; at each end of these rows stand giant stone eagles and lions. Amongst the statues, look out for those of the self-proclaimed god Antiochus, of Tyche (the goddess of fortune), of Zeus (the king of the gods), of Apollo (the god of the sun), and of Herakles (a demigod). While on their original thrones, the statues stood as high as nine

meters but, following a series of earthquakes, their heads, which were as tall as an average human being, tumbled down. They still lie on the ground today.
You can climb Mount Nemrut in the afternoon to see the sun setting. Alternatively, if you don't mind your teeth chattering, you can always hit the road at two in the morning, wrap yourself in a blanket and be there to salute the rising sun. Afterwards, why not try the additional treat of heading on to Diyarbakır by boat across the Atatürk Lake? For ferry information phone (0532) 65156 87.

© Saffet Emre Tonguç

HOW TO **TRAVEL?**

Coming from İstanbul or Ankara it would be wise to fly to Adıyaman airport. Otherwise, there are buses to Adıyaman from most large towns, and then local buses on to Kahta.

Popular three-day tours to Mt Nemrut are offered by several travel agencies in Göreme, in Cappadocia.

WHERE TO **STAY?**

About half an hour from Adıyaman, Kahta is one of the better places to stay if you are planning a hike up Mount Nemrut.

Zeus Hotel, Kahta
Phone: (0416) 725 56 94
www.zeushotel.com.tr
A decent hotel, which even has a pool.

WHERE TO **EAT?**

Sofra Restaurant, Adıyaman
Phone: (0416) 216 32 21
Great kebabs.

Peri Hanımeli Sofrası, Adıyaman
Phone: (0416) 214 44 40
It may come as a surprise around here, but the owner is a woman named Nimet Peri. The local dishes are delicious. You must try their specialty, "meyir", made from ayran (yogurt and water drink), crushed wheat, eggplant, and green peppers.

Neşet'in Yeri, Kahta
Phone: (0416) 725 76 75
If you continue straight on from Kahta, you will come to an establishment beside the lake, which is probably the best and most interesting local restaurant. As you tuck into your fish, you might want to take a peek at the owner's collection of antiques.

Papatya Restaurant, Kahta
Phone: (0416) 726 29 89

MOSQUES AND CHURCHES BEHIND HIGH WALLS

100 Diyarbakır

Saffet Emre TONGUÇ

Hidden behind its black basalt walls, old Diyarbakır is full of surprises. With its narrow, maze-like streets, mosques, churches, hans, and lovely old houses, it seems to belong to another, much more oriental world.

A street vendor on a Diyarbakır back street.

Saffet Emre Tonguç

Diyarbakır's existence is mentioned in sources dating back 5,000 years, which makes it one of the world's oldest known settlements. Ruled in turn by the Urartians, Assyrians, Persians, Romans and Byzantines, the town was right in the center of upper Mesopotamia. What was Amida (Amedros) to the Byzantines, later became Diyarbakır, which means the Land of Bekr, and commemorates the Arab Bekr tribe that captured the town in 638. Punctuated by 72 towers and four major gates (Dağ, Urfa, Mardin and Yenikapı), six kilometers of black basalt walls encircle the city; they are in excellent condition and are said to be amongst the longest such walls in the world.

Intended to replace the Byzantine Church of St. Thomas, the Ulu Camii (Great Mosque) was commissioned by Melik Şah in 1091. The Mesudiye Medresesi, built in 1198, was one of Anatolia's first universities. Paid for by a scion of the Akkoyunlu dynasty, the Nebii Cami dates back to the 15th century. Still used as a bazaar and filled with carpet and jewelry stores, the 16th-century Hasanpaşa Hanı makes an interesting place to shop. If you prefer something more modern, there is also a large mall called Diyar, which more or less duplicates the shopping centers in other big towns.

Old Diyarbakır has two sorts of houses – those intended for summer living and those intended for the winter.

Mosques and churches

The 16th-century Safa, Behram Paşa and Kasım Padişah Camiis are all beautiful examples of Islamic architecture; the latter is also known as the Dört Ayaklı Minare because its minaret

The church of the Syrian Orthodox faith.

stands on four legs. There are also many churches belonging to different Christian denominations dotted about the old town, an ever-present reminder of the religious harmony of the past. Although they have only very small congregations, the Chaldean Keldani Church, the Armenian Surp Giragos Church, and the Syrian Orthodox Church of the Virgin Mary are well worth seeking out. During weekly services, the priest of the Syrian Orthodox church reads the Bible in Aramaic, which is believed to be the language spoken by Jesus. This alone is enough to make you want to learn more about the rich history of your surroundings.

The home of the renowned poet Cahit Sıtkı Tarancı (1910-1956) is now a small museum, as is the home of the famous nationalist poet Ziya Gökalp (1876-1924). Other attractions to look out for include a Roman Bridge and Diyarbakır Archeological Museum. On the outskirts of town, the On Gözlü Köprü (Bridge of Ten Niches) over the River Tigris (Dicle) provides a marvelous view of the city.

While you will often hear people saying "başım gözüm üstüne" (which means roughly "with great pleasure") as you walk around Diyarbakır, you should still keep an eye out for young pickpockets.

The Malabadi Bridge straddled the trade route between Diyarbakır and Van. It was built during the Artukid period in 1146.

Saffet Emre Tonguç

WHERE TO **STAY?**

Büyük Kervansaray Hotel
Phone: (0412) 228 96 09
Close to the Mardin Kapı, one of the gateways into the city, this hotel, in a restored caravanserai, has a pool and hamam (Turkish bath).

Class Hotel
Phone: (0412) 229 50 00
www.diyarbakirclasshotel.com
In an extremely central location, opposite the Ulu Camii.

Dedeman Diyarbakır
Phone: (0412) 229 00 00
www.dedemanhotels.com

Prestige Hotel
Phone: (0412) 229 50 50

WHERE TO **EAT?**

Diyarbakır is famous for its gigantic watermelons. If they are in season, be sure to try one.

Kaburgacı Selim Amca
Phone: (0412) 224 44 47
www.kaburgaciselimamca.com
With three other branches in İstanbul, Kaburgacı Selim Amca was established in Diyarbakır in 1982. If you eat there, you might want to try bumbar (rice and meat sausage), poached içli köfte (meatballs wrapped in bulgur) or stuffed ribs.

Gazi Köşkü
Phone: (0412) 226 33 33 /226 34 93
On the road to Mardin, the Köşk Sofra Salonu is housed in the lovely Gazi Köşkü where you can eat lunch overlooking the Tigris river. Its specialty is stuffed kibe-bumbar; to make it they chop up tripe and stuff the intestines of a lamb.

Çarşı Konağı Izgara (Grill)
Phone: (0412) 228 46 73
The grilled meat dishes are good and the prices reasonable.

Dağkapı Ciğercisi
Phone: (0412) 224 10 15
If you like liver, this is a great place to come.

Ben-ü Sen Meyhanesi
Phone: (0412) 224 16 55
The name comes from those of the master and apprentice who competed on the construction of the walls. It's a great place to get tipsy.

CITIES OF HONEY-COLORED STONE

101 Mardin, Midyat and Hasankeyf

Saffet Emre TONGUÇ

Located in the middle of the vast Mesopotamian plain, Mardin is a city built out of glorious honey-colored stone. With a handful of ancient churches and a lively bazaar, it has a real whiff of the orient about it. The same is also true of old Midyat, which keeps a low profile behind a seemingly uninviting modern town. Hasankeyf gained a certain notoriety, as the world learned that it will be drowned, when a dam is built on the River Tigris.

Mor Gabriel Monastery, Midyat

Mehmet Çabuk

Zeynel Bey Tomb, Hasankeyf

Following early Assyrian settlement, the Arab conquest in 640, and repeated Mongol attacks in subsequent years, Mardin was finally added to the Ottoman Empire in 1517. Its name is thought to be derived from the Aramaic word "Merdin," meaning "fortresses."

Right in the centre of town, the bazaar is absolutely enchanting, with artisans hard at work on every corner. Modernity hardly seems to have penetrated the back streets, and walking around the bazaar feels like entering a time warp. Here you can still watch craftsmen making felt and packsaddles, two crafts which are rapidly dying out elsewhere. Buy some filigree jewelry, some peksimet (a type of biscuit), some fresh badem şekeri (almond candy), some roasted chickpeas, and a bottle of Syriac wine. Look out, too, for glass paintings of the Şahmaran (a monster with the face of a woman and the body of a snake) at Kadir Özcan's shop in the Bakırcılar (Coppersmiths) Bazaar. When you get tired, take a break in the Marangozlar (Carpenters)

Coffee House, which was once a synagogue. While you're quenching your thirst, you can check out the posters of Turkish actors from the '70!

As you wander around the bazaar, you are likely to come across large white donkeys who work as street cleaners on the Municipality payroll; because vehicles can't squeeze down the steep and narrow streets, the donkeys had to take over the task!

Before you leave you should try to attend a service at the Forty Martyrs Church, also known as Mor Benham, which serves as the bishopric of Mardin. The old wooden doors and bell tower are interesting, as are the hand-painted curtains that drape the interior. While the Syrian Orthodox Christians in Mardin speak Arabic, those living in Midyat, just an hour away, prefer to use Syriac in daily life.

Other places to visit include the 14th-century Latifiye Cami, the 12th-century Ulu Camii (Great Mosque), the Kayseriye Cami, and the 14th-century Sultan İsa and Zinciriye Medreses. The Akkoyunlu Dynasty ruled Mardin in the 15th century, and the lovely Kasımiye Medresesi is a masterpiece that survives

Mardin's Ulu Camii (Great Mosque)
Asude Akınlı

The Mardin houses are beautiful examples of traditional stone craftsmanship.

Bünyad Dinç

The historic bridge over the Tigris (Dicle) River, Hasankeyf

Saffet Emre Tonguç

from this period. It's a great place to come to watch the reflection of the setting sun in its courtyard pool. In a gorgeous 19th-century building on the main square, the Mardin Museum houses archaeological artefacts dating back to 4,000 BC as well as an ethnographic collection that showcases details of local life.

Midyat and Dayrülumur

From Mardin, you can easily visit Midyat and Hasankeyf. In Midyat, where the fabulous Syriac artistry is reflected in the carving of the stonework, you will be mesmerized by the filigree jewelry sold in the stores. As the church bells toll alongside the sound of the ezan (call for prayer), you can offer up a prayer for religious tolerance and peace.

Dayrülumur Monastery is a beautifully restored Syriac complex, 24 kilometers from Midyat, near İdil. Built in 397, the main building still boasts beautiful mosaics. The second church was constructed for Emperor Justinian's famous wife Theodora, probably the most influential woman in Byzantine history. As a tourist, you may not care for many of the local toilets. Those at the monastery are the cleanliest in the area.

Deyrulzafaran Monastery, Mardin

Serhan Güngör

Hasankeyf

Once you get to Hasankeyf, you should climb straight up to the top of the hill, passing all sorts of ancient structures along the way. From the summit you can watch the river Tigris, which is mentioned in the Bible, flowing past Hasankeyf, as it has done for thousands of years. If it's lunch-time, go straight back down to the river and eat at one of the restaurants built on stakes embedded in the water. As the Tigris flows by, you can sit at a table with your feet in the river and enjoy this pleasant break from normal workaday life.

HOW TO **TRAVEL?**

The most practical way is to fly to Mardin and then rent a car. It's roughly 1,600 kilometers from İstanbul to Mardin. Mardin is about 95 kilometers from Diyarbakır and 65 from Midyat.

WHERE TO **STAY?**

Artuklu Kervansarayı, Mardin
Phone: (0482) 213 73 53
www.artuklu.com
The building, dating back to 1275, is spectacular, although the fabulous stonework would be better displayed without the kitsch objects. The rooms are nicely decorated and the food delicious. The next-door mosque is lit up at night and looks breathtaking.

Erdoba Evleri, Mardin
Phone: (0482) 213 76 77
www.erdoba.com.tr
A constantly expanding establishment in the center of town with pleasing stonework in its lounge. There is a spectacular view of the Mesopotamian plain from the restaurant.

Büyük Mardin Hotel, Mardin
Phone: (0482) 213 10 47
This modern hotel is out of the town center but offers views of the Mesopotamia plain.

Öztürk Ailesi Evi, Savur
Phone: (0482) 571 21 27
About 50 kilometers out of Mardin on the way to Midyat, you will come to pretty, unspoilt Savur ("Little Mardin") where the Öztürk family welcomes guests to their 200-year-old house.

Nezirhan Hotel, Nusaybin
Phone: (0482) 446 34 16
Four-star hotel in the middle of nowhere, with a lovely stone konak in the grounds.

Midyat Konuk Evi (State Guest House), Midyat
Phone: (0482) 462 13 54
Accommodation in a finely restored Syriac house.

Matiat Hotel, Midyat
Phone: (0482) 462 59 20
www.matiat.com.tr
Spacious, clean rooms.

WHERE TO **EAT?**

Cercis Murat Konağı, Mardin
Phone: (0482) 213 68 41
www.cercismurat.com
Kişk soup, sembusek (covered lahmacun), ikbeybet (boiled içli köfte), irok (fried içli köfte) and kiliçe (Mardin patty) are just some of the local dishes to try here. The view of the Mesopotamian plain is as fabulous as the food on your plate. Definitely the best restaurant in town - makes you wish owner Ebru Baybara would open a branch in your hometown.

Gelüşke Hanı, Midyat
Phone: (0482) 464 14 42
The restaurant serves up kebabs inside an historical building in the Kuyumcular (Jewelry) Bazaar.

Yolgeçen Hanı, Hasankeyf
Phone: (0488) 381 22 87
Literally meaning an inn where many people pass through, "Yolgeçen Hanı" is a Turkish idiom which suggests an excess of people coming and going as they please. It turns out to have come from the name of a cave in Hasankeyf. The stone-cut Yolgeçen Hanı sits underneath Hasankeyf citadel, with an entrance on the Tigris river side; there is even a secret passage inside the cave to access the fortress. The atmosphere is relaxing, with the soft sound of running water everywhere. The food is excellent and smiling faces come a dime a dozen.

WHAT **TO DO?**

You must see Nasra Hanim's hand-painted church curtains decorated with scenes from the Bible. Her house is near the Diyarbakır Kapı
(Phone: (0482) 212 17 65).

Grab a seat at the Şehidiye Coffee House and end the day gazing out over the pancake-flat Mesopotamian plain. When you turn your head, the lights of Mardin Castle will offer an altogether unforgettable sight.

Four kilometers outside Mardin, Deyrülzafaran Monastery takes its name from the saffron crocuses that were supposedly used in the mortar. It served as the seat of the Syrian Orthodox Patriarchate until 1932; the Patriarch, who bears the title "Patriarch of Antioch (Modern city of Antakya)", now lives in Syria. The monastery is a definite must-see with an EU-funded café and gift shop attached.

Tour the villages of the Tur Abdin (the area surrounding Mardin and Midyat), which have quietened down considerably after most of the Syrian Christians were forced to emigrate. This under-visited area is spectacularly rich in ancient monuments. Thought to be one of the oldest churches in the world, the Church of the Virgin Mary in Anıtlı (Hah) village dates back to the 4th century and should definitely be visited. İzbırak and Gülgöze villages are equally interesting.

On your way to Nusaybin, visit the ruins of Dara, roughly 30 kilometers out of Mardin. According to historians, this is where Alexander the Great fought King Darius (Dara) of Persia. Deep below one of the houses lurks a vast cistern which is still only partially excavated. It's an extraordinary sight.

Mırra coffee

Asude Akınlı

What is "travel writing"?

The internet encyclopedia Wikipedia defines travel literature, or travel writing, as recording "the people, events, sights and feelings of an author who is touring a foreign place for the pleasure of travel". Naturally, if a few of these articles are combined, and if they are long enough, they can be regarded as a travel book.

Aydın Kudu

In January 2006, the prestigious Australian newspaper The Sydney Morning Herald published an article on travel writing by former Lonely Planet editor Andrew Bain. "Guidebooks are both loved and hated, but they have been the essential traveling companion for centuries," wrote Bain. The same article also mentioned Pausanias, who wrote history's first travelogue in c. 150 AD. The author's 10-volume set could serve as a reference book, even for modern travelers. Although they were not travel writers per se, the works of Homer of Smyrna, Strabo of Amasya, and Herodotus of Halicarnassus, the Anatolian forefathers of literature, geography and history respectively, have also proved to be important guides for travellers. However, although they often assist people in their travels, guidebooks can also be abused. For example, the officer in charge of the German Luftwaffe that bombed England in 1942 picked up one of the best guidebooks of our times, Baedeker, and put all the important buildings mentioned in the book on his target list. The end result? 50,000 demolished buildings.

But why would someone else's travel experience interest anyone else? If traveling is such a personal experience, why would we want to read anyone else's travel journal?

The best answer probably comes from Ahmet Haşim, an influential early 20th-century Turkish poet. In his prose work Gurebahane-i Laklakhan (The Hospice of Chatter), Haşim beautifully describes how subjective travel experiences enchanted him as a child: "I am very familiar with the pleasures of travelogues - I spent an entire childhood reading them. As the wind blew outside on cold winter nights, the light from the gas lamp was reflected in my pupils like two golden flecks. Few works of literature have given me the same taste I acquired from the innocent and candid styles of African and American travelogues read in a comfortable chair…"

One of the first examples of a travelogue is, without doubt, the work of the medieval Venetian traveler Marco Polo, in which he depicts his journeys through Near Eastern and Central Asian lands. His book has been translated into a number of languages. Another famous name is that of the 14th- century Arab traveler Ibn Battuta, who traversed Anatolia, Central Asia

and Persia, and left beautiful descriptions of the lives of the local people in his writings. The early 16th-century Ottoman admiral and cartographer Piri Reis also provided his readers with a splendid account of the Mediterranean in his Kitab-ı Bahriye (Book of Navigation).

The travelers of Turkish literature

The first known Turkish travelogue is Seydi Ali Reis's Mir'ât ül Memâlik (Mirror of Countries, 1557). In this work, Ali Reis brilliantly describes how he hit shore after a typhoon, as he was fighting the Portuguese, and how he reached Edirne via Afghanistan and Central Asia. In turn, Katip Çelebi left a colorful depiction of numerous cities of the sprawling Ottoman Empire in his Cihannüma (Pinnacle). However, when speaking of travel writing in Ottoman and Turkish literature, the first name that always springs to mind is that of Evliya Çelebi. His 10-volume Seyahatname (Book of Travels) includes sections both on the Ottoman lands, and on Austria, Abyssinia (modern Ethiopia), Egypt, and Dagestan, and remains a major reference book to this day. His surprisingly clear language is often interspersed with, presumably, exaggerated descriptions. An anecdote, such as "In Erzurum, as he was jumping from one roof to the next, the cat froze in mid-air, for it was too cold, and then with the arrival of spring he thawed out and resumed his jump," not only puts a broad smile on the reader's face, but also leaves a vivid trace in his memory.

Yirmisekiz Çelebi Mehmet Efendi's Paris Sefâretnâmesi (Paris Travelogue), which he wrote in the 18th century, while serving as an Ottoman ambassador to France, is regarded as one of the first travelogues to describe the "West".

Ahmet Mithat Efendi's Avrupa'da bir Cevelan (Wandering in Europe) describes a long train journey through various European cities. After the 19th century Ottoman Tanzimat reforms, Turkish authors turned their eyes more towards the West, and Paris cafés became more and more familiar to their readers. Ali Bey's Seyahat Jurnali (Travel Journal) and Cenap Şehabettin's Avrupa Mektupları (Letters from Europe) are among the "best-seller" travelogues of the period.

Of the Republican travel writers, one of the best known is Falih Rıfkı Atay; his Denizaşırı (Overseas), Tuna Kıyıları (The Banks of Danube), Taymıs Kıyıları (The Banks of the Thames), Hind (India), Yolcu Defteri (Notebook of a Traveller), and Bizim Akdeniz (Our Mediterranean) are just as pleasant to read now, as they were at the time they were written. Reşat Nuri Güntekin's observations, collected in Anadolu Notları (Notes on Anatolia), as well as Saik Sabri Duran's Akdeniz'de Bir Yaz Gezintisi (A Summer Excursion in the Mediterranean) and Şükufe Nihal's Finlandiya (Finland) are classics, which also enjoyed considerable popularity when they were first published. Sadri Ertem, Burhan Arpad and later Azra Erhat, Haldun Taner, Melih Cevdet Anday, and Bedri Rahmi Eyüboğlu have also opened doors onto a whole different world for their readers.

Saffet Emre Tonguç

EPILOGUE

Book in the bag...

As soon as they have a moment to spare, one of the first things most people think about is a holiday. But then they have to decide "where, how and doing what?" The answer lies in a good travel book. Well, now that you have that book in your bag, your compass is already pointing in the right destination.

Vacations are often limited to 15 short days of annual leave, or come with a fixed budget. If you are lucky, you have two weeks' holiday; if you're born lucky, you have a few thousand dollars. What's best?
Should you try and see a bunch of places, or put down roots and become part of one particular place? Should you immerse yourself in art, or study a culture in greater depth in a faraway land?

The decision is yours to make, of course, but a book to help you is a must! Preferably a book with inspirational pictures; a book that describes that "special place" with all its smells, its exotic dishes, and its different way of looking at life...

In The Art of Travel, Alain de Botton shares his ideas about the "art" of traveling with his readers. Traveling may be freedom, he says, but it also brings with it certain obligations on the part of the traveler. By definition that traveler is bound to be on a voyage of discovery.

Yes, traveling is freedom.

Yet it is a painstakingly acquired freedom, one for which you may have to fight to make space amid all the complex arrangements, the endless calculations, and the limitless choices in day-to-day life.

You have to take time to do travel justice. A bit of preliminary research, a good guidebook, but most of all a free spirit are all prerequisites for the best travel experiences. A good guidebook will tell you what to eat in which restaurant and where to catch the best view, as well as which museums you should visit, which fountains you should photograph… In fact, a good guidebook may even suggest how you should be feeling. It sets the mood and blends the right ingredients, then sets them to simmer over low heat. There's no doubt about it - a good guidebook is absolutely essential. It will lead you in the right direction, cut down on wasted time, and offer suggestions for how to combine practical solutions with budget restrictions. What is more, it should help to encourage a more active mode of travel, with quick tips about the places to be visited en route.

Alain de Botton's "The Art of Travel" contains wonderful essays on his experiences of traveling…

This is exactly the kind of book we have tried to create for you with "101 Must-See Places in Turkey". A little bit of guidance, but not so much that you are drowning in it… A book that leaves room for your own discoveries; one that tells you something, but not everything; one that prompts you but doesn't force you…

The rest is up to you.